Nature

The Other Earthlings

Nature
The Other Earthlings

by James Shreeve

Macmillan Publishing Company   *New York*

Collier Macmillan Publishers   *London*

Macmillan Publishing Company
866 Third Avenue, New York, N.Y. 10022
Collier Macmillan Canada, Inc.

Library of Congress Cataloging-in-Publication Data

Shreeve, James.
    Nature: the other earthlings.

    "The first of a series of companion volumes to
the Nature television program"—p.
    Includes index.
    1. Zoology—Miscellanea. 2. Natural history—
Miscellanea. I. Nature (Television program)
II. Title.
QL50.S55 1987   508   86-21740
ISBN 0-02-534920-1

Macmillan books are available at special discounts for
bulk purchases for sales promotions, premiums, fund-
raising, or educational use. For details, contact:
    Special Sales Director
    Macmillan Publishing Company
    866 Third Avenue
    New York, N.Y. 10022

10 9 8 7 6 5 4 3 2 1

PRINTED IN THE UNITED STATES OF AMERICA
Design by Antler & Baldwin, Inc.

Contents

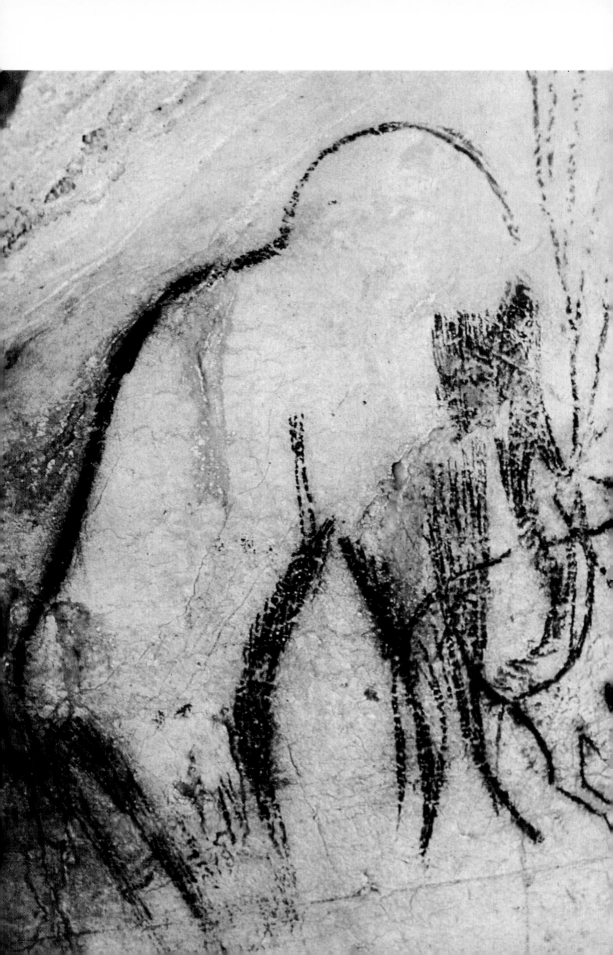

Foreword

Rather like a clumsy imitation of a Silurian dragonfly, the last helicopter had lifted off, vanishing into the rapidly dwindling twilight along the Madre de Dios River. Through the courtesy of an American company exploring for oil in the Peruvian Amazon, the World Wildlife Fund group had made the trip from the technological termite mound that is Manhattan to one of the remotest spots on earth in less than forty-eight hours.

Jaguar and harpy eagles patrolled the rain forest of the Manu Park. Upriver there was a less-than-friendly Indian tribe, and at higher elevations, the elusive spectacled bear. For a nineteenth-century naturalist the trip would have taken months and been an expedition in the truest sense of the word. And to underscore the comparison, we soon discovered the absurdity that we had inadvertently been left with the oil camp's entire weekend supply of ice cream (strawberry, chocolate, and vanilla, of course). The latter part of the twentieth century is, in a sense, a golden era for field biologists like myself, as well as for those less fortunate who are not *paid* to pursue their passion for nature and faraway places.

Jet-age speed and the other wonders of our technological society unfortunately obscure the fact that we really know very little about life on earth. This exciting phenomenon, of which we are very much a part, exists only on this planet, so far as we know. More than 1.6 million species have been described by science, and probably millions more remain unknown.

7

So poorly explored is nature that cameras for the *Nature* public television series sometimes uncover new knowledge before the field scientists.

We are humbled by our rudimentary knowledge of life on earth when we recognize the *complexity* of living systems, and particularly so when we consider the complexity in relation to the simplicity of the inanimate world. Harvard zoologist E. O. Wilson estimates that the amount of information contained in one chromosome of a domestic mouse is equivalent to that found in all editions of the *Encyclopaedia Britannica* combined. Imagine, then, the complexity that must exist even in a roadside verge, let alone in the great tropical forests with, for instance, hundreds of tree species in just a few acres.

Yet technology, like a shimmering mirage, distracts us from the biological essence of our existence, leading us to believe it will solve our problems. This same technology that makes remote wilderness accessible combines with the sheer weight of human numbers to engender destruction of the natural world at a rate, and to an extent, unparalleled in human history. Almost everywhere nature is in retreat, either obviously through habitat destruction by axe or bulldozer, or insidiously through agents like acid rain and chlorinated hydrocarbons. Hundreds of thousands of species are threatened by extinction, and conspicuous among them are the great mammals celebrated in this companion volume to *Nature*.

I often think of the great mammals dramatic enough to inspire culinary form as the animal-cracker animals. Neither they nor we (the gingerbread-man animals) run this planet, appearances notwithstanding. It is the squirmies and the plants that are in charge, and we, in the last analysis, are just along for the ride. That more and more of the great mammals are on lists of endangered species is a matter of greater concern than might be obvious, for their imperiled status indicates that many less spectacular and even unknown species will soon follow. The great mammals tend to be among the first to feel the environmental pinch, but they are in no sense alone.

Indeed the field naturalists of today who, aided by technology, can see so many natural wonders, will be the last to see many of them. This is a sobering thought that impels those of us in conservation to work ever harder. A really top-priority world crisis is upon us—severe impoverishment of our faunal and floral heritage and all its potential for human society.

It is my ardent hope that the *Nature* series and companion volumes like this one will use modern technology to break into our ever-increasing self-centeredness and isolation from nature. There is one great force on our side, namely, a basic affinity for and curiosity about nature. It runs far deeper than the fear of snakes or insects sometimes instilled in us in childhood. If people would stop long enough to give themselves a chance, they would discover what joy and wonder awaits them in the natural world. Some, happily, are already doing that—the number of bird watchers has swelled enormously in recent decades, and Kenya, for example, receives vital foreign exchange as people flock to see her wildlife wonders.

I wish that more widespread enjoyment of nature would in itself suffice to avert the looming loss of so many plant and animal species. It is only a first step, however, because so many threads of human existence are woven into the great vector of extinction. But it is a necessary first step to prevent what those of us aware of the problem would see as a new irreversible age of loneliness, of perpetual lament for the great mammals and other lost species. Animal crackers might still be made, but rather than filling the void, they would remind us of our loss.

—Thomas E. Lovejoy,
Nature Scientific Advisor,
World Wildlife Fund–U.S.

Introduction

In my office there is a handmade valentine which arrived during the second season of the public television series, *Nature*, unsigned and with no return address. A red heart bordered with paper lace bears the message "Thank you for the beauty you have brought into my life. I love *Nature!*"

This valentine is my favorite. It says, in effect, that *Nature* touches people in some very personal way. The common theme in all the correspondence we receive is that *Nature* helps viewers appreciate the natural world and the interdependence of all life on earth.

Nature premiered on PBS on Sunday, October 10, 1982. It was an immediate hit with viewers and critics, and in one season became the highest rated weekly series on PBS.

We were very nervous before *Nature* went on the air in 1982 as an anthology of natural history films unlike any others offered regularly on American television. They were slowly paced and sparsely narrated, and the sounds of nature dominated the occasional music. Films tended to be lingering looks at some aspect of the natural world or a serious history of scientific inquiry. *Nature* was *not* fast-paced or action-filled.

I am often asked why I think *Nature* is so popular. It amazes me that millions of Americans sit for an hour and watch a film about a single tree in a Central American rain forest or a pile of rocks in Africa's Serengeti plain. Or why would so many people, during "prime time," watch Wolfgang

Bayer's study of a cactus plant growing in the American Southwest in "Saguaro—Sentinel of the Desert"? Or Hugh Miles' film about a particular female otter and her family: "On the Tracks of the Wild Otter"?

Could it be that these natural history films are just another form of televised escape? After all, they do take the viewer to some of the most exotic and still unspoiled corners of our planet. Could it be that life in the wild, brutal and beautiful but always fascinating, is a welcome relief from the constant barrage of information, fact and fiction, about the confusing and often depressing affairs of man? I suspect that *Nature*'s appeal has something to do with both of these factors but I have a strong sense that something much more profound is at work.

Man has struggled to dominate nature, to bend her to his will. Man's extraordinary ability to rise above the real dangers of the natural world, to tame it and to exploit its resources grew slowly but relentlessly until nature didn't have a chance. In evolutionary terms, this ability to harness nature was the key to man's survival, and he was so successful at mastering natural forces that eventually he became the planet's dominant species. But many of us *homo sapiens* now realize that in the process of achieving and maintaining dominance we lost something very precious.

We have reached the point where contemporary humanity in the industrialized nations has very little, if any, contact with nature. We are prisoners in great cities of asphalt, concrete, glass, and steel; as our numbers expand, the natural world—those few wild places unaffected by man and his machines—is shrinking at an alarming rate. And so, perhaps, when we have an opportunity to experience nature, even vicariously *via* television, we seize it. Perhaps these programs awake some deep memory of a time when man and nature were more in balance, a time when man was part of nature but not its ruler. We think critic John Corry of *The New York Times* was right when he wrote about *Nature* that "spiritual impulses seem to be at work."

As we work on the *Nature* series, I sometimes have the sinking feeling that we are compiling a film archive of what little is left of the natural world as the twentieth century rushes to a close. Most days I'm an optimist, however, and remember my anonymous valentine. I prefer to think our television series and this first companion book to *Nature* will encourage a growing recognition that the preservation of our beautiful little planet, and therefore of all its life in all its forms, is the single most important issue facing us.

In this book, James Shreeve tells wonderful stories about mammals in a warm and personal way. I hope you will agree that his love for his subjects shines from every page and brings us closer to those magnificent creatures which still roam the wild places of our home, the third planet orbiting a star we call the sun in a planetary system where, to the extent of our present knowledge, we and earth's other life-forms are alone.

—George Page
WNET/Thirteen
Nature host

Prologue: Denning in New Jersey

One day in the spring of 1982, a male black bear weighing 465 pounds walked onto a patio in Passaic County, New Jersey, and ate the food left out for the family cat. A bear so large would raise some eyebrows even in the backwoods of Maine, let alone in the suburban backyards of the Garden State. His temerity, however, was hardly unprecedented. In 1981, a bear crashed a barbecue party in nearby Sussex County, and when the guests scattered, it followed its nose to the grill and made off with the franks. A third ursine Jerseyite, this one in Morris County, even closer to Manhattan, shuffled into another backyard and removed some wash from the clothesline. The bear played with the children's swing for a while and then sexually mounted a ceramic deer, breaking it in the process. The owner of the property quickly called the authorities, fearing that his antique automobile, black like the bear, might be the next recipient of the bear's amorous attention.

Americans love wildlife, but we generally prefer to meet it under more managed circumstances. American zoos, in fact, attract more spectators annually than do major league baseball, football, and hockey games combined. Our national parks receive over seven hundred thousand visitors per day. And since its inauguration in 1982, the *Nature* television series has been one of the most popular regular programs on public television. All over the country, millions of us put aside human concerns for an hour on

15

Sunday evening and turn our minds to the feeding habits of crocodiles and kinkajous, the sex lives of the Arctic fox and the Arctic rose, the hoots, howls and silent signalings of life lived beyond the borders of common experience. So long as the natural world is safely contained by a television screen, a park boundary, or a concrete moat in a zoo, we relish every opportunity to poke around in its mysteries.

Wildlife, however, doesn't always stay in the wild. In the last ten years, bears and humans in New Jersey have become increasingly intimate with each other's habits. The foregoing instances were among many noted by nature writer John MacPhee, himself a New Jersey resident, in an essay published in *The New Yorker* magazine. After being reduced to a handful in the early seventies, the state's bear population has now swelled to well over 100. All told, there were 266 bear sightings in New Jersey in 1985. Most of the time the bears are encountered in rural areas, violating more our preconceptions about New Jersey landscapes than of typical bear habitat. But bears make their appearance in well-tamed country too. Bears in Princeton near the university. Bears in the suburbs of Trenton, noses deep in trash cans. Bears ambling down the median strip of the Interstate, crossing over, visiting shopping malls. In nearby areas of Pennsylvania, bears have discovered that with a little digging and leaf hauling, the basements of some newly occupied development homes can be finished into comfortable winter dens. Pennsylvania bears even venture into cities. A few years ago a young male wandered through the lobby of an office building in Williamsport (population 33,401) and sat down behind a desk.

Bears, of course, do not belong in downtown lobbies. The unfamiliar smells and hard shapes worry their senses; they fear the echoes tossed down from the ceiling and the people perched on hind legs, pressing in. A bear grows confused in such a place; its claws clatter and skid on polished tiles. Naturally there would be a panic on the other side too. Even ordinarily fearless people would admit to having a queasy feeling at seeing a bear where it's not expected to be. Its intrusion suggests that something has gone wrong somewhere; that the borders of normal experience have been breached, letting in a strange and undismissable new presence.

The bear in the Williamsport lobby was soon disposed of—drugged and whisked away by the Fish and Game people. No doubt the office workers were relieved to have things back to normal, but one can imagine a lingering wonder, a shared thrill among the onlookers, as if their blood all beat now to one pulse, quickened by the bear's proximity. Strangers talked animatedly to each other, coins chimed through the lobby pay phones: "Honey, you won't *believe* what just happened. . . ." All the workers were late getting back to their desks, and nobody cared.

Close encounters with bears are indeed extraordinary. Over the past several millennia, and especially during the last five centuries, humankind has gradually distanced itself from most animals. We have defined ourselves as extranatural, distinct from mere flesh, and regard earth's other animals

Two faces filled with wonder and not a little ambivalence: an Australian girl and a common brush-tailed possum share a most unnatural moment.

as inhabitants of a separate, lower plane of existence. Our ability to manipulate nature has made us unable to survive without controlling it, keeping other animal life back behind high fences and city walls. The price of our triumph is a singular loneliness, a sense of having once been richer for the chance encounters with wilder lives. Our love of zoos and nature films and bears in lobbies are all fueled by a common source, what C. S. Lewis called "the longing for other bloods." More recently the sociobiologist E. O. Wilson has bestowed upon it a genetic origin and called the longing *biophilia*, which he defines as an innate tendency to gravitate toward other life-forms.

"To explore and affiliate with life is a deep and complicated process in mental development," Wilson writes. "To an extent still undervalued in philosophy and religion, our existence depends on this propensity, our spirit is woven from it, hope rises on its currents."

If one knows just a little more about the black bears of New Jersey and eastern Pennsylvania, their presence on porches or even in lobbies is not so surprising, and certainly does not constitute a threat to human welfare. First of all, there is plenty of prime black bear habitat in the Poconos, and in the valley associated with the Kittatiny ridge in the northwest part of the state. Black bears prefer dense, coniferous forest and swamp, which provide both cover and food. Their diet consists mostly of succulent vegetation—tubers, fruits, berries, nuts, and young shoots—spiced now and then with honeycombs (bees included) and an occasional squirrel. When natural foods are scarce, garbage appeals greatly to bears, as does corn and the various snacks left out deliberately by bear-lovers.

According to Gary Alt, Pennsylvania's chief bear biologist and promoter, the steady supply of food from human sources accounts for the phenomenal health of bears in that state. Pennsylvania bears are larger than average, reach reproductive age sooner, and have bigger litters than black bears in any other part of the world, including the most remote wilderness. In New Jersey, meanwhile, Dunkin' Donuts supplies wildlife biologists with day-old bear enticers. According to Pat McConnell, who heads the state's bear project, the animals have discriminating tastes. One bear dislikes plain doughnuts—put out a bag and he'll defecate on it, then trample the doughnuts to pieces. But the same bear finds cream- or jelly-filled ones irresistible. Another bear hates chocolate, and carefully nibbles a doughnut out from beneath its chocolate icing.

The fact is, black bears are among a number of large mammals who can easily abide humans dwelling nearby, so long as they don't stir up trouble with poisons, guns, and bulldozers. Deer populations explode when they can feed effortlessly on the fringes of farms. Until recently, the fifteen-hundred square miles along New Jersey's northwestern border harbored the highest concentration of wild deer in North America. Raccoon and skunk long ago became adapted to human environments and human garbage. All over the world the animals live in our traces after dark. Red fox birth their litters in the Back Bay fens off Boston's Beacon Street. Coyote loop their trails through the traffic patterns of Los Angeles. In Italy, wolves, for so long the most feared enemies of civilization, tread softly down the roads leading to Rome.

As far as being a danger is concerned, black bears in the East have a disappointingly uneventful history. They are shy and easily frightened. Except in extremely rare cases, they attack only when cornered, remaining remarkably blasé even when their cubs are threatened. (Usually the mother will run away from where her cubs are hidden, apparently trying to distract the intruder.) Only one attack has been reported in New Jersey, and in that case the bear delivered only some superficial scratches as it scrambled to escape. No bear attacks have been reported in Pennsylvania for at least one hundred years.

"We have almost seven thousand bears in this state and twelve million people," says Gary Alt. "In literally thousands of encounters every year there has never been a single case of a serious injury."

Those are some of the bear facts. Our ambivalence toward wildlife, however, is a very ancient and potent force that had its beginnings before humanity itself, when our prehuman ancestors still foraged for fruit and tubers in the forest or on its fringes. Like other herbivores, these early hominids probably took little notice of other plant-eaters, amicably sharing territory with antelope, horses, and grazing elephants. There was much to fear, however, from lions, leopards, and other large predators. Lacking sharp teeth, strong antlers, or swift hooves, the hominids may have begun to evolve a greater intelligence partly as a way of outwitting predators. The early human who learned to build the safest sleeping nest high in a tree or develop cooperative defenses with companions would stand a better chance of passing on its genes for mental agility to the next generation.

Meat-eaters have even left their mark on our nightmares. Most carnivores stalk the night. Separation from one's parents once meant almost certain death. Human children in all cultures still fear being left alone in the dark, an "irrational" terror today, but one that made perfect sense in a darkness bristling with claws and curving teeth. The young ones who cried out survived to pass on the wisdom that predisposed them to beware the dark. (Fearless children donated their DNA, along with their body proteins, to feed the big cats.) The predators have vanished over time, but it will take many millennia to scour the human psyche of such a deeply embedded dread.

Some two to three million years ago, a change in our ancestors' diet utterly transfigured our relationship with the animals. In his book *The Cult of the Wild*, Boyce Rensberger discusses this as the first of three such transformations. Following some now-silent calling, for unclearly understood reasons, some hominids came out onto the plains and joined the ranks of the carnivores. Aided by their superior intelligence, they gradually became adept at scavenging and hunting, especially as they moved into virgin territory where unsuspecting prey species—which now included some former predators—were unfamiliar with their exceptional prowess. In North America, for instance, fossil evidence suggests that about thirteen thousand years ago human beings pushed south from Alaska a "wave of extinction" of mastodon, mammoths, and other large mammals.

Back then, there may have been very good reasons to beware of bears. Human beings had been inhabiting the Western Hemisphere long before this time, but their presence was negligible, in spite of the existence of a land bridge linking Alaska to the more densely populated regions of Asia. According to Valerius Geist, a zoologist at the University of Calgary in Canada, humankind's conquest of the continent might have been impeded by a giant "bulldog bear" *(Arctodus simus)*, a fearless superpredator as big as a grizzly but with the long, ground-swallowing legs of a cat. Humanity simply had to wait in Siberia until the unassailable bear disappeared, a victim of changing climate patterns.

With their enormous brains, the human hunters would certainly have been able to perceive that the animals they killed for food were featured like themselves and behaved very much the same, often living in family groups, with the mothers nursing their young just as human mothers do. They therefore had no reason to believe that the animals did not share the same thoughts and emotions—protective love of their young, anger, and tenderness, for example. It was reasonable to assume then that they would be immeasurably vengeful against a species like *Homo*, who killed so much. Because of this assumption, according to sociologist Richard Lewinsohn, humans began to pay homage to animals as a means of placating their wrath. This tendency to anthropomorphize them utterly altered our relationship with wildlife; from then on, animals lived a separate existence in the mind of humanity, giving shape and extension to our awakening self-awareness.

The recruitment of animals into myth and religion progressed steadily; there has not existed a culture without its animal totems and icons. Humankind's second transformation, however, added a new, bitter note to our songs of nature. Between ten and twenty thousand years ago, human societies began to grow their own food. As soon as we developed the techniques to cultivate some plants as crops, all others became weeds to be burned back and torn away. With the domestication of sheep, cattle, and other hoofed animals, our rival predators henceforth became deadly enemies.

Life on earth is not naturally patterned to accommodate farming. The hunger of a wolf is not the least bit changed by a fence between him and his prey; to an aphid, a leaf tastes the same whether it grows in a meadow or a hothouse. But as soon as we became dependent upon manipulating nature for our survival, Nature lost her innocence. Inoffensive co-tenants of the planet, such as the rat and the crow, suddenly were defined as vermin. After thousands of years, the redefinitions continue wherever we are still cutting into the wilderness. The African elephant, largest of the land mammals, each day gives up more of its natural habitat to farmland, retreating to national parks. Elephants consume trees faster than they can grow back on the reserved land; hence the parks have to deal not only with elephants, but with "the elephant problem." Should they return to the cultivated fields beyond the park, the elephants become large and and recalcitrant pests.

Human beings in wilderness areas still confront wildlife on this deeply competitive level. In much of the rest of the world, and certainly in the developed nations, our relationship has already passed long ago through a third transformation: a movement into villages and cities that effectively cut us off from any contact with wild animals in their natural milieu. Except for some domesticated guests and some rather placid hangers-on, those of us who dwell in cities and suburbs have virtually cleared our lives of any contact with our closest relatives on earth. It is now entirely "natural" for a man or woman to spend days, or even weeks, pursuing the imperatives of existence (seeking food, shelter, companionship, mates) without encountering another animal larger than a pigeon.

As Boyce Rensberger points out, this third transformation made it possible for humans to invest an animal with any attribute they wished, since there was no longer any opportunity to check the belief against reality. The popular notion of a lion, for instance, is that of a proud and noble hunter, when in fact lions are more typically scavengers, with a penchant for murder much greater than our own. Likewise gorillas—shy vegetarians in the wild—were easily transformed in the public eye into bloodthirsty monsters. From *Aesop's Fables* to *King Kong*, the animals came to serve, rather than excite, the human imagination.

Within the past three decades, humankind has taken the initial steps toward our final detachment from the rest of earthly creation. Technology has extended our reach to the point where we can seriously consider our place, not only on this planet, but in all that is beyond it. The word *extra-terrestrial*, as E. O. Wilson writes, "evokes reveries about still unexplored life, displacing the old and once-potent *exotic* that drew earlier generations to remote islands and jungled interiors."

Against the supposition of life beyond our planet we throw a new image of ourselves as "earthlings," equal not to the inhabitants of the earth, but of the sky—of gods, of life-forms yet to be apprehended and understood. Implicit in the word is the assumption that we alone have come to stand for earth, that when the stars yield their finer organisms, their new voices, their deeper intelligences, they will come for *us*, and we will go forth to meet them as the culmination of life on this planet. The other species are mere prototypes, alternative models that did not fulfill their promise. They are rapidly becoming expendable, even in our fictions. The new foils of our imagination, the aliens, may have exaggerated hat sizes, but otherwise we imagine them remarkably human—hairless beings that walk on two legs and express a lot of complicated emotions. Who needs fur in space? For those with their eyes on the heavens, a bear in the backyard is a reminder of how bound we still are to purely terrestrial concerns.

In this version of our future, the animals will shrink to historical artifacts. At the present, human-accelerated rate of extinction, some one million animal species could vanish before the turn of the century—approximately one species gone every hour. Every year an area of tropical rain forest the size of the state of Maine is leveled for cultivation. The destruction of animal habitats has led to the prospect that in the next century virtually all exotic wildlife will exist only in zoos, managed by captive breeding programs.

Against such powerful trends, does it make any difference that a few new bears turn up in New Jersey? That they *do* matter has something to do with that quickening of the senses, the common, "biophilic" thrill we feel at the thought of them among us, sleeping peacefully through the winter in our foundations. There are better illustrations of the interdependence of human life and animal life, but few more explicit or closer to home. New Jersey is about as thoroughly humanized a place as one can find.

Nose-to-nose with nature. Like its cousins in the backyards of suburban New Jersey, this black bear in Alberta's Banff National Park has little fear of cross-species contact. These human nature lovers, however, may be getting more than they bargained for.

Toward New York City to the east, the factoried flatlands lie sore and exposed, overlaid with decades of soot from acrid smoke. The population of the state is 90 percent urban—a richly varied human milieu, but one not accustomed to other large mammals with the freedom to roam. The bears' existence in New Jersey is forever tenuous, depending much on human concern, human whim. Even the bear country to the northwest is largely a by-product of a grand human project gone awry, the collapse of the Tock Falls Dam project in the 1960s.

Until a few years ago, the New Jersey bears were thought to be only visitors, restless males that swam the Delaware or trotted over a bridge at night from Pennsylvania. But lately they seem to be settling down for a longer stay. In 1983 a graduate student named Richard Pais reported the discovery of birthing dens, the first in the state in modern memory. The bears have settled in, their population growing with a steady trickle of immigrants and born-and-bred New Jersey black bears. For whatever the reason, the bears are among us, depending upon us.

This book is mostly concerned with large, globe-striding earthlings like the bears, animals with whom we share the top of the food chain on land. In a superficial sense they are the dominant life-forms in their environments, by virtue of the fact that no other species eats them. The great bears, the tigers and wolves and human beings are the end products of countless biological transformations, of energy held in the temporary custody of one organism and freed from its cellular confinement by death, only to fuel the life processes of another organism further up the chain. But from another point of view, these are the least significant of creatures. If the earth were to lose the large mammals, life would adjust and adapt. Compared to the silent assimilations, the unceasing munching going on at the other end of the food chain, all the bone-gnawing carnivores in the world contribute next to nothing by their living and dying. A large mammal nearing extinction is probably a sign that an ecosystem is suffering some deeper distress farther down in its workings. If species at the base were to disappear—the blue-green algae, or the plates of marine plankton—the whole edifice of life on earth would collapse like a torn beach ball.

By what measurement, then, do we define our own domination over the other species? The truth is we don't even know what they are. It has recently been discovered, for example, that the forest canopy of the tropical rain forest holds such an abundance of unknown species that we have to completely revise our notions of the diversity of life. Previous estimates called for between three and ten million species on earth; now some scientists say that there may be as many as thirty million species of insects alone. Nevertheless, a single bulldozer can go a long way toward eliminating a measurable number of those species. Doesn't that argue well for our domination, if not our common sense?

Not really. Quite a different animal—the termite—benefits much more from our "slash-and-burn" methods of land clearing than we ourselves do, undergoing a population boom every time a new acre of rain forest is opened to the sky. One expert, Pat Zimmerman of the National Center for Atmospheric Research, estimates that there may be two hundred quadrillion termites on earth, three-quarters of a ton of termites for every human being. Every one of these insects is a tiny factory for methane gas, a product of the digestion of cellulose. If Zimmerman is correct in his estimates, the termites account for a hundred million tons of methane poured into our atmosphere each year—enough, perhaps, to have a significant effect upon the composition of the upper atmosphere and to alter the climate of the earth.

In the long run, the termites' influence upon the planet earth may have even greater consequences than our own. But, strictly speaking, the insects themselves cannot claim responsibility for the methane. Unable to digest the wood particles they ingest, the termites have evolved a symbiotic arrangement with dozens of species of protozoa. These one-celled creatures swim about in the insect's hindgut, digesting the wood for the benefit of themselves and their host. To produce the methane, however, at least some of these microorganisms need help from even tinier creatures. As Sidney Tamm of the Boston University Marine Program at the Marine Biological Laboratory in Woods Hole has shown, one species of protozoan found in the gut of a Florida termite cannot move about without the aid of rod-shaped bacteria aligned on the protozoan's outer membrane. Whirling their propellerlike tails in unison, the bacteria push the protozoan through the termite's gut like so many tugboats nudging the *QE2* through a crowded harbor.

Where, among such spirals of interdependence, is there space for a concept like domination? When man is put back where he belongs, as a part of the movement of life rather than a self-appointed benefactor and overseer, then the word "earthling" takes on new meaning. It must include *all* of earth's inhabitants. As we journey through space, we journey together. On the scale of the stars, we are all part of the same life-form.

Over the past few decades, at the same time that we have been developing the technology to bring the universe closer within reach, field biologists—trained biophiliacs, one might say—have been studying the nature of animals in a completely new light. Beginning with the work of people such as Clarence Ray Carpenter and Frank Fraser Darling in the 1930s, scientists have made it a passionate concern to observe—over a long period of time and with as little interference as possible from the observer or from human preconceptions—animal behavior as it exists in natural habitats. In so doing they have brought us closer in understanding to our co-tenants on the planet than we have been since humankind still lived among them.

This book, the first of a series of companion volumes to the *Nature* television program, is a journey to these mammalian worlds. Relying on the most recent evidence of biologists in the field, it is an attempt to reestablish, through science, something of the ancient bonds. From the backyards of New Jersey we will move away from human habitats to the floating realm of the black bear's cousin, the polar bear. As we travel geographically from ice to forest to desert and beyond, we will also travel up progressive levels of biological organization—from the physiology of bear fat to the politics of life in a wolf pack. The book is not intended to be an encyclopedia of animals, and there are numerous species scarcely mentioned or not mentioned at all that offer just as splendid alternatives to our own evolutionary course. With one enormous exception, all life-forms on earth exist in a sort of raucous interdependence with all others. Each animal has evolved to become, gloriously, itself. Certainly humankind cannot abandon its course as the "dominant" species, any more than a tree shrew or a house cat can assume it. But by exploring the lives of other earthlings, perhaps we can penetrate our isolation and return from the journey more human than before.

CHAPTER ONE

Creature of Light

I

Truly ambitious travelers, from Dante to Dorothy of Oz, begin their journeys by getting lost. We too should set off on less familiar ground, in a place not quite so tangled up with the affairs of human beings. Some two thousand miles north of New Jersey, the human population thins out considerably, and a little farther still, approaches zero. This is the domain of the white bear—a great, tumbling collar of ice encircling the top of the globe, confined on one side by the permanently frozen polar cap, and on the other by abrupt intrusions of islands, continents, and the open sea.

Slow violence works upon the face of

27

the polar world. Unyielding masses of ice are thrown against each other by currents and tides. Vertical ice sheets called *pressure ridges* are thrust upward, their rising accompanied by long, eerie shrieks, as if the earth were protesting another scar on its countenance. Pressure ridges may climb six stories into the air, catching the wind like sails, setting in motion pans of ice the size of Manhattan. Though a large floe drifts along at only two or three miles per day, several billion tons of ice do not have to move very fast to make a dent in anything it meets. All around, the grumbling of ice against ice merges into a continuous complaint. Collapsed ridges lie about like ruined temples. Ribbons of water called *leads* cut through the pack, opening and closing haphazardly. Along shore leads, where the pack ice shoulders up against stable, landfast ice, the terrain changes with every shift in the tide. Such places should be avoided by those who treasure security and order. Finding your bearings can be unsettling when the landscape slides into the sea before your eyes.

In winter, with temperatures falling to forty degrees below zero, one can trek over several horizons worth of solid ice without encountering visible life. But even in the pack there are places that never freeze, areas of open water called *polynyas*, thought to be caused by the power of wind, tides, and currents. Polynyas vary in size from a few hundred yards to several miles across. Some famous ones, such as the North Water Polynya between Canada's Ellesmere Island and Greenland, are as large as the largest lakes on earth.

A small polynya in the distance is revealed by the mist rising from it, a vague stain on the horizon. Even such a modest patch of open water, a few hundred yards across, bristles with life. Polar cod and other coldwater fish feed on schools of tiny crustaceans, and in turn contribute to the diet of seals. Walruses scout the bottom for shellfish and shrimp. In winter, when the walruses mate, the water rings with the calls of the bulls, their repeated patterns of thumpings and clicks. Above, ravens circle around the stripped carcass of a seal left behind by a white bear. The birds await their turn while an Arctic fox tears at the seal's flesh. Occasionally the black pool ripples with the silver flukes of narwhals, sounding in unison, or a pod of surfacing belugas; sweet-tempered, whistling whales with large brown eyes.

The winter winds have cleaned the banks of the polynya free of snow, and with no shadows to lend it definition, the terrain seems to swell and recede, softly opaque. The water's surface is mottled with a drifting jumble of floes. A hundred yards down the bank a plump ringed seal lies on the ice, its acrid, musky scent identifying it as a sexually active male. The seal has hauled up on the ice for a rest, but his motions are restless and un-resolved, like an insomniac busy adjusting pillows and bedcovers. His ner-vousness is fully justified. Ringed seals are the favorite prey of the white bear, another frequent visitor to the polynya. The seal twists over on his side, scanning the dim horizon. Another of his kind surfaces a few yards from the bank. The seal sniffs the air peevishly and rolls over on his other

side. For a few moments he lays his head down on the ice and closes his eyes, but half a minute later is up again. The other seal has disappeared. The bull peers into the gray distance and scratches his flank with a hind flipper.

Suddenly a bright shaft of sun carves through the bank of clouds overhead, and all around the ice breaks into color. The surface of the water shifts from black to emerald, as if someone has thrown back a curtain, and each angle of drifting ice catches the sun and declares its own bold shade of azure and aquamarine. The banks around the pool, given back their shadows, fall crisply into the water. The terrain beyond distills into a textured, rippling patchwork of white shapes, all aglare—save for one, small, cream-colored hummock a hundred yards away that remains curiously opaque and then seems to vanish altogether.

Closer to the shore, the seal takes full advantage of the sunlight, stretching showily on his belly like a small-town playboy by a public pool. With the wind fairly still and the air temperature rising, he lets his long lashes close over his eyes and slips into a nap. He would have been safer had he taken one last look over his shoulder. The unobtrusive, cream-colored mound of snow has reappeared, only this time it is only fifty yards from the seal and slowly creeping closer.

The domain of the ice bear covers an enormous swath of territory. It was once thought that the bears of the Arctic comprised one large, scattered population of animals, wandering at will around the circumpolar collar. Biologists have since identified several discrete populations, each returning in the fall to established denning areas and exhibiting certain coherent characteristics. In Canada and Alaska, for instance, the polar bears seem to be physically larger on average the farther west one travels. The bears seldom travel far inland, so geographical features such as mountain ranges and rivers have little effect on their wanderings. Naturally, bear populations migrate across man's political borders that nominally define polar geography. A bear summering north of Prudhoe Bay in Alaska might winter in Canadian waters to the east. One who spends the cold months killing seals near Wrangel Island in the Soviet Union might turn up later along the Alaskan coast, foraging for seaweed within a few meters of a corporate oil rig.

Bear experts believe there are several loosely defined polar bear population centers: one around Wrangel Island and eastern Siberia, others in western and northern Alaska, and another scattered among the islands of northern Canada. Further east, populations surround Greenland and link Norway's Svalbard archipelago, the Soviet Union's Franz Josef Land, and central Siberia. However, for all the acreage it enjoys, the polar bear is as rigidly confined as a turtle in a pond. Its range is limited, first of all, by the range of the ringed seal. Polar bears are the most carnivorous of the bear species, and though they embellish their diet with a variety of other food, they must rely on seal to survive. Where ringed seals are scarce, so are

Polar bear migration patterns are often monitored from aircraft and even from satellites. In 1977 a female bear fitted with a radio collar was tracked for 228 days by a NASA satellite. Released in June near Point Barrow, Alaska, the bear headed east briefly, then abruptly turned around and trekked to Siberia, covering a total of 820 miles.

bears, and where seals flourish, so do their predators. Ringed seals, like all marine mammals, require oxygen to breathe, so they frequent areas where they can find open leads or polynyas, or where they can carve air holes in relatively thin, young ice with the heavy claws on their foreflippers. Thus the polar bear thrives best on the shifting, broken, half-frozen sea, where the seals are most accessible.

There is another reason for the polar bear's natural confinement to the Arctic ice. The presence of some populations many miles from the seal-rich shore during summer suggests that in the past the species' range was not necessarily restricted to the broken edge of the frozen sea. Long ago the white bears roamed much farther to the south; only in the last 250 years have their ranges and numbers been severely reduced by the advance of European hunters and whalers. In the seventeenth century, bears lived on the northern island of Japan, and are still occasionally reported as far south

as Labrador and the southeastern coast of Alaska. Healthy populations, protected by inaccessible swamps, can be found along the lower Hudson Bay
and James Bay in Canada. In fact, every now and then some Newfoundland
farmer steps outside on a fine July morning to find a great white bear
grazing placidly among his cows. Perhaps the lone bear drifted south on a
floe and took to the water when the ice melted beneath him. Almost invariably, such drifters are quickly shot, leaving the people, now out of
danger, to decide just how dangerous the bear might have been.

How much of a threat are they? Gruesome reports of bear-beheaded
sailors repeatedly surface in the chronicles of early explorers. The man-
hating fury of the bears was exaggerated, but modern encounters show that
an excessively hungry or sick bear will attack a person. Starving subadult
males are the most serious threat. When bears are angered they stand stiff-
legged, upper lip protruding, and utter a soft "chuffing" sound. Researchers
on Cape Churchill complain of having had their observation tower impa-
tiently shaken by a bear, as if to pry loose the human fruit from above.
Since 1967 two people have been killed by bears in the Churchill area.

Most bears are aware, however, that human beings are far more dangerous to them than they are to humans. Bears unfamiliar with men might

*Ferocious white bears were common in nineteenth-century depictions of the hard-
ships of Arctic exploration. In fact, only a sick, starving, or cornered bear will
attack a man. Here a gang of bloodthirsty, man-eating bears mounts an amphibious assault on a boatload of desperate whalers.*

have their curiosity momentarily aroused, but only rarely their appetite or anger. With no rivals to their domination of the Arctic, and reluctant under most circumstances to work up a heat under their heavy fur, most bears incline toward an easy-going *noblesse oblige*. They save their energy for hauling seals out of water, fighting for mating privileges, and defending cubs. In general, the grizzly bear, and perhaps even some western black bears, pose a greater danger to man. Jack Lentfer, one of Alaska's leading polar bear researchers, points out that these other ursines have caused several human deaths in Alaska in recent years, while the polar bear has killed no one. Scientists like Lentfer performing mark-and-recovery studies dread an iced-up airplane engine carburetor more than an unprovoked bear attack.

The polar bear is nevertheless a formidable presence. Males of the species often weigh in excess of half a ton. In 1984 a giant, sixteen-year-old male was tranquilized from a helicopter near Coral Harbour on Canada's Southampton Island. Too big to hoist onto the helicopter's scales, the bear's weight was estimated by his enormous girth to be 1,766 pounds—the largest polar bear on record. But the mass of the animal is as much a mark of sound energy management as of carnivorous intent. The greater one's mass, the less surface area one has exposed to the air in relation to total body volume. Most Arctic species are larger than their southern counterparts because bigger bodies conserve more heat.

There is something else about this bear that stirs our deepest apprehensions. Everyone knows that the animal's fur is white, a great shaggy disguise. No other land animal exists so large and so clean of color. Perhaps it is this emphatic whiteness, wrapped around such power, that sets the animal apart in our imaginations. The polar bear is the largest predator on land, yet it possesses an almost indecent ability to *blend in*, its white-shrouded shape disappearing against the cold geometry of the ice pack. In *Moby-Dick*, Herman Melville turned to the bear to borrow horror for his mythic whale: It was the polar bear's "smooth, flaky whiteness" that so inspires our distrust, "an abhorrent mildness, even more loathsome than terrific." The bear seems an eerie contradiction, a superfluity of muscle lodged in nonconscious form, as if a chunk of hardened snow were to suddenly break off an iceberg, come alive, and charge across the drifts.

In the Arctic, of course, it pays to be white, for predators and prey alike. The polar bear acquired his color fairly recently, perhaps as little as a hundred thousand years ago, when *Ursus etruscus*, the ancestor of both polar and brown bears, ventured north onto the ice. The ice and the cold and an awakening taste for seal molded a creature distinctly different in form and habit from its cousins to the south. The brown, or grizzly, bear *(Ursus arctos)* has a massive head and a concave facial profile. Its high shoulders produce a sloping back, emphasizing the animal's robust build. The polar bear has a more aristocratic profile—a long neck tapering to a smaller, V-shaped head. It carries itself low to the ground, out of the wind and out of sight.

In spite of their great bulk, polar bears are extremely agile on the broken sea ice. In short bursts, they can run as fast as twenty-five miles per hour.

The carnivorous polar bear may in fact be something of an evolutionary throwback. Bears share their early history with dogs. Fossil evidence suggests that twenty million years ago a diminutive bear about the size of a fox branched off from the canine line. This so-called Dawn Bear was probably strictly carnivorous. Gradually, however, the succeeding species of bear adapted more and more to an omnivorous diet of tubers, berries, small rodents, and fish. To fashion a meat-eater again from a brown bear required some important adaptations. The brown bear's long blunted claws, well-suited for digging in soil, were tightened over time into needle-sharp curves, the better to cling to ice and clasp tight to struggling prey. The surface of the brown bear's flat cheek teeth, adapted for chewing vegetable matter, grew longer and turned jagged and sharp—adaptations for tearing hide, blubber, and flesh.

The sea and the ice, meanwhile, worked their own changes. Like seals and whales, polar bears wear a bulky layer of blubber beneath their skin that keeps them warm even in near-freezing water. They are exceptionally strong swimmers. Fishing boats have reported bears paddling along, without apparent distress, thirty and forty miles from the nearest landfall. Jack Lentfer once came across a bear in the open sea, a hundred miles from the nearest ice. Under water, the bear's beady black eyes are no more powerful than those of an entirely terrestrial mammal, suggesting perhaps a fairly recent accommodation to a marine environment. Up on the ice, however, the bear's vision appears to be good, especially at night when the tapetum, a layer of tissue behind the retina, backlights the retina.

Polar bear fur, meanwhile, did more than change color to adapt to the Arctic. Like that of most cold-weather mammals, the bear's pelt consists of a layer of tough guard hairs protecting a thermal blanket of finer hair beneath. One of the best insulating materials against cold is air, and each fiber of the polar bear's pelt is a hollow tube which traps air within it. In water, the pelt loses over 90 percent of its insulative value. Polar bear cubs, not yet supplied with their load of subcutaneous fat, have to ride on their mother's back when she paddles across a lead.

Despite all the adaptations for thermal protection, polar bears must still take cover in a severe winter blizzard, when the wind throws the snow about in piercing sheets and the wind chill sends the apparent temperature down to −100° F. Virtually all animal life scurries for shelter under such conditions, digging holes into drifts, cowering in rock crevices or under boulders. Only the musk ox, a small, stocky creature more closely related to goats than to cattle, can face up to an Arctic storm without protection. The guard hairs of the musk ox, covering all but its lips and nostrils, protect a luxurious mat of underwool. Called *qiviut* by the Eskimos, this fiber is longer than cashmere and only two-thirds the diameter. The *qiviut* needed to knit a dress weighs as little as four ounces.

The musk ox is the northernmost of hoofed mammals, surviving through the long winter on sparse grasses, which it finds by pounding through snow with its forefeet. The animal is believed to have originated on the tundra of Asia, where it evolved a curious method of defense against predators. At the first sign of danger the herd will run to high ground or into shallow snow, where the adults form a tight line so that any attacker is immediately confronted with a solid wall of horns. The calves fall in place behind, and if more predators attack, the line closes around the calves to form a circle. From this phalanx, individuals launch furious counter-charges, the other oxen closing ranks behind. Once in formation, each musk ox in the herd will continue to fight until the attacker is repelled.

Such a strategy works well against wolves, and presumably was effective against now-extinct northern feline predators. The defense is pathetically insubstantial, however, against even a solitary human hunter. Apparently, primitive man drove the Eurasian musk ox to extinction with nothing more than bows and arrows. The animal's habit of loyalty to fallen herd members also does little to help the species survive against human predators. Before a hunter can capture the pelt of a single animal, the whole snorting mass of them must be shot. When only two remain they

Musk oxen, relatives of sheep, rely on a cooperative defensive strategy—a snorting, steaming phalanx—to protect themselves from their enemies.

will fight on, rump to rump; when only one is left, it will back up against a boulder or drift, or if nothing else presents itself, even a little rock.

In the past, the North American musk ox provided food for Eskimos, but the population rapidly crumbled before the firearms of European hunters. Only a 1917 Canadian pro-hibition of killing the animal saved it from extinction. Recently, efforts have been made to domesticate the musk ox for its fine wool. The last naturally occurring populations in northern Canada and Greenland are recovering, and populations have been successfully reintroduced into Alaska and Norway.

Musk ox fur is dark brown, even in winter, when a white coat might be a better defense against predators. Perhaps the evolution of a cooperative strategy of defense dispensed with the ancestral musk oxen's need to change colors with the seasons. Camouflage aside, it would certainly be an advantage in the cold northern climate to have as dark a coat as possible, the better to soak up energy from the sun. Desert animals face the opposite necessity; most have evolved light-colored coats to ward off intense solar radiation.

Then what are we to make of the polar bear's pale disguise? Has the bear sacrificed body warmth for killing efficiency? Surprisingly, polar bear fur isn't really white at all. Under a microscope, the hairs are revealed to be transparent and free of pigment. They appear white to us (and to seals) only because they catch and reflect all of the visible wavelengths of light. According to biologist David Lavigne of the University of Guelph in Canada, the bear enjoys a sort of personal "greenhouse effect." The gigantic shaggy pelt is really a forest of needlelike crystals, bouncing the sun's brilliance among their surfaces, soaking up the meager Arctic heat and holding it close against the animal's skin. The longer, heat-producing wavelengths of energy are trapped by the transparent cover of hair, just as the glass roof of a greenhouse keeps warmth from the soil from escaping. A too-dark coat might actually place its Arctic owner at something of a disadvantage: Warmth would be caught on the *outside* of the pelt, where it could be lost to the wind and body movements. The best place to be dark is underneath.

Indeed, under its white outer coat, the polar bear's hidden skin is as black as shadows. If Melville had been aware of the polar bear's true color, perhaps his loathing for the animal would have been tempered. In a sense the polar bear is an apparition; what we see is not the animal itself, but a creature of light, an animated, tangled surface of radiant energy. Regarded thus, the bear's magnificent pelt renders him far more awe-inspiring than Melville could have imagined. In that carpet of prisms that he wears upon his back, the polar bear captures and commits to his use the sun itself.

Lord of the land of the midnight sun. The polar bear survives the Arctic deep freeze beneath a coat designed to trap heat in an undercoat of fine hair next to its black, energy-absorbing skin.

Return now to the polynya. The sun slants off the facets of drifting ice, tossing scraps of rainbows about in the vapor rising from the pool. The male seal still basks in the relative warmth, while a creamy mound of stalking polar bear approaches downwind. The bear, a mature female, keeps her huge form low to the ground, lifting each paw from the ice with the delicate patience of a cat creeping through dry leaves. Her hunt began three hundred yards away, its progress disguised by the jumbled field of white shapes behind her. Taking advantage of every rough outcropping of ice for cover, the bear inches forward, eyes fixed on the seal. Sometimes she crouches so low that she must drag herself along by her forepaws.

Abruptly, from twenty yards away, the bear rushes forward, arriving at the napping seal's side at approximately the same time that the seal lifts his head for another look around. His view is obstructed, fatally, by a paw the size of a hatbox, and in less time than it takes for his brain to register an image, the seal's skull has lost all its integrity and shape. The bear grips her dead prey about the neck with her jaws and carries him a few yards from the water's edge. Immediately she stoops to eat, clipping the flesh from the fat, using her pin-sharp incisors like dainty shears. Curiously, she consumes only the hide and blubber, leaving the meat behind on the ice for the foxes and seabirds.

The ringed seal accounts for some 85 percent of the polar bear's diet. The remainder is made up of catches of bearded seal—a relatively enormous cousin to the ringed seal weighing up to eight hundred pounds and reaching a length of nine feet—as well as feasts of carrion, occasionally a narwhal or beluga, and a sampling of vegetation and small mammals for bears who summer on the land. On average, a bear will kill a seal once every five days, or some fifty over the course of a hunting season.

Ringed seals are one of the smallest of the pinnepeds, about four-and-a-half feet in length. In appearance they are difficult to distinguish from the familiar harbor seals, whose playful sociability in zoos endear them to human beings. Ringed seals are not quite such an attraction in captivity, since they are extremely hostile to each other. Their lack of cooperative social life has much to do with their bear-beset circumstances in the wild. According to Ian Stirling, a polar bear specialist who has also written extensively about seals, while there could be some advantage to the seals if they maintained communal breathing holes and kept a mutual watch for bears, the liabilities of such an arrangement outweigh the benefits. When a bear attacks, there is no time to stand in line waiting to get back through the hole and into the water. In winter ice, each ringed seal excavates its own collection of breathing holes, staunchly defending them with both sham and real attacks from any other ringed seal who might be rising for a bit of air. Underwater, they bark threats at each other. On the ice, dominant seals might even deny younger individuals a chance to reenter the water, once they've hauled out for a rest. The hole then freezes over, forcing the juvenile to find another route back to the water. Meanwhile, it is a morsel served up on a platter for any passing bear.

A full-grown ringed seal.

The ringed seal's breathing holes, known to the Eskimos as *aglos*, may be only a couple of inches wide at the surface, but in winter the seal must scratch and gnaw through as much as ten feet of solid ice to keep that slim channel open. As the winter progresses and the ice thickens, the *aglos* will gradually take on an inverted funnel shape, broadening to several feet at the base. The more breathing holes a seal builds, the greater will be its fishing area, and each seal will maintain as many holes as the temperature will allow. Late in winter, a seal will be hard-pressed to keep more than a half dozen holes open at one time. If the seal loses track of his *aglos*, or if they should all freeze over, cutting off his route to the surface, he will surely suffocate.

The seal's breathing holes thus figure very importantly in the polar bear's life as well. "Stalk hunts," such as the one described above, actually make up only 20 percent of the bear's hunting attempts, and more often than not end in failure, with the seal scurrying to safety over the bank. The most common and presumably most reliable hunting tactic is the "still hunt," or ambush. Aided by a sense of smell believed to be among the most acute on earth, the bear first locates a breathing hole, often buried under three feet of snow. Then the bear simply plops down on its hind-quarters to wait. The colder the temperature, the fewer *aglos* the seal will be able to keep open; consequently the chances are greater that the seal will surface to a hole with a bear hanging over the rim. Late winter and early spring are the best times to catch seals in this manner. Though the

Apparently accomplished in the science of the "still hunt," this very fat, 1,500-pound male keeps his huge bulk low against the ice to avoid detection.

wait may be long, odds are the owner of the *aglo* will eventually return for air. Charles Jonkel, a bear expert now studying grizzlies farther south, remembers coming across an iced-over breathing hole sprayed with blood. Next to it were four dish-shaped depressions melted in the snow: one where the bear's forepaws and snout lay together, one each for the hindpaws, and one for the anus.

When a seal surfaces to its *aglos*, it lets forth a loud and foul-smelling gush of air from its lungs. If a bear is waiting, the seal has probably breathed its last. The bear plunges its forearm into the hole, and in one motion smashes the seal's skull and drags the whole corpse onto the ice. If the seal is larger around than its breathing hole, the bear will simply break as many bones as necessary to squeeze it through. Using its teeth, a bear can pull from the water a bearded seal weighing as much as the bear itself.

Usually, a successful hunter will quickly devour most of what it wants of its kill, since there is always the danger that some larger bear will happen along and commandeer the catch. Polar bears rarely leave the table without washing up, and after feasting on the seal for twenty or thirty minutes, the bear will typically stand over the water, dipping in its forepaws and licking its muzzle clean. Reports that polar bears exult after a kill, rolling around in the snow and waving their paws in the air, are much exaggerated. All their thermoregulative equipment is needed to conserve body heat, and the least exertion puts a bear at risk of overheating—another reason, perhaps, that the bear prefers still-hunting to a strenuous stalk.

During late February and early March, ringed seals prepare birthing chambers in the snow above their breathing holes, giving birth in mid-March. This is a good time of year to be a polar bear. Birthing chambers are nearly indistinguishable by sight, but a bear can smell them out with chilling precision. Creeping up to within a few yards, the bear rushes forward and smashes the snow roof with both forepaws. If the lairs are protected by compacted layers of snow, the bear may adopt a sort of piledriver approach, pounding repeatedly on the domed top of the birthing chamber.

Ringed seal pups are a favorite prey of bears in spring. Young seals come into the world wearing a creamy-white birth coat that molts after a few weeks and is replaced by the silver-ringed pelt of the adult.

Not all individuals are large enough to gain entry to the lairs by such brute force, and there is one case of a bear, weighing only two hundred or three hundred pounds, who may have used its wits instead. A smashed-in *aglo* was discovered with a fifty-pound chunk of ice within it. A trail of bear tracks and drag marks led to a larger mass of ice, whose jagged contours matched those of the piece in the breathing hole. Apparently the bear, having failed to beat in the seal's chamber with its paws, dragged the ice over and heaved it through the *aglo*. There was no blood on the snow, however, so whatever tactic the bear may have used, the seal seems to have escaped.

Over the past century there have been numerous accounts of polar bears heaving chunks of ice about or using other tools to aid their hunt.

Legend has it that a stalking polar bear will obscure his prominent black nose by pushing a piece of ice along with his snout. It is more likely that the bear keeps his dark nose exposed, so that at a distance it would appear to the quarry as nothing more threatening than another seal resting on the ice.

The most common involve the polar bear's relationships with its "arch foe," the walrus. Polar bears and walruses are pretty equally matched, but according to the reports of early explorers, bears were seen to tip the battle in their favor by first lofting an iceball at the walrus's head. No modern

When feeding, bears are occasionally interrupted by both larger bears and smaller competitors, so they've learned it is always best to gobble up the best parts quickly. Here a flock of herring gulls waits while a mother bear and her cubs finish their meal.

researchers have been able to confirm such behavior, and most are skeptical. Zoo bears, however, have been known to throw large chunks of ice and other objects around in their cages, and one bear feeding on a mound of musk ox carrion was seen to keep an annoying bunch of huskies away by pitching hunks of meat at them.

In 1910 a naturalist named Manniche reported the extraordinary discovery of a polar bear den composed partly of neatly carved blocks of ice. Another bear, or perhaps the same one, apparently piled similar blocks around a stash of seal meat.

Because the ability to manipulate tools is touted as one of the best indications of intelligence in animals, human beings snap to attention when they hear such unexpected reports. We are a lonely species, always eager to hear that other earthlings are more like us than we thought. But Manniche was probably mistaken. Bears do not *need* to go to such extremes to build dens or cupboards. Illustrations of animal intelligence are more interesting (and believable) when they show the animal making sense on its own terms, in situations that demand ingenuity. An investigator working with Charles Jonkel, for instance, once came upon a foot snare that had been neatly defused by a bear. By all indications, the bear had piled rocks on the trap until it sprung, whereupon the bear, unharmed, made off with the bait.

Historical accounts of bears beaning walruses, meanwhile, only slightly outnumber reports of walruses skewering bears, or the two of them found locked in an embrace of death. These reports may also be biased in favor of a good story. A full-grown walrus would make short work of a polar bear in the water, though it is hard to imagine what would provoke such an attack. On land, the situation is changed. While polar bears will keep their distance from an adult bull, they have been known to stalk the occasional calf or even a female hauled out on the ice away from her companions. Usually the bear charges the herd in the hope that a calf will be left behind in the rush for the safety of the water.

Walruses may be particularly wary of bears in polynyas and other areas where their route of escape is limited. Ian Stirling reported one example of a large group of walruses around a polynya in the high Canadian Arctic who were able to ward off a threatening bear by what appeared to be a well-coordinated defense. After several unsuccessful charges at individual walruses, the bear threatened a group of six, who quickly took to the water, swimming out into the middle of the pool and watching the bear circle around them on the ice. One of the walruses swam toward the bear, who retreated from the water's edge. The bear made several more attempts at other groups, but each time they seemed to anticipate her approach, as if they had somehow been forewarned. Suddenly a couple of dozen walruses surfaced and charged. Two of them rose up in the water, and rolling forward in a dive, smacked their hind flippers on the water's surface. The sound was as loud as gunshot, and the bear quickly turned on her heel and fled. Dr. Stirling surmises that the walruses may have been communicating the bear's position to each other with underwater vocalizations.

Polar bears share their northern domain with walruses, but the two great mammals only rarely pose a threat to each other. Walruses spend much of their time submerged—eating, courting, and mating in the water, and hauling up on the ice only to rest. Water conducts heat twenty times better than air, and for the animal to live in both worlds demands very specialized adaptations. When the walrus dives underwater, its blood supply is pulled inward, its blood-drained blubber providing a thick blanket of insulation. A surfacing walrus is bleached white. Air temperatures above 0° F. quickly trigger a process called "vasodilation," in which the warm blood surges back to the skin where it can be cooled. The walrus then assumes its reddish-brown complexion.

The walrus's handsomest features are its arching tusks, second only to the elephant's in length and quality. Until recently it was believed that the tusks were used primarily to rake the sea bottom for clams and other shellfish. It now appears that the walrus relies on its sensitive snout to muzzle around in the dark for food, consuming thousands of clams each day, along with a salad of shrimp, crabs, sea cucumbers, sea squirts, and even an occasional seal. Shellfish burrowed deep in the sea bottom are drilled out with a powerful jet of water squirted from the walrus's mouth.

Tusks are used as weapons and sometimes to help the walrus drag his bulk out of the water. But their primary purpose is to determine each bull's status in the highly gregarious

Each summer the appropriately named Walrus Islands in Alaska's Bristol Bay attract thousands of male walruses who haul out on the shores to rest in the warm sun. Their thick hides protect them from injuring each other with their tusks.

walrus society. Well-endowed bulls display their tusks at every opportunity, moving unopposed into the most comfortable positions in the hauled-out herd. Tusk size is particularly important to the males during breeding seasons. Actual fights are rare, occurring only when two males find each other's tusks about equal in length. The walrus protects itself in such battles with a knobbled layer of skin three inches thick about the neck.

As the sea ice breaks up, polar bears reveal their amphibious natures, swimming with ease among the floes.

As the days become warmer in late spring, the pack ice begins to "puddle," offering additional opportunities for the seal to surface out of reach of bears. Patience will yield fewer and fewer fruits, and the great bears increasingly turn to their wits to survive. Only the seal's breathing holes have swelled to a few yards, some clever bears swim under them and turn over, so that the seal, darting back into the water, will find himself instead diving into a bellyful of white fur.

Another technique is an aquatic variation of the stalk hunt, an enterprise that proves again this massive beast's ability to render itself lethally vague.

Having spotted a seal napping on a floe, a bear slips backward into the water like a cautious bather entering a pool. With all but its black snout submerged, there is little to betray his approach but a hushed, V-shaped ripple not much bigger than the wake of a duck. If for some reason the seal grows apprehensive, the bear can dive and continue the stalk under-water for up to two minutes. Reaching within ten yards of the prey, the bear surfaces for one last look at the seal's position, dives again, and ex-plodes out of the water alongside the seal. In the same motion he springs up on the ice and lunges for the prey. Water stalking, however, requires considerable skill, and it is unlikely that any but the most experienced hunters are consistently successful at it. Ian Stirling once watched an adult female bear perform a curiously individualized stalk. Instead of keeping her body totally submerged except for the snout, she thrust her hindquarters vertically into the air, as if to fool the seals into mistaking her for a bit of floating ice. Apparently, the seals seemed unalarmed by this hairy iceberg, but still managed to escape at the last moment.

As the proportion of open water to ice increases, the advantage in such contests turns toward the seal. While bears are strong swimmers over long distances, they are no match for a seal in speed and agility. Some seal species are known to swim at speeds of six hundred yards a minute, and can remain submerged ten times as long as a bear. Ring-necked seals have been seen swimming circles around a polar bear as it lumbered through the water. One can hardly imagine a seal enjoying a more gratifying sport.

II

The coming of warmer weather brings a new abundance of large life to the Arctic—narwhals and their relatives, the white belugas, swim in through the open leads in iridescent formations. They are followed soon after by gigantic bowhead whales, creatures reaching sixty-five feet in length. All of these whales have long been essential resources to the Eskimo, and until recently were taken in great numbers by commercial whalers. Like its southern cousin, the right whale (so-named because it was the "right" prize for early European whalers to catch), the bowhead is a particularly corpulent animal, carrying as much as two feet of blubber around its flanks. Both species are examples of baleen whales, which filter their food through a comblike structure of plates attached to their upper jaws. The bowhead's baleen plates sometimes exceed fourteen feet in length. In the last century, these flexible slats—which so exquisitely outfit an animal weighing thirty tons to feed on the larvae of tiny crustaceans—were removed from the butchered animal and turned into "whalebone" corsets.

The narwhal is best known for its bizarre tusk, which protrudes up to ten feet from the left side of the male's upper jaw. Grooved in a counter-clockwise spiral like a backward corkscrew, the tusk is something like a tooth gone mad: The corresponding tooth on the right side of the jaw remains embedded, as do both teeth in the female narwhal. Such asymmetry is extremely rare in nature. Narwhal tusks were once thought to possess magical powers, especially effective in detecting and preventing poisoning. In the fifteenth and sixteenth centuries the tusks were valued at ten times their weight in gold, and often served to settle debts. The narwhal's habits, however, usually kept it well out of the reach of whalers, and it survives today in good numbers.

No one knows why the animal is so curiously endowed. Some early naturalists believed that the tusk was used to poke breathing holes in the ice or to flush out bottom-dwelling fish. More recently, two dental anatomists suggested that it might be a sort of cooling coil, allowing the well-insulated narwhal to release excess body heat. It has even been suggested that the tusk might somehow focus or amplify acoustical signals sent out by the narwhal to navigate and find prey, much in the manner of bats.

Most scientists today believe that the narwhal's tusk serves primarily as a sort of cetacean epée in jousts over mating privileges. Males have often been observed with tusks crossed, and in one study more than half the males examined showed deep scars around the head that could have been tusk-inflicted. One animal had the broken tusk of another embedded in its jaw, and others have been found with a sheared-off tusk tip neatly corking the broken end of their own tusk. Since the tusks undergo a spurt in growth when the narwhals reach sexual maturity, they may well serve to attract mates and intimidate rivals, much like the antlers of a stag.

The beluga is a close relative of the narwhal and frequents the same Arctic waters. There is scarcely a more beautiful sight than a pod of these pure white whales sweeping through a narrow estuary on a spring day. Like the narwhals, belugas are highly gregarious whales, sometimes forming pods of as many as ten thousand individuals strung out over a distance of several miles. Deriving its name from the Russian word for white, the beluga averages about seventeen feet in length. Its whistling exhalations long ago inspired whalers and fishermen to dub it the "sea canary." Scientists have poetically compared the beluga's vocalizations to bells ringing, women screaming, lechers wolf-whistling, as well as to a barnyard-full of animal noises. Belugas supplement their vocabulary with a range of body and facial expressions unsurpassed under the sea, including an abiding smile as serene as the Mona Lisa's. Belugas supposedly mate vertically, belly to belly, their heads poking modestly above the water's surface.

Polar bears and whales rarely encounter each other because whales, unlike seals, do not bear their young on land or ice, and therefore seldom venture within paw's reach of a terrestrial predator. Both belugas and narwhals will venture into the maze of drift ice in winter, and occasionally a sudden freeze or shift in the pack ice can cut off their route to the open ocean, trapping the whales in a gradually shrinking hole. Whales need constant access to air, and the surface of a shrinking pool boils with their frenzied attempts to escape. When the whales "blow," the fountain of water they exhale quickly freezes, further constricting the hole and deepening

A curious beluga surfaces in the midst of its pod. There is scarcely a more beautiful sight in Arctic waters than a pod of these pure white whales sweeping through a narrow estuary on a spring day.

their plight. Some observers have reported seeing narwhals and belugas thrust into the air by the struggle of their companions.

Lucky polar bears have been known to add live whale to their diet. Bears can subdue a beluga five times their own size, killing it with a blow to the head and plucking the whale from the water as easily as we might pull a stubborn tuber out of the soil. Even the greediest bear becomes satiated on a fraction of such a kill, and the remainder provides food for a host of other bears, sea birds, and foxes.

One reason a beluga might enter a narrow lead in the first place would be to escape a more dangerous predator, the killer whale. The largest of the dolphin family, killer whales, or orcas, frequent all oceans, but tend to avoid narrow channels and estuaries for fear of injuring their delicate dorsal fins. Their sleek bodies are black above and white below—a color scheme that renders them barely visible to animals looking down into the depths or gazing upward into the sun-tinted surface. Armed with powerful flanks and thick jaws equipped with pairs of curved, interlocking teeth, orcas have no serious adversaries in the sea. They feed primarily on fish such as salmon and herring, but commonly eat warm-blooded whales, seals, and dolphins as well. The stomach of one individual was found to contain thirteen porpoises and fourteen seals. Orcas, in pairs, are said to kill whales twice their own size by swimming up on either side of the prey and slowly squeezing the life out of it. Another source has them harrassing the flukes, fins, and lips of huge bowhead whales, so exhausting their victim that its tongue lolls out. The bowhead's tormentors then grab hold of the tongue and commence to eat it, along with parts of the head, leaving the meticulously mangled prey to die a slow death.

Despite these stories, the orca's reputation as a bloodthirsty killer is quite undeserved. Like social carnivores on land they will hunt cooperatively when the occasion demands. Commonly, a hunt begins with "spy hopping," the whales hovering vertically with their heads out of the water, searching for signs of distant schools of fish. Once a school is located, the adult males and females and the older juveniles spread out in a line, slapping the surface raucously with their flippers and communicating to each other with a variety of honks, squeals, and clicking sounds. While the younger whales playfully mimic their elders' actions, the pod slowly herds the fish into a tighter and tighter cluster, swallowing the confused prey as the trap closes.

The same technique is used to corral seals, and on occasion perhaps orcas do kill more than they can consume. (This is also true of other social carnivores, including wolves and lions.) What is impressive about their predation is not its wanton excess, however, but its restrained intelligence. In the drift ice, orcas sometimes catch seals trying to escape across a floe by heaving their weight onto the edge of the ice and tipping the floe so that the prey rolls back into their waiting jaws. Perhaps their reluctance to predate upon humans is equally intelligent, given the swift revenge we impose on any species that limits our freedom of movement on the planet. On the other hand, the orcas may simply find us distasteful.

Like many marine mammals, orcas and belugas are intensely social. They chatter to each other through open seas, plan strategies, and live for generations in closely knit groups. Belugas even enjoy games together. Sometimes a male surfaces, swinging a loop of seaweed in his mouth; the game is tag, he's it, and the others give chase. Another whale emerges, balancing a stone on his head. The object of this game is to bump the stone from the whale's brow. The water erupts with commotion.

Pacing the ice, the white bear is alone. All bears tend toward solitude, but the polar bears most of all. Both the grizzly and the black bear have fairly well-defined territories which they will defend against intruders. Sea ice, on the other hand, has no boundary. Polar bears don't avoid each other's territories; they avoid each other. A big, heavy-clawed male defines his territory by his mere presence.

Bears must socialize, of course, in order to produce new bears. The polar species mates in late spring, when thick blankets of vapor rise from the newly opened pools and leads. A female comes into heat, or estrus, only once every three years, so her readiness to mate is of enormous interest to males in the area. The enticement of her scent wafting over the ice may lure half a dozen males to her tracks. Commonly, a single male latches onto her scent, and the two travel across the ice hummocks for days, the male following at a discreet distance. Courtship among bears involves much mutual circling and tentative approaches, the male bobbing his head low to the ground, the female keeping her distance at first, pausing now and then to perfume the snow with urine. She stands still and grants her suitor a lingering sniff at her crotch or some other such intimacy, only to slough off his advances and leave him to lope balefully along behind. Next she turns and muzzles up to him. The male might then take advantage of her boldness and lead her to some secluded place, away from the threat of intrusion by other males.

The female's behavior might appear to us as decidedly fickle, but there is more to it than whim. Most bear biologists believe that bears are among the animals for whom ovulation must be induced by a rise in the level of a hormone, estrogen, before copulation can take place. All the head-bobbing, urine-sniffing, and other foreplay stir up the female's hormonal levels to the point where she is ready to conceive.

Since the female into estrus so infrequently, the male bears compete viciously for the chance to copulate. Rivals for a female's attention stretch up on their hindquarters, snarling and lashing out at each other's faces and necks. Larger bears naturally have an advantage, and can usually intimidate younger individuals without much trouble. These encounters seldom result in mortal injuries, but almost every sexually mature male wears scars on his muzzle from such brawls.

It has long been believed that polar bear mating in natural conditions is tumultuous, even violent. Where bears have been seen courting, the snow was later found to be considerably churned up. Like the males of most species, polar bears possess a bone in their penis called the *baculum*, and an occasional bear turns up in an Eskimo hunter's catch with a broken penis bone. But if this is evidence of violent sex, it is slim indeed. The truth about polar bear unions remains unknown. If it is anything like the mating of grizzlies, partners couple quietly over long stretches of time, the male thrusting only in short bursts.

Polar bear couples may stay together for several weeks, the male defending his interest against new arrivals. If a larger, stronger bear comes within range of the female's scent, he may succeed in chasing off the first male and mate with the female himself. Again inferring from the grizzly behavior, the fighting between the males may enhance the female's own excitement, and mating with the new, victorious male proceeds with far less sniffing and circling.

The bears' relationship ends with the passing of the female's estrus, and they drift apart, once again to travel in solitude across the snow. In her uterus, the female's egg develops through only a few cell divisions, and then suddenly stops. It will float in her womb in this dormant state for several months, its implantation on the uterine wall delayed until fall.

For bears accustomed to life on the ice, the coming of warmer weather poses some problems. Depending on their circumstances, some stay with the sea ice as it retreats to the north, while others head for solid land. A few find themselves adrift on a floe heading south into the open sea. Some bear populations, such as those that inhabit Canada's Hudson Bay, have no options: The pack ice disappears entirely from the bay, so the bears are forced to summer ashore. In contrast, many bears of the Chukchi Sea off the northern Alaskan coast never touch land, and their lives change little during the summer.

Summer bestows no largess on an earthling partial to ice. Most bears on land rarely enjoy seal, their winter staple. Nothing is predictable, however, and there are exceptions. While conducting some studies in 1978 at Wager Bay in the Northwest Territories, biologists Donald Furnell and David Oolooyuk sighted a good-sized male polar bear swimming in shallow water near the shore, while its intended prey, a medium-sized ringed seal, bobbed its head up some fifty yards out from the bank. The bear paddled off toward the seal, which promptly dove underwater. Immediately the bear stopped, floating motionless. When the seal once again came to the surface for a look around, the bear stealthily paddled up behind. Five times the seal sounded, each time surfacing a little closer to the bear. Finally the seal poked up only a couple of feet from what it may have thought was a drifting floe. With an easy lunge the bear grabbed him by the neck and carried him off.

For nourishment in summer the bears ashore rely on their own reserves of fat, supplemented by whatever they can forage. Grasses and berries make a welcome snack. In August, when the purplish bilberries ripen, some bears on Canada's Southampton Island stain themselves so thoroughly with the fruit that they earn distinction as the world's only blue polar bears. Seaweed, marine invertebrates, and other gleanings from the coastal shallows make up a small part of the summer diet. A polar bear will rarely trouble to hunt a large mammal such as a musk ox or caribou, but voles and other small rodents that scurry in the undergrowth are available for the bears deft enough to catch them. Some bears on Twin Islands in Hudson Bay have developed the technique of cruising under flocks of long-tailed ducks and snatching them from below. Those inhabiting the mountainous shores of the Svalbard archipelago occasionally climb steep slopes to snatch eggs from the nests of kittiwakes, black guillemots, and other seabirds.

A dead whale washed up in the shallows is a far more common meal in summer than a living one plucked from the brine in winter. The scent of such a find draws bears to the scene as predictably as ants scurrying to a scoop of ice cream tumbled from a cone. Nothing engrosses a bear more than free food. Hunters and explorers have often flushed a contented, blood-

The Arctic fox is a constant companion to the polar bear in the high Arctic, scavenging meat from the bear's kills.

stained polar bear from deep inside a whale carcass. The bears abandon their normally solitary habits to follow their noses to such carrion. They are joined at table by a host of ravens, gulls, and Arctic fox.

The Arctic fox is the polar bear's white shadow. One or two attach themselves to a bear in winter, trailing at a discreet distance and cleaning up the scraps from each kill. If the bear is a good hunter, its shadow will not go hungry, and the trim little canid has only to keep an eye out for an occasional angry swipe of a paw.

Like all Arctic mammals, the fox boasts a selection of unique adapations to the climate—short, rounded, furry ears to minimize heat loss, a thick white coat to provide warmth and disguise, and hair on the pads of its feet for additional insulation on the snow. Foxes are not picky eaters, gladly consuming the eggs of seabirds—as well as the birds themselves if they can be caught—rodents, fish, carrion, ground squirrels, berries, and seal pups, not to mention trap kills, pilfered wolf caches, and garbage. In summer, when food is relatively abundant, the fox will sequester tidbits in rock crevices and under boulders. A single one of these stashes near a den might contain scores of lemmings, a few dozen eggs, or thirty or forty little auks, all neatly tucked out of sight.

Lemmings are favorite fox food. During "lemming years," when the population of these mouselike rodents explodes to as much as a hundred times its normal level, a fox lives high, pouncing on lemming after lemming through the sunlit Arctic night, snapping their necks with a quick bite. No one is sure why the lemming population fluctuates so wildly, with an explosion every three or four years, but a baby boom among the foxes is sure to follow the next

Arctic foxes come in two color types—white and silvery blue. The white foxes turn grayish brown in summer, while the blue foxes change to a chocolate color. The Arctic fox is supremely well-adapted to withstand severe cold, and will not begin to shiver until the temperature drops below −70°C.

year. Many of these will later die of starvation when they enter a world that is not as lemming-rich as it was for their parents.

With litters averaging eleven whelps the species claims the distinction of being the most fecund non-marsupial mammal on earth (litters of up to twenty-two have been recorded in the Soviet Union). Such fertility is yet another adaptation, probably tied to the extreme variability in the foxes' sources of food. An average fox family requires up to a hundred lemmings a day to sustain itself. Most of the lemmings are hunted down at night by the male parent, who ranks as one of the most attentive providers in the dog family, and by the time the whelps are ready to leave the den, the family will have consumed as many as four thousand of the little creatures. In lean years, the parents may be forced to desert the whelps, or the young may fight and kill each other, thus reducing the family's food requirements to a manageable level.

The vast majority of polar bears roam alone on the sea ice year-round or come ashore on remote islands. But there are exceptions, and like all exceptions, they attract attention and soon people are mistaking them for the rule. The summering bears of Churchill, Manitoba, well documented on film in recent years, represent the largest congregation of *Ursus maritimus* in the world. Yet they remain an unusual group, doing very unusual things.

Every fall, some six hundred polar bears mass along the one-hundred-mile strip of coast between the Churchill and Nelson rivers, waiting for Hudson Bay to ice up so they can set off after seal again. As many as eighty bears may congregate on the narrow spit of sand extending a mile into the intertidal zone off Cape Churchill. The situation poses something of a "bear problem" for the citizens of Churchill, just a few miles away. Every time somebody slaps some bacon on the griddle or revivifies the dump with another load of garbage, a keen snout may catch the aroma and lead its owner to the source. The bears have been gathering on Cape Churchill at least since the beginning of recorded history in Canada. Aside from a few early traders, humans didn't appear on the scene in any appreciable numbers until 1942, when a military base was established there. One has to wonder which of the two groups poses more of a problem to the other.

In any case, the bears of Cape Churchill offer a fascinating glimpse at the social behavior of confirmed loners thrown together with time to spare. Most females head inland to seek denning sites, but the males stay near the shore, root around in garbage dumps, share food freely, chase each other about, and engage in other sorts of frolicsome behavior. Such playfulness among adults rarely occurs even in much more social mammals. The bouts of exuberance last as long as fifteen minutes, after which the bears stretch out on the snow to cool off, only to rise up in a little while to play some more. Sometimes, as October turns to November, unrelated

These two Cape Churchill bears are just tussling in fun, but when the mating season comes they may fight viciously for the privilege of mating.

polar bear playmates may even become polar bear friends, enjoying numerous sessions of play-fighting, resting near each other, and even sharing makeshift beds hollowed out of the snow.

How can we account for such unusual ursine intimacy? Some biologists believe that play-fighting prepares the combatants for more serious battles later, especially in a species such as the polar bear, whose males must compete intensely to reproduce. Another theory suggests that play between adults helps establish social hierarchies, in which case the behavior would perhaps be a throwback to a time when polar bears did frequent each other's company more routinely. We really do not know the rules for sojourning bears. Full-grown human beings, especially younger males, toss balls around or otherwise engage in behavior more common to their children—but only when they have the time. Leisure is a condition rarely found in the lives of other earthlings. Perhaps the long wait by the shore helps release the bears' lighter spirits. While biding their time on land as the ice slowly accumulates depth and integrity, the bears may simply be having fun.

To a pregnant female, the coming of cold weather in the fall inspires more conventional polar bear behavior. Prompted by the long-delayed implantation of the fertilized embryos on the wall of her uterus, she seeks

On Cape Churchill in summer young males like these two swimmers are the most likely to spend their time in play.

out a place to den. Landed bears, such as those in the Hudson Bay region or on Wrangel Island in the Soviet Union, will begin to wander farther inland. Though they usually settle within five miles of shore, some polar bear dens have been reported as far as fifty miles from the sea. The Svalbard bears of Norway prefer to den high up in the mountains, where the slopes provide good protection from the wind. Bears committed to the ice pack will find good denning spots in the lee of a hummock or pressure ridge, and drift with the floe as it moves south through the winter. A pregnant female holed up a few miles offshore in November may find herself four hundred miles out to sea when she emerges in the spring. No matter: At that time of year the sea ice offers plenty of seal, and she and her cubs will not go hungry.

Whether on land or on the ice, the choicest spot for a maternity den will be a thick, well-ventilated drift, not too icy, but hard enough to maintain its integrity as the bear digs deep into it. Den construction seems to be a matter of personal taste. Some bears excavate cavernous apartments with half a dozen separate rooms, while others are content with a simple chamber scooped out of the snow. Wind, not temperature, is the enemy of life in the Arctic, and the female faces her den entrance to leeward. To conserve heat within the den, the living quarters are built *above* the tunnel communicating to the outside.

Once inside, the female may have to worry more about heat than cold. Her own body warmth can maintain an interior temperature 35° C. above that outside—any warmer and her snow house might start to melt. (Refrozen icy snow makes for bad insulation.) Throughout the denning period the bear must adjust and monitor the den temperature, usually by digging ventilation holes to the outside or by scratching away some of the snow's weight above the den. Should the prevailing wind direction change during her hibernation, she and her newborns may be suddenly exposed, and she will have to excavate some temporary structure as quickly as possible. A den gone to ice may also be abandoned.

Consider for a moment what it means to hibernate. Most animals require a constant intake of nitrogen-rich foods to synthesize the proteins that support the whole cascading chemistry of cellular life. Deprived of an external source of nutrition, an organism quickly begins to consume its own muscle tissue as the only available source of protein—in other words, it begins to starve. The synthesis of proteins also produces a host of poisonous waste products such as urea, ammonia, and creatinine. So long as there is water in the system, the kidneys process these wastes and expel them as urine. Human beings are particularly poor at enduring starvation. Without food, a plump human might last a couple of months. Deprived of water, however, a human dies of uremia or dehydration in about two weeks, poisoned by the toxins produced by his own metabolism.

A hibernating animal, on the other hand, can go for months without food or water and still avoid such a fate. "Deep hibernators," such as ground squirrels or woodchucks, survive by virtually shutting down their energy demands. With their body temperature lowered close to that of the surrounding air, they enter a sort of deathlike torpor. A hibernating ground squirrel could be plucked from its nest, placed on a truck with a faulty muffler, and driven through a pep rally, without stirring in the slightest. In order to survive, however, the squirrel still needs to rouse itself every week or so to eat, drink, and relieve itself of wastes before falling back into its near-frigid sleep.

Though the survival techniques of the deep-hibernating earthlings are fascinating, the ursine species accomplishes something even more marvelous. Bears are hunger artists, dietary wizards. For months at a time a hibernating bear (black, brown, or white) lives in its den at close to its normal body temperature, burning four thousand kilocalories *daily* without eating a thing. Nor does the creature drink, urinate, or defecate. During that time the bear even manages to *increase* lean-muscle weight slightly, and at the same time avoids uremia, keeps body temperature up, stays awake for needed den repairs, and if disturbed, springs up alert and ready to defend itself.

If the denning bear is a pregnant female, she also has to deal with the matter of giving birth. All summer long and into the fall her embryos have floated in her uterus, held suspended in what is called the blastocyst stage of development. With no growth taking place in the embryos, the female has been able to husband her fat reserves for the time when she will need them most. As soon as the blastocyst attaches itself to the wall of her uterus, its cells begin to divide again, feeding on her stockpile of nourishment, while her own body falls into an undemanding lethargy. Gestation takes only six to ten weeks—any longer and the needs of her fetuses would outdistance her body's ability to satisfy them. One can also imagine the difficulty of giving birth to large and well-developed twins or triplets while dangling groggily between sleep and enforced starvation. Once the cubs are born, the mother must also produce enough milk to feed them for months, still without leaving the den or eating anything to replenish her own nutritional stores.

Dr. Ralph Nelson, a professor of nutrition with the Carle Foundation at the University of Illinois, has spent years unraveling the biochemical mysteries of bear hibernation. According to Nelson, a bear falls into a hibernating state weeks before it actually enters its den, having gorged itself beforehand in order to build up a reserve of fat. This fat supply fuels the bear's hibernating metabolism, and the synthesis of proteins does not slacken in the least. On the contrary, as Dr. Nelson has shown, the remaking, or turnover, of proteins gears up to five times its normal, nonhibernating rate. Protein turnover, however, is composed of two complementary processes: *catabolism*, the breakdown of complex protein molecules into simpler compounds that can be utilized (as well as into waste products, that cannot), and *anabolism*, the rebuilding of complex molecules from simpler amino acids, a process necessary to keep the body in good repair and to sustain such demanding activity as the growth of a fetus. Catabolism unsupported by the intake of nutrients would gradually drive an animal to the edge of starvation. Our hibernating bear, however, is able to juggle its fat reserves so that anabolism keeps slightly ahead. Meanwhile, urea and other toxins produced by catabolism are quickly broken down, and the resulting nitrogen is reenlisted to form new amino acids. In a sense, the sleeping bear recreates itself moment by moment, losing nothing in the process but a load of extra fat.

Among the three ursine species, the white bear emerges as the true master of metabolism. In summer, when the seals have disappeared, the polar bear's diet offers very little chance to fatten up and many seem to consume next to nothing. One study showed that the Churchill bears spend less than 3 percent of their time eating during summer and early fall. In winter, on the other hand—when black and brown bears retreat to dens—the polar bears' food supply is more abundant. Pregnant females make their way to dens, but most of the others stay awake and walk the ice, searching for seals.

Recall now the polar bear's preference for seal blubber over seal meat.

Fat provides quick energy in a cold climate, but there is more to it than that. If the bear were to eat quantities of meat, where could it find the water needed to flush away the toxic products of protein metabolism? Licking snow is a dead end; the bear would have to burn about two thousand kilocalories per day just warming up the snow to its body temperature. The breakdown of fat, however, produces no noxious by-products; instead it leads cleanly to carbon dioxide and *water*. Splendid bear! The seal blubber provides both food and drink, and the bear's droppings, lie few and far between, crisp and dry. This earthling has gone her relatives one better, striding about the top of the world in a state of perpetual hibernation.

According to Nelson, we could learn a lot about ourselves if we could figure out how the bears pull off this triumph. Already he has applied his findings toward a diet for humans suffering from kidney failure that postpones their need for kidney dialysis and transplantation. He believes, moreover, that the symphony of reactions in the hibernating bear must be orchestrated by some hormonal mechanism, and if a "hibernating hormone" can be isolated, it could be used in the treatment of obesity and anorexia nervosa.

The bears' metabolic virtuosity, finally, might even help our efforts to reach other worlds. Space flights lasting months would require immense stores of food and involve the serious problem of disposing of wastes. "A polar bear can go nine months without eating or drinking," Nelson points out. "From a theoretical (and perhaps practical) aspect, it would be the best mammal to send on long-term space flights."

No doubt we will reserve the greater glory of space exploration for ourselves, but we can still carry aboard some ursine wisdom. Manipulating the right combination of protein and water intake during flight would minimize the need for water and the production of wastes. Further, adipose tissue—fat, in other words—is a far more concentrated source of calories than food, and what better place to stow sustenance than on our own bodies? To prepare for space hibernation, then, human earthlings would have to emulate the bears and store up on fat before takeoff. But is America ready for roly-poly astronauts floating across the TV screen, waving good-bye like balloons in the Macy's parade?

At the nadir of the polar night, while the denning polar bear lies suspended in hibernation, two blind, nearly hairless balls of quivering life fall from her onto the den floor. The bear cubs are utterly helpless against the cold. (In December 1978 some cubs unexpectedly born aboveground to a captive bear quickly died, and an autopsy revealed that they had almost no fat layer of their own at birth.) Even the near-thawing temperature of the natural den is too bitter for the naked cubs, and the mother quickly scoops them to her breast, curling around her newborn and sheltering them with her own abundant fat. The cubs grope for their mother's teats in the dark. Once at the breast they will be well provided for. Polar bear milk is the richest in fat among land mammals—33 percent as opposed to approximately 5 percent in human milk—and it is this fortifying fluid, tasting like cod-liver oil and smelling of seal, that enables the cubs to survive and double their weight every couple of weeks.

The mother sits back on her hips, leaning against the wall of the den with her forelegs protecting her young as they suckle. Within a month they will have their eyesight and some rudimentary sense of hearing. In another month, weighing about twelve pounds, they suddenly begin to mature, and sniff and prowl about the den, climbing clumsily over each other and digging their own narrow tunnels deeper into the snowbank. Their mother meanwhile remains lethargic; all her energy reserves are concentrated on the production of milk for her cubs.

On some sunny day in early spring, the new family breaks out through the snow covering their den—first the mother emerges and sits groggily at the den entrance for two days or so. Then the cubs tumble out, falling over themselves and each other, poking cold black noses into the air. Once outside the den, the mother will still have to keep her strength up with little food for about two weeks, until her metabolism returns to its non-hibernating pace. Most of her time is spent resting, or walking to and fro near the den entrance, with her head hung low and swinging from side to side as she searches for scraps of vegetation left from the previous summer. The cubs may invite her to play, running up and jumping for her nose, but she responds with only a touch of her snout. Rambunctious displays of affection will only drain her meager reserves. Mostly she sleeps, cradling her infants in her forelegs as she leans against a rock.

For the cubs, these two weeks outside the den are a cram course in the pure excitement of being alive and a bear. Like most infants their attention span is short, and they will hop from one activity to another, chasing and nipping each other and playing a sort of king-of-the-castle game on a hummock, or sliding down a slope on their bellies again and again. In such play one can see the blueprints of hunting and fighting, and there is no question that much adult behavior is based on inherited traits. But bears rely greatly on learning to sculpt and define their gifts. In the middle of their revels, a soft call from their mother brings the cubs obediently back to her side. As she forages in the snow, they too bend their noses to the ground, and if she pokes out her tongue or scratches her fur, they too poke and scratch, imitating her movements with solemn concentration, the helter-skelter abandon of their play forgotten.

By the time the new polar bear family is ready to leave the denning area for life on the ice, the cubs have locked onto their mother as provider, protector, mentor, and guide. Often covering as much as twenty miles in a day, in spite of frequent stops to rest, the mother heads unerringly for seal. She navigates her way using senses so far known only to bears. Perhaps she is pulled seaward by her keen nose. Bears denning in Manitoba, on the other hand, strike out for Hudson Bay in a northeasterly direction, even

A female and her cubs foraging together on a warm July day near Cape Churchill, Manitoba. Polar bears are not always confined to the remote sea ice, and can tolerate temperate climates reasonably well in spite of their thick coats of blubber and fur.

though a more direct route to the bay lies due east. Similarly, the bears of Ontario farther south will eschew the warm, seal-poor waters of James Bay, and instead head overland directly north toward Hudson Bay. Perhaps the female is also guided by memory. But once on the ice, she and her cubs must cover many more miles over a terrain that never existed before, and still the mother heads steadfastly north, until she and her cubs are safe again among the seals.

"We don't really know how the bears navigate to and from their denning areas," says Ian Stirling. "Maybe we never will. But why should a bear, or any other animal, be entirely comprehensible?"

In time, the cubs will learn from their mother most of what they need to know to survive on the ice—how to keep low and approach downwind from a seal, how to deblubber a kill, where to find a good denning spot on the leeward side of hillock just south of a certain bend in the river, and to remember the place for seasons to come. The mother bear is a strict and demanding teacher, and when she perches above a seal's breathing hole, she will brook no fooling around by her cubs nor any of their fumbling attempts at hunting that might spoil her own chances of success. When it comes time to build a temporary den again next winter (all polar bears will hole up in extremely bitter weather, though only pregnant females will den for extended periods) she will not tolerate her yearlings' attempts to help her dig. They must stand, watch, and learn.

This long association with the female parent accounts for the wide variation in bear personality and style. If the mother has chanced upon a new twist in the hunting routine, her cubs might use it too. If she has witnessed, or felt herself, the crippling sting that follows the report of a gun, her students will be gun-shy as well. But if she has grown up without having enjoyed much contact with humankind, the sound of a gun echoing over the ice may receive no more attention than the crackling report of a floe smacking into landfast ice. The noise may even appear, tragically, to be an interesting sound worth investigating.

For two years the bear cubs will be totally dependent on their mother, not only for sustenance, but for the lessons in survival they will need in order to hunt for themselves.

For the next two years the cubs will wander with their mother, never venturing more than a hundred meters or so from her side. She will continue to nurse them as they develop their hunting skills and taste for blubber, and will ferociously attack anything she considers a threat to their safety, be it a male bear out to cadge an easy breakfast of cub, or a human being who stumbles upon the family while emptying his garbage. If threatened by the sound of a helicopter full of bear specialists, she may even reach up and try to pull the copter down from the sky.

Her rigorous devotion is not difficult to understand. Since a female bear is able to mate only once every three years (two in some southerly populations), each cub life is deeply precious, a measurable percentage of the future of beardom. Eventually, however, the mother will grow impatient with their demands for milk, their nips and pawings and clamoring for attention. When once again she feels the stirrings of estrus, the mother chases off any cubs who haven't already left. The young bears will set off across the ice to seek their own seals, leaving her free to mate again.

In Praise of Prey

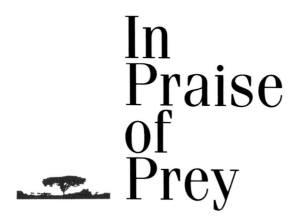

Everybody loves a predator. There seems to be something hypnotically important in predation, in the solemn rhythms of hunt, chase, kill, and feed. We bestow on the polar bear its out-sized epithets—Lord of the North, King of the Ice—not only because it is large and powerful and intelligent, but because it exploits these qualities to secure live prey. There are some twenty thousand bears stalking the Arctic ice, hunting some five million ringed seals, who in turn feed upon countless millions of char, halibut, cod, and herring. The fish themselves take their nourishment from several billion tons of shrimp and other crustaceans inhabiting the Arctic ocean—a swarm of life vastly outweighing all the predators on the food chain above it. Nevertheless, one seldom hears the Arctic referred to as the Kingdom of Shrimp.

However gruesome its details, there is nothing inherently vicious about predation, and nothing unhealthy in our admiration for the predator. To live by the hunt demands skill, planning, and experience, the ability to respond to new situations, anticipate the prey's movements, and cut off their escape. Predators tend to be more intelligent than the animals they feed upon. This is no slight to the prey, for whom too much intelligence might be a disadvantage: Thinking takes time, precious milliseconds. Imagine a rabbit trying to decide how best to manage a mountain lion about to drop on its back. Prey animals tend to rely more on uncalculated, stereotyped responses to danger, most often by fleeing.

64

The next chapter explores the habits and behavior of the tiger, another of the great predators. But it is worth pausing first to pay respect to prey animals, and their place in the scheme of things. In our fascination with the predators, it is easy to mistake prey animals for passive, innocent victims, rather than the resourceful creatures they are, well-supplied through evolution to defend their grip on life. An animal's position on the food chain has nothing to do with its success as a species. On the level of species, in fact, predators are more at the mercy of their prey than the reverse: A shift in the migratory pattern of a herd of wildebeest, for instance, could mean starvation for a pride of lions. If the population of lions in the area is already fragile, such change could lead to a local extinction.

The vulnerability of predator species is implicit in the energy dynamics of the food chain. When one animal eats another—let's say a tree shrew devours an earthworm—part of the prey is assimilated by the predator, and part is lost to the environment as waste. Much of the portion of earthworm at the shrew's disposal is burned up fueling the shrew's metabolism, while the remainder is funneled into new tissue growth. If a cat eats the shrew, only the fraction of the worm-energy that has been turned into shrew tissue will benefit the cat; the rest was dissipated or burned away. Therefore, a predator population invariably represents a smaller "total biomass"—the combined weight of all individuals—than the species below it on the food chain. Since the predators also tend to be larger than their prey, their absolute numbers will be smaller. As one moves up the ladder, populations decrease in size and a species' hold on existence grows ever more precarious. Huge, powerful carnivores like the bear and the tiger are the animals most vulnerable to any disruption in the ecosystem surrounding them. When human intervention disturbs an environment, their absence will be among the first to be noticed.

Predators and their prey are partners engaged in a fluid, mutually responsive relationship, a dance whose rhythms and measures extend through generations. In order to survive, a prey species constantly evolves new feints and disguises, innovations of form and behavior to confound its pursuers. One of the best ways to avoid being eaten, for instance, is to avoid being detected in the first place. Camouflage is a common evolutionary tactic of prey throughout the animal kingdom. The fur of the Arctic hare, for instance, is as white as that of the Arctic fox. Small prey animals can take advantage of their size to hide in thickets. The diminutive duiker of southern Africa, for example, derive their name from the Afrikaan word for "diver," from their habit of diving into cover at the least sign of danger. Hiding from a predator's keen sense of smell might be more difficult than just keeping out of sight, but it can be done. In Canada and the northern United States, wolves rely substantially on their noses to sniff out moose and other prey. Normally, newborn animals of a species are the most vulnerable to predators, and the female moose must often leave her young alone while she forages. But moose calves (alas for the wolf) are relatively odorless.

Natural selection has set in motion a perpetual race between predators, such as the cheetah here, and prey, both evolving new ways to outwit, outrun, and out-compete the other.

Predators must keep pace with their prey's adaptations and evolve countermeasures—new talents and strategies to keep the prey within reach. If your prey can smell you coming, learn to stalk from upwind. If your intended meal can escape with a burst of speed, grow fast through generations—or grow extinct. Speed alone may not determine the outcome of the chase. The cheetah is the fastest animal on earth, reaching speeds of seventy miles an hour. But the cheetah tires after only a few hundred yards, and its long, straight legs make it hard for the cat to turn quickly and follow an antelope's zig-zagging flight. Sometimes the race goes not to the swift, but to the most cooperative. The same antelope, chased not by a solitary cheetah but by a pack of wild dogs, might zig away from one pursuer only to zag into the jaws of another, who has veered away to cut off its flank. Flight is nevertheless the most common and effective predator defense. Prey can outrun their predators, most of the time.

"When spider webs unite," says an Ethiopian proverb, "they can halt a lion." Large deer and antelope—the caribou, wildebeest, impalas, and the like—cannot play hide-and-seek as successfully as their smaller cousins like the duiker. Instead, these species congregate in large groups, a situation which multiplies their ability to detect a predator's approach and sound an alarm. With so many eyes, ears, and noses on the alert, each individual can spend a greater percentage of its time safely grazing, its head down. If a gazelle or deer catches the scent of a predator or hears a suspicious rustling in a bush, it may also give a soft snort or bark, alerting the herd to the danger. When a predator does plunge into their midst, herds tend to scatter in all directions at once, confusing the attacker and making it difficult for it to focus on any one victim.

Such explosive scattering is not necessarily an indication that the individual animals are acting in some conscious fashion "for the good of the herd." Each gazelle or wildebeest flees for its own life. All this solitary panic nevertheless ends up in a confusing jumble that ultimately benefits the herd, and the disposition to scatter continues through generations. The tendency to congregate in large clusters in the first place is influenced by decidedly selfish motives. Since a predator tends to hone in on one of the closest prey animals, there is a very important, individual advantage in pushing toward the center of the group in order to keep as many other bodies as possible between oneself and the predator. The herding instinct, however, can sometimes backfire on its most successful practitioners. When a large herd of prey is attacked by a lion at a water hole, for instance, those closest to the center of the herd might have to wait for the surrounding animals to depart before they can move. By then it could be too late.

Outright counterattacks are not as common among mammals as they are among bird species, but in certain circumstances, mammalian prey will take the offensive. Groups of elands—giant African antelopes often reaching two thousand pounds—will sometimes stop in their tracks when chased by a lion and charge their startled pursuer. Ground squirrels are a com-

Many prey species, such as these impalas, rely on each other to detect the approach of a predator and sound a general alarm.

mon prey to snakes in North America, and in some areas the squirrels take matters into their own paws by chasing the snakes, kicking sand on them, and pouncing on their backs. Wisely, the squirrels are much less inclined to be aggressive in places where the snakes are poisonous.

Not surprisingly, the most ferocious prey individuals are females defending their young. If a jackal attacks a Thompson's gazelle and her fawn, the mother often charges the jackal, lunging at it with her horns. Sometimes another female, most likely a sister, will set upon the intruder as well. Hans

Every summer a herd of wildebeest a million strong migrates across the Serengeti Plain in East Africa to greener grazing in the north, returning south again in November. Along the way, thousands will be drowned in river crossings or killed by lions, but the sheer mass of the herd ensures that the population will survive.

Kruuk, a biologist working in East Africa, often observed "tommy" females attempting to distract an approaching hyena from their young by repeatedly cutting across the hyena's path to the fawn. Occasionally as many as four other females would join in to protect a single fawn. Their efforts, however, rarely seemed to break the concentration of the hunting hyena, who made off with the fawn in half of the cases Kruuk witnessed.

A little help from one's relatives can nevertheless be the saving grace to a beleaguered animal. The photographer and naturalist Hugo van Lawick once saw a pack of wild dogs separate a zebra mare, her foal, and her yearling away from the rest of their herd. The dogs surrounded the trio, while the rest of the zebras disappeared over a rise. The dogs bit at the foal, while the mare and her yearling lunged back at them. For several minutes they held the dogs off, but van Lawick could see that they were tiring, even as the dogs grew bolder and more frantic.

"The end seemed inevitable," van Lawick wrote, "and the end is always much worse to watch when the prey has bravely defended itself or its young one. But suddenly I felt the ground vibrating and, looking around, I saw, to my amazement, ten zebras fast approaching. A moment later this herd closed its ranks around the mother and her two offspring and then, wheeling around, the whole closely packed group galloped off . . ."

If a prey species is harassed continually by specific predators, it may be advantageous to dodge the enemy, not only over plains, creeks, and canyons, but through the dimension of time. Recall for a moment the relationship of the bear and the ringed seal, out on the ice. Ringed seals are among many prey species that are afforded protection by breeding seasonally—in their case, all the females give birth in late March and April. Their well-timed deliveries are a distinct survival advantage. If every weak newborn arrives on the scene at the same time, the predators will benefit in the short run; but with more seal (or deer, or wildebeest) available than the predators can eat, some of the young are certain to survive past the critical, defenseless stage of infancy.

This influence of predators upon the reproductive cycles of a prey species is called "the Darling effect," after the pioneering ethologist F. Fraser Darling. In studies of seabirds off the English coast, Darling discovered that the presence of its mate alone was not enough to excite a female to breed, lay her eggs, and rear the young. She also had to be stimulated by the presence of other nearby members of the species who were also going through their reproductive cycles. Synchronizing reproductive cycles would serve the species through time much as the herding instinct functions in space: The individual herring or seal who ignored the stimulus to breed in season would be in the same vulnerable position as a water buffalo with a penchant for wandering on the margins of the herd. Through natural selection, fewer and fewer females would breed at the "wrong" time of year, when the predators were hungrier, and eventually everyone's reproductive cycle would coincide. Remove the individual from the group, however, and her breeding cycles take their own course. To counter the Darling effect, a predator would have to evolve some way of stocking up on nutritional reserves in order to survive the leaner seasons when newborn prey, the easy catches, are not to be found. We don't have to look very far for an example: Polar bears are remarkably well-equipped to pass a seal-less summer without a great deal of strain.

In order to outdo a predator through time once and for all, a prey species would have to evolve some means of "disappearing" beyond reach for such a long period that its predators could no longer fix on it as a stable source of food. No mammals have yet acquired this art, but one noisy insect has. Cicadas, familiar to residents of the eastern United States and Canada, spend most of their lives underground as "nymphs," existing on organic matter in the soil. Once every seventeen years (thirteen years in some species), the cicada nymphs emerge as adults and take to the trees. The timing of their return, after so long in the ground, is astoundingly precise. Whole populations, consisting of millions of individuals, rustle up through the leaf litter on a single night, most within a span of *two hours*. Once aboveground, the cicadas employ additional predator defenses. It has been suggested that their loud rasping sounds scramble the communication systems of birds that prey upon them, while their large size serves to quickly satiate the predators. But the cicadas' escape into time remains their most dazzling defense. No predator has yet matched them, step for evolutionary step, by committing itself to a period of hibernation Van Winklish in duration.

CHAPTER TWO

Tiger with Deer, Tiger with Tigers

I

On this earth, survival demands change. The only time an animal achieves its final form is at the moment of extinction. Through long, humanless centuries the predators and their prey chase each other, the deer nipping at the tiger's heels as much as the reverse, both calling forth new speed, finer senses, and greater caution from the other. Every animal is the creation of such past encounters. William Blake's famous poem nonwithstanding, the tiger of today was shaped not by immortal hands but by the hooves of elk and wild pig,

73

which have long ago turned to dust. Its stripes found their pattern in yesterday's sunlight slanting through reeds, and its burning eyes penetrate a darkened forest millions of years old.

Within living memory, eight subspecies of tigers roamed through Asia, from the wooded plains of central Siberia west to the edge of Arabia, and to the east through the oak and poplar forests of eastern China, and the jungles of Southeast Asia. Each subspecies has adapted to the conditions of its habitat. The Amur, or Siberian tiger, is still fairly well-suited to a cold climate, increasing its winter bulk with an inch or two of fat and a thick, silky pelt. It is also the largest of all the big cats. To the south, tigers have adapted by decreasing slightly in size, their coats darkening to a tawny gloss, their hair so short in the Indonesian varieties that the black stripes seem painted on.

Tigers are solitary and deeply territorial animals. Their requirements for territory posed no problem to the species so long as there were ample forests. In the last one hundred years, however, human populations in the tiger's range have increased drastically. In marked contrast to the empty expanses enjoyed by the polar bear, the tiger's remaining habitats border some of the most densely populated places on earth. Consequently the world population of tigers has plummeted in this century from 100,000 to some 6,000 individuals, including 2,000 of the three Indo-Chinese subspecies, 800 Sumatran tigers, a smattering of the Chinese tiger farther north, and the remains of the Amur population, mostly found in nature reserves. The Balinese and Javan subspecies are almost gone now, as is the Caspian subspecies—all of these extinctions having occurred within the last few decades. The most familiar subspecies, the Indian, or Bengal, tiger, fell to a low of 1,800 animals in 1972, but has almost doubled since. Its recovery is due to a massive conservation effort known as Project Tiger, which now protects one quarter of the remaining animals in India in fifteen parks and reserves.

Straddling the border of Bangladesh and West Bengal in India is the great mangrove swamp of the Sunderbans, home of the largest concentration of tigers on earth. This forest lies at the juncture of two huge and violent ecosystems. From the north and west the melting snows of the distant Himalayas and the Tibetan plateau join with the monsoon rains. The water collects first in tiny rivulets which feed into streams, thence to larger rivers. The tumult of soil-laden water rushes into the great Ganges, the Brahmaputra, and Meghna rivers. Finally, this gathering watershed of a half million square miles descends into the largest delta in the world, fertile and densely farmed.

From the south and east, meanwhile, come the storms. From March to November the winds and rain punish the coastline and its animals and people. The cyclones produce waves well over a hundred feet high that are sucked up the estuaries over crops and forest. In November of 1970 a cyclone that struck at high tide killed two hundred thousand people in

Dominated by the ruins of an ancient fort, Ranthambhor Park in northwestern India is one of fifteen tiger reserves established by the Indian government since 1973. Ranthambhor is home to tigers, leopards, sloth bears, crocodiles, and a host of prey species and waterfowl.

Bangladesh; in 1984, fifty thousand died in another storm. Were it not for the protection afforded by the fringe of swampy forest—the Sunderbans— many thousands more would have been killed.

The cyclones represent the most dramatic impact on the Sunderbans from the saltwater ecosystem of the Bay of Bengal. But the influence of the bay is constant. Twice a day saltwater tides sweep up the long, muddy rivers of the forest, their force driven by the compression of the banks and the density of salt water against fresh. When the incoming tides hit the ebbing flow coming out, a wave forms, driving the salt water farther into the swamp.

The vortex of this meeting of ecosystems is a humid labyrinth of channels, forested islands, and muddy creeks, known as *khals*, some one-and-a-half-million acres in extent. Only the mangrove trees can survive in such an abundance of salt and water. Some mangroves, like the sea date and the tall kripa farther back in the swamp, stand poised on roots like stilts, their pencillike pneumatophores protruding above the tides. The gnarled goran, kankra, and baen, stunted above the surface, send out long, semisubmerged roots studded with knobs and knees.

The water is dark and brackish, full of scurrying life. Giant crabs climb up the trees. At night, the canals glow with luminescent plankton, and the forest pulses with fireflies. Crocodiles glide through the khals, their excrement fed upon by larval insects and arthropods, which are eaten by small fish and fry; these, in turn, feed the crabs and turtles and goggle-eyed gobiid fish, which then fall prey to the dolphin and otters, the big fish, and water snakes. Finally, the crocodile eats the fish and the snakes and the mammals—and occasionally a man—and returns it all as fodder for the larvae. Fishermen in the Sunderbans look upon the crocodile as a competitor for their catch. Yet if the crocodile were driven from the swamp, the food chain would be broken and the fish would grow scarce.

In the midst of all this fecundity, crouched behind an umbrella of mangrove root, there is a young male tiger, not yet in his prime, but by the look of him already weighing over four hundred pounds. In repose, his bunched muscles show prominently beneath his swamp-slickened coat. The tiger blinks, looks up at a buzzing horsefly, blinks again. There is something about him both terrible and terribly familiar. Looking at a tiger's face, one can see cat's eyes, cat's whiskers, cat's nose, cat's maw—but all of this tame recognition is undone by the size of the features. The jaws are scaled to clamp down on the necks of deer and pig; the muzzle deep enough to harbor two-inch canines, the nose tip as wide as a child's hand.

Each tiger's face, lit by two swaths of white above its eyes, presents its own indelible pattern of black blotches and bars—a hypnotizing design as enigmatic and intriguing as the inkblots of a Rorschach test. The eyes burn as bright as cold fire. Some biologists believe that the tiger's pale iris is fashioned to achieve the highest contrast with the black pupil. Each pupillary movement—a glow of dilation or a sudden shrinking to a tiny black point—communicates another change in the tiger's mosaic of mood. Much of what a tiger communicates, of course, is lost on us, leading some to attribute the tiger's glassy stare to plain stupidity. But in its aspect, at least, the tiger not so much lacks intelligence as disdains the need for it. What is thrilling about this feline face, framed in the mangrove roots, is the absence of *becoming*, an expression of a state fully attained but empty of meaning, as if the tiger had long ago thought through the ineffable truths of the universe, and knows that none of them are of the slightest consequence.

The tiger blinks once more, turns, and climbs up the bank of the stream. With a liquid grace he picks his way among the knee roots and pneumatophores to higher ground, to a path where the footing is sure and the dew-sodden branches only occasionally slap against his long flanks. Occasionally he seems to vanish, then reappear. In pure artfulness, the tiger's striped camouflage outdoes even the polar bear's disguise, mimicking the play of light as it trembles through stalks of grass, with ribbons of

shadow between. An animal with a solid coat could stalk effectively only in similarly colored terrain, but the tiger's broken bars slip by unnoticed in a variety of backgrounds. In dry reeds, the tiger can be mistaken for a sudden, inconsequential thickening in the cover. Down by the river, mingled in green grass, it can seem like nothing more than a mound of earth.

In wooded hills, even a sapling's few skinny twigs and leaves can be enough to confuse the careless eye, erasing the presence of a tiger standing broadside behind.

On either side of the path, the ground falls off into vaporous pools. At this hour, shortly before daylight, the dew falls steadily from the canopy of leaves, as loud as rain. Though he is hungry, the tiger walks without hurry, stopping now and then to sniff a solitary bush or tree trunk. At one point he turns his back to a tree and lets fly a spray of urine. Soon after sunrise he pauses to defecate, dropping the feces conspicuously on the path. He scratches the soil with his hind paws, leaving a mark that gives further evidence of his passing.

As the light begins to harden, it pulls shapes out of the dark vapor—garjan trees, squat and ugly, their knobbly roots poking up from the black water like startled ghosts. Beyond, there is an opening in the cover where a grassy meadow penetrates the swamp from the seaward side, just behind the protection of the dunes. The tiger knows this is good hunting ground. The meadow supplies food for the deer, and the bush that surrounds it makes for good hiding and hunting. By the meadow's edge the tiger pauses, concealed in a thicket of reed. Farther along the rim of forest he spots a herd of five chital, or spotted deer, grazing on the dew-soaked grass. When

A herd of chital, or spotted deer, grazes in the morning sunlight penetrating the sal forest of India's Corbett National Park.

one large buck looks up, the tiger crouches and freezes, even though he is well out of range of the buck's unexceptional sight. The buck wades deeper into the meadow. The tiger stays motionless for several minutes, then steals back into the bush. He hurries toward the deer, keeping himself hidden in the damp root life; when he has gone a hundred yards, he leaves the bush again and drops down into the reeds.

From his vantage point, the tiger can see the meadow, still tipped with fog, and there, just to the right, stand the herd of deer. In the new morning the spots on their flanks shimmer like dappled sunlight. The big buck, his lyre-shaped antlers held high, lets go a hoarse bellow, a signal of his rut. The tiger doesn't flinch. The chital's alarm call, which would have betrayed the tiger's presence, is an entirely different sound, short and grating. This buck is too interested in announcing his own sexual state to be aware of the predator. Slowly, the tiger begins his stalk.

All tigers—from the swamps of the Sunderbans and the jungles of Sumatra to the deciduous forests of the north—are united by their taste for deer. In northern Asia the tigers follow the herds of wapiti and sika. Those on the Indian subcontinent prey on the majestic sambar, the bara-singha with its prominent throat ruff, and the somewhat smaller, elegantly spotted chital. A tiger is capable of killing larger prey, including wild buffalo and gaur—a huge species of cattle weighing up to two thousand pounds—but before attacking such beasts, the tiger must assess the risk. Wild boar is another favorite prey, especially in central Asia; but boars too are aggressive and well-armed, and the tiger who takes on a four-hundred-pound boar may regret it. If the occasion arises, the tiger will eat smaller animals as well—the tiny hog deer and tinier muntjac, the langur monkeys that abound in most tiger habitats, as well as pangolins and porcupines, pythons, frogs, turtles, various birds, and an occasional leopard. In spite of its reputation as a man-eater, tigers seldom attack human beings for food.

Throughout history tigers have suffered from a homicidal reputation, promulgated mostly by hunters. A man is more justified, and certainly more glorified, if he kills an animal who would in turn kill him given the chance. Females will attack in defense of their young. (A bird-watcher in India's Corbett National Park was killed in 1985 when he dashed into a thicket to get a closer look at a rare forest eagle owl and surprised a tigress with her cubs.) But the tiger's malice is mostly fiction. For every tiger sighted in the forest by a human being, there are probably hundreds of human beings scrutinized and left unmolested by tigers. In most areas, tigers are aware of human beings only so that they can better avoid them.

There are a few places, however, where tigers have earned their reputation for man-eating, and the Sunderbans is one of them. In the Tiger Project area itself, covering some twelve hundred square miles, officials estimate that roughly three dozen people are killed and eaten by tigers annually, and more are probably attacked in the surrounding forest areas. (Estimates of bodies taken away and consumed by a tiger in dense swamp will always be rough.) Many of the victims are woodcutters and honey-collectors venturing alone into the forest. Normally tigers are wary of anything that walks on two legs, but according to ecologist John Seidensticker, the honey-collectors and woodcutters of the Sunderbans might unwittingly excite a tiger's interest every time they bend down on all fours to peer through the elevated roots of the mangrove trees. There are also well-documented accounts of tigers swimming out to fishing boats at night, where they climb on board and take their pick of the sleeping fishermen.

Why the Sunderbans tigers prey on so many human beings is somewhat of a mystery. Some studies suggest that a tiger turns to man-eating in the harsh mangrove habitat because it finds it difficult to secure more conventional prey. Since human beings and tigers both move about on established paths tracing the higher ground, they are more likely to encounter each other. Human flesh is apparently an acquired taste, and an accidental killing might add another confirmed man-eater to the population.

In an indirect way, the Sunderbans habitat itself is responsible for the conflict. The waters of the delta are abundantly rich in fish, and the forest holds a wealth of honey, especially in spring. In contrast, the human population of the delta is achingly poor. The lure of the swamp, even with its tigers, is too great a temptation to resist. According to a report of the Bombay Natural History Society, "The local people of the Sunderbans have a firm conviction that death is an inevitable phenomenon and occurs as decreed by the Tiger-God and there is nothing one can do about it."

Recently, conservation officials in the Indian Sunderban tiger reserve have taken a more active approach to the problem. They plant dummy woodcutters and fishermen in the swamp, dressed in used clothing to make them smell human, and wrapped around with wire attached to a 12-volt car battery. Any animal that attacks a dummy receives an electric shock.

"By moving the dummies around to places where the tigers are troublesome," says Pranabes Sanyal, director of the reserve, "we hope we can spread the message that humans are dangerous targets."

A very wooden woodsman.

In the Sunderbans, the tiger's favorite prey is the chital. This is a beautiful, gracefully proportioned deer, reddish brown in color, with one black stripe along its spine. Each white spot on its flanks is swept backward, hazy on the edges, giving the impression that the animal is speeding away even when it stands quite still. In a footrace a chital, or any deer, will quickly outdistance a tiger. But speed is only the final, desperate defense against a charging cat. The deer's senses of hearing and smell are highly refined. As a member of a herd, the chital gains from the constant surveillance of all the herd's members. At the slightest scent of danger the grazer raises its head from the grass and freezes erect, head up, tail up, alerting other chitals with its poised-sentry posture and irritable stomps of the forefoot. In areas where spotted deer abound, its short, doglike bark of alarm is one of the most common sounds in the forest. The herd grazes through a meadow or river grassland all in a single direction, and when on the move the deer fall into single file. In this way, they are less likely to stumble upon ambushing tigers and leopards.

Normally, the chital prefer to graze in open areas, free of any cover

Langur monkeys, safe as long as they stay in the trees, become extremely vulnerable to tiger attack when they descend to the forest floor.

An ambitious Bengal tiger plunges into shallow water in hot pursuit of a sambar calf. The sambar buck in the foreground doesn't seem to realize the danger. After a painstaking stalk, a tiger needs only a few ground-swallowing bounds to reach its prey. However, unless the tiger has crept to within fifty feet or so of the prey without being detected, the attack will probably fail.

that a predator might make use of. Yet the chital must balance its fear of the tiger against a fairly constant hunger for grass. In the course of a morning's feed, a deer often passes close by thickets or bushes deep enough to hide a big cat. So long as the tiger remains motionless, the chital cannot see him at any real distance. If the tiger is detected before it has crept to within fifty feet or so, it is stripped of all hope of a kill: The chital bark, "I see you!" and relax their viligance. The tiger pulls its weight up from the grass and stomps off, without the slightest pretense of stealth, carving a corridor of squawks and screechings through the forest. Sometimes, it must suffer the indignity of actually being tailed by a herd of chital endeavoring to keep it in sight.

In addition to their own warning systems, chital are particularly well-tuned to any sudden change in the voice of the forest—the screech of a jungle babbler or red-wattled lapwing, some jungle fowl flushed from a thicket, or langur monkeys bleating alarm from above. The langur's position in the trees provides a better view than that of the deer, and an especially beneficial alliance often forms between a troop of foraging monkeys and a herd of chital. The deer become the monkey's nose, the monkey the eyes of the deer, and both bark their fury at the tiger. The benefits of the relationship, however, are not precisely balanced: The chital also cozy up to the langurs for the seedpods and other greenery the langurs let fall during their feeding.

For the young male tiger in the Sunderbans, it has been a long and hungry night. Low tide has made traveling hard, even for such a sure-footed animal. The herd of chital locked in his vision are the first he has come even close to for several days. The tiger keeps low to the ground, eyes burning with the bright, depthless glare common to all cats on the stalk. He lifts each leg gingerly, and places it back down again with even greater care. If his paw encounters a dead leaf, he slowly crushes it into pulp rather than allow it to rustle. He is now only forty feet from the buck, with the does a bit beyond, farther out in the tidal meadow. Like all tigers, he has made his approach to his prey from the direction offering the most cover, regardless of which way the wind is blowing. This time the air is completely still, his scent trapped in the thick vapor. The buck looks up briefly, but returns to his feed.

Suddenly the tiger raises his head from the thicket and catapults himself at the buck. At the same moment, a fly happens to land on the buck's face, looking to cadge a drink from the rim of its eye. The distraction is slight, but enough to tip the balance in the tiger's favor. The buck hears the rustle of danger in the grass, but a fraction of a second too late. The does bolt at the sound, their hooves falling quickly into synchrony, touch and leap, touch and leap, as if escaping from a tiger were the grand finale of an ancient ballet. The buck bolts too, but there is already a horrible weight upon his back and a burning pain deep in his shoulders.

There is something chillingly inevitable about the kill, as if the tiger were by nature quite incapable of making a mistake. Even the deer seems

The tiny, elusive hog deer is prey to tigers, but the cat prefers to hunt much larger game.

to concede his life as soon as the tiger has his grips in place. Every killing pounce is launched from behind or from the side, the tiger's hindfeet never leaving the ground. The work is accomplished with muscle-packed, prehensile forelegs tipped with needle-sharp retractable claws. His grip cannot be shaken. As the buck begins to topple, the tiger, tail held high, ducks under its chin to avoid the hooves. Before the prey has hit the ground, the tiger has flipped around and seized him by the throat. If the animal were smaller—perhaps a fawn, or a full-grown hog deer—the tiger might dispatch it with a single, chomping bite to the nape of the neck to crush the animal's cervical vertebrae. But for the larger, preferred prey, a suffocating throat hold serves best.

For several minutes the two lie quiet, perpendicular, joined at the dying animal's throat. There is little commotion; they almost seem to be resting. The buck makes one attempt to rise, his antlers digging up mud. The tiger merely shifts his jaw and grabs onto a little more flesh. Three minutes later the tiger lets go and stands up. He bends to sniff at his kill, licking a bit at the blood from the shoulder wound. For a few moments he straddles the deer, panting from his exertion. Picking the buck up by the neck, he drags it back into the bush. The 150-pound body, hooves dragging in the mud, is an easy load; a hunter once watched a tiger jump up a fifteen-foot high streambank with a similar kill in its mouth. Another tiger, having killed a goat set out as bait by some researchers, found his efforts to make off with the kill thwarted by the tether around the animal's neck. The tiger simply gave a good pull and separated the goat's body from its head, leaving the latter behind, still bound to its stake.

With the buck dragging between his legs, the tiger descends deeper into the forest, away from the open meadow. From the night before he recalls a secluded freshwater pool, and sets off to find it again. Eating buck is thirsty business, and with the pool close by he will not have to trouble himelf to look for water later. The seclusion is even more important. No tiger likes to feed in the open, and will often drag its kill great distances to dense cover if the terrain permits. By the edge of the pool the tiger drops the buck, then drops down himself beside it.

The tiger works into the carcass, pulling the meat free with jerks of his head. Invariably a tiger addresses the first few bites to the meaty rump of the animal. Each kind of cat, in fact, has its own favorite place to begin the feed—jaguars opt for the forequarters and chest, leopards start at the abdomen, and cheetahs zero in on a thigh. Lions invariably begin with the viscera and the fat surrounding them. A feeding lion has to contend with the snarling intrusions of other lions, so perhaps it is best to go at the softest, most accessible regions first, before someone else steals one's place at the carcass.

For the young tiger in the Sunderbans, the first quarter hour of feeding goes by in splendid solitude. Having worked well into the rump, the tiger rips the carcass open from anus to rib cage. The entrails and stomach tumble onto the ground. Unlike the polar bear, who eats only the seal's blubber, the tiger is not choosy about the flesh it eats, swallowing mouthfuls of gut and muscle, chewing up small bones. He is a pure carnivore nonetheless, and when the buck's rumen falls out, containing a half-digested meal of grass, the tiger fastidiously moves the rest of the carcass away from it and resumes his feed.

The tiger's complacence at the kill does not last long. Having satisfied his initial hunger, he stretches to an upright position and paces around the buck, then scratches the ground, as if attempting to cover his prize with dirt. A tree pie, a pretty orange-and-black bird ubiquitous in the Indian forest, attempts a landing on the buck's ear. The tiger chases him off with a snarl. The bird would take no more than a few tiny beakfuls of flesh, but the tiger seems to suffer the anxiety shared by all who succeed: He now has something to lose.

Considering its frightening advantage in strength, a tiger's defense of its prey might appear slightly hysterical. One similarly jealous tigress was seen to leap up from her resting place and charge twenty feet to scare off some crows sitting on a branch above her kill. Another tigress, having left a half-eaten buffalo in a ravine, returned to find the carcass covered with vultures. She stalked to within a hundred feet, then pounced on the birds, plucking one out of the air with her forepaw and killing it with a swat. Vultures are a real threat to the tiger's stash. They would surely devour any kill left unguarded and uncovered. There are, besides, larger scavengers in the forest, including leopards and other tigers. Given the difficulty of ob-taining the food in the first place, the tiger's possessiveness makes good sense.

Finding no convenient way to cover the buck's carcass, the tiger drags it closer to the pool, into a patch of muddy shade. He takes a drink and cleans the blood from his muzzle. The fog has lifted from the forest, and hazy, midmorning sunlight lies in heavy patches all around. There will be no more feeding for a while. Close by, a peacock utters the first in its long, weary chain of calls, each one a pair of rising syllables, too loud, too long, as if the bird has some personal complaint to make to the jungle and has ceased even to care that nobody listens. The tiger settles down by the pool on his flank, one paw laid over the rigid foreleg of the buck. The tiger's eyes close, while the buck's stare blindly into the canopy above.

II

The Sunderbans forest is a fine habitat for harboring tigers, but a difficult place for tiger research. Wild animals do not pick a convenient spot to make a kill and schedule demonstrations of their prowess. Field biologists must have the freedom of movement to go to where the animals live and stay there, observing behavior as it occurs in the context of long, often tedious routines, measuring the individual animal's actions against that of entire populations. To do research in the Sunderbans requires a

A sated hunter relaxes beside its sambar kill. Unless a scavenger finds and picks it clean, a carcass of this size will keep the cat well fed for several days. Except for the large bones, the rumen is the only part of the deer that the tiger will not consume.

large and expensive boat—seventy-five feet or more—to cope with the enormous tides. There is also the matter of the storms off the Bay of Bengal, violent enough to sink a smaller vessel. So far, no one has penetrated the Sunderbans and returned with the full story of the tigers living there.

In the mid 1960s, zoologist George Schaller found more accessible terrain to study tigers in the meadows and open forests of Kanha Park, in the Indian state of Madhya Pradesh. Before Schaller, the natural history of the tiger "had been studied predominantly along the sights of a rifle." His work provided the first detailed portrait of the tiger and its relationship to its prey. More recently, investigators such as Chuck MacDougal, Mel Sundquist, and David Smith have expanded on Schaller's study, focusing their research in Chitwan National Park in Nepal. Over time, their investigations have uncovered a fascinating pattern of interactions between members of this seemingly solitary species, a design woven of scent signals and guttural roars through the forest, matings and gatherings, births, battles, deaths, and dispersals.

Formerly a hunting preserve, Chitwan Park is located in a richly forested valley in the Siwalik Hills—gentler country than most of Nepal, and because of a particularly deadly form of malaria, protected up until a quarter of a century ago from widespread human encroachment. With a rainfall of ninety-five inches per year, the valley is exceedingly lush. Winter days are pleasant, but the nights throw a frigid shroud of mist over the terrain. In early spring the temperature begins to climb and the humidity to fall. By the end of May the place is as dry as a desert, the brain-fever bird earning its name with its maddening crescendo, "It's too hot, it's too hot, IT'S TOO HOT!!" The monsoons arrive in June, suddenly and spectacularly, and the rivers are transformed overnight into flooding torrents. There is little relief from the heat, however, until October.

In the 1950s the poverty of farmers in the hillier areas forced them down into the valley in search of more productive farmland. They were aided by an effective malaria control program, and within a decade the area north of the Rapti River filled with people, who removed most of the forest, grassland, and wildlife to plant their crops. Fortunately, King Mahendra of Nepal declared the area south of the Rapti a rhinoceros sanctuary. In 1970, responding to the sudden worldwide realization of the tiger's dwindling populations, the king expanded the sanctuary into a tiger reserve as well. With international support, the reserve became Chitwan Park in 1973, and now includes over a thousand square kilometers of some of the finest tiger country in the world.

The best way to travel in Chitwan is by elephant. The lowlands of the park along the rivers and marshlands are covered with a patchwork of high grasslands and riverine forest, a tapestry of brilliant emerald and jade. Along the banks of streams and near lakes and ponds, the grass never browns, even in the heat of the dry season. Stands of *Saccharum* rise twenty feet or more in height. In one swath of grass running along the edge of the river, a person can ride an elephant for two days and never see over the top. Rhinos lace their trails through the grass and sequester young in the thick stands along streams. In the tapestry, one has to imagine the hidden tawny flecks of tigers, who use the grass and forest as cover to stalk chital, sambar, hog deer, and wild hog. The hills, meanwhile, are given over to dense expanses of sal trees, whose trunks rise seventy feet before the first branches flare out to form a sun-perforated canopy. Beneath, the forest floor is relatively open, with no layer of shrub to attract prey.

Tigers make three demands of their habitat: It must have dense vegetation to hide in, an adequate population of prey animals, and access to some permanent sources of water. Needless to say, these three factors are not static entities; they are threads braided together in a dynamic give-and-take. The tiger's habitat shifts with time and the seasons, and is never predictable. Inexplicably, female tigers prefer grasslands in the cool season, while the males keep more to the riverine forest. In Chitwan, a tiger might do ninety percent of its hunting in the grassland and riverine forest, but it

The tiger's tawny coat keeps these two cats well-hidden in dry grass. Some researchers think its black stripes mimic the play of light and shadow.

still spends a third of its time wandering in the sal-tree forest above, where the hunting is relatively poor. Perhaps tigers do not trust in momentary abundance. Deer are fickle; the herd of chital by the riverbank might disappear tomorrow, and perhaps then the sal will provide a meal in the form of a solitary sambar, a larger, forest-dwelling deer. The habitat itself cannot be trusted; the grass might stand tall one day, and the next morning villagers come in, swinging their scythes and burning, rendering that hunting ground useless until new shoots entice the ungulates back again. Over the years, more drastic alterations can occur. An epidemic disease of deer can rapidly, and catastrophically lighten a tiger's prey biomass. Storms, floods, and the leveling of forest tracts all work their changes in the character of a habitat.

The balance of ecological requisites will help to determine how many tigers an area can support, but it is not the whole story. Tigers are firmly territorial. A resident male secures an area containing more prey than he needs, yet he will rarely suffer another adult male to linger within his boundaries. In a rich habitat like Chitwan, a male occupies a range of from fifteen to forty square miles. The male's territory embraces the smaller ranges of several females, who likewise defend their territories against intrusion from other females. (In open country, where prey might be dispersed over many miles, tiger territories extend great distances and tend to overlap more.) This puts a further limit on the number of tigers any given locality can support. Chitwan currently holds some 50 to 60 breeding tigers with territories; the rest of the total population—150 animals—is made up of cubs, "subadults" not yet of breeding age, and disenfranchised wanderers.

The word "territory," when applied to tigers and other wild animals, must not be confused with human notions of property. We cannot know how a tiger perceives of geographic space at all. It is possible, however, to watch how the tiger *behaves* in relation to other tigers in its region—where it wanders, how it makes its presence known, and what it does to defy intruders. It may seem like a subtle difference, but tigers do not behave the way they do in order to maintain territories; rather, the territories are a result of the behavior. Territorial actions need not be conscious. A tiger puts down a scent mark, for instance, not like a farmer erecting a fence post, but more like a man checking into a hotel room. He empties his pockets onto the bureau top, throws his overcoat on the bed, and otherwise establishes the room as his own with his possessions.

Along one edge of the tapestry of Chitwan, one might encounter an old resident male, a savvy and battle-proven beast, well-established in his territory. His northern boundary might be formed by the Rapti River as it meanders through a floodplain. To the south, low but rugged hills establish another natural border. To the east and west, and all between, the tiger defines his range by his presence alone. The tiger is almost constantly on the move. In the past, it was thought that these restless wanderings were yet another measure in the dance of predator and prey: If a tiger stayed too long in any one neighborhood, the deer would become increasingly alert to its presence, and the odds of making a successful kill—already nineteen to one against the tiger—would tilt even further in favor of the deer.

Now it is believed that the solitary tiger is urged on more by social pressures than by hunger. In order to maintain a territory, a tiger must obey the maxim, "Use it or lose it." Any portion of his range that he does not exploit will quickly be taken over by some other tiger. Tiger territory, in fact, is something of a paradox. The old tiger, by virtue of his exclusive habits, is constantly brought into contact with others of his kind. In a given night, he might travel twenty miles or more, checking up on the doings of the females in his territory, and of other tigers along the fringes of his range, even as he pursues the deer. What's happened to the lame male encountered last week in the rise of woodland? What about the young one who lives on the island in the river—has he been creeping up the bank again? Who's that roaring in the far hills? Who's scent mark is this? Is that the smell of a cub? It's best to go and find out, keep on the move.

Obviously, in an area of twenty-five square miles or more, not even the fleetest, most peripatetic individual could patrol all borders at once. Instead, the resident leaves behind a collection of markers, traces of himself, that serve to define the limits of his territory. The most common form of communication is scent-marking. As the resident male leaves a path that forms the boundary of his range, he backs up to a distinctively gnarled tree and lets loose a spray of urine. For many days thereafter, the tree will smell pungently of tiger, an odor rather like that of buttered popcorn. He needn't bother fringing the border of his territory evenly with scent marks. He concentrates on the places where thin vegetation makes access easy for intruders, or where the boundary takes a turn. Depending on the season, the tiger might also leave behind two other kinds of messages: a pile of feces dropped conspicuously on the path or in some other open area, and a characteristic scrape mark—two scratches dug into the ground with the claws, parallel to the tiger's direction of travel. In the wet season, when feces quickly dissolve in the rain, the tiger scratches more often, and lets his excreta drop with no message implied.

The shower of scent left on a bush or tree contains a wealth of infor-mation about the tiger who left it behind, including its identity, how long ago it left the mark, and in the case of a female, her sexual state. The freshness and density of marks in an area is a good indication of when the tiger is likely to return. All of this is of utmost importance; for tigers, knowledge is power. When another tiger senses the mark, or even if the same tiger returns to the spot, it bares its teeth in a nonaggressive grimace called a "Flehmen response." Like many mammals, the tiger possesses what is called a Jacobson's organ—a region of chemically sensitive cells on the roof of the mouth. It is thought that Flehmen exposes the Jacobson's organ to chemical stimulants, called pheromones, contained in the tiger's marking fluid. In this fashion, the animal obtains a chemosensory portrait of the tiger who left the mark.

The use of pheromones— chemical messages that signal to others of the same species across distance—is frequent in nature. Each species uses chemical signaling for its own purpose. Pack-dwelling animals like wolves and hyenas, for instance, recognize each other and identify strangers by their scents, while life-forms as diverse as moths, lobsters, and deer employ pheromones as sexual lures. Human beings also have the equipment to catch pheromonal messages from the opposite sex, though there is some question whether we still find them stimulating, or in our odd refinement prefer perfumes based on the secretions of other animals. Human females show a curious sensitivity to the glandular excretions of the musk deer and civet cat, strikingly similar in their chemistry to the musklike compounds found in both human males and in boars. The synthetic musk odor used in one study could only be perceived by sexually mature women, who were themselves much more sensitive to the odor during ovulation.

Some animals, including many species of insects and fish, release a pheromone when mutilated to warn others of their kind to the danger of attack. If wounded on a patch of skin barely one-hundredth of a square millimeter in diameter, a minnow will release a pheromone from the injury powerful enough to cause the entire school of minnows to flee. The normally stationary sea urchin, alerted

to threat by an alarm pheromone from a crushed urchin nearby, will race away on its spines at the astonishing urchin-speed of one foot every ten minutes.

The marking fluid of the tiger is designed to be durable in the hot Indian climate. The pheromone itself is composed of volatile molecules, but to preserve its pungency over several days, the odoriferous part of the fluid is bound with a less volatile chemical formation called a lipid,

The heavily scratched bark indicates that this tree is a well-used boundary marker for the local tiger population. This tiger leaves its scent on the tree trunk by rubbing the bark with its chin.

which prevents the odor from being quickly dispersed, even in heavy rains. The tiger releases its scent on an object about a yard aboveground, where wind currents can carry it twice as far as a scent dropped at ground level.

With the placement of scent marks, fecal mounds, and a few scrapes, the forest begins to take on tigerish definitions, a frame on which the slowly revolving design of tiger interaction weaves itself. The roaring across the jungle, the feces scattered on the road, and the fluent chemistry of scent-marks are not meant to challenge, but to inform. The old resident male approaches the decaying stump of a silk-cotton tree. Smelling his own odor upon it, he turns around and freshens his mark. Two days later, a younger, stronger male stands over the stump, grimacing in Flehmen. He can tell by its fading blush that the scent is old, and he proceeds further into the resident's territory looking for food. In the early morning he catches a langur monkey by surprise, and eats it on the spot. By daybreak, however, he is back across the boundary, wandering fitfully in search of some place free of the scent of other males.

Someday, the younger animal may decide to stay, and the old resident will have to either fight him off or abandon the scene himself. But in spite of the tiger's constrained habitat and the number of transient animals, outright battles over territory are not common. The reason may lie in the vulnerability explicit in the life of the solitary hunter. If a wolf, a hyena, or even a lion suffers an injury, they can still survive on the killings made by others in their group. But according to Chuck MacDougal, tigers "cannot afford the luxury of uninhibited aggression." A tiger lives by his own prowess. Even a slight injury—a broken foot bone, an infected blister—can hobble the tiger's ability to bring down prey. In Chitwan, an emaciated male once walked into the kitchen of a guardhouse and collapsed. A single porcupine quill was embedded in his shoulder—apparently enough to slow the sweep of his paw or weaken his grip. The tiger died of starvation the following day.

More common than battles over territory are fights to determine sexual privilege. A tigress in heat announces her condition by scent-marking heavily throughout her territory and by moaning, sometimes insistently, as she paces through the forest. In most cases, she will succeed in attracting the resident male. If she lives on the fringe of his territory, males from nearby territories, or even transients, may also be lured by her signals. The system favors matings between residents, who are thus much more likely to pass on their genes. Fights erupt only as a last resort; usually the less dominant animal will quietly withdraw. If the competing males decide to press the issue, the fights are bloody and sometimes fatal, occasionally to both parties. In one case in Chitwan two males were so incapacitated by a fight that neither one was able to respond when a third male arrived and made off with the tigress.

If one could ask a tigress what her preference in a mate would be, she would probably list familiarity near the top of his selling points. Tigers are polygamous, but they seem to avoid mating with strangers. Before copulating, a variety of courtship rituals build or reestablish trust, the pair sparring and playing together, often with a deceptive churlishness that helps to break the ice. The tigress lies low in the grass, for instance, her eyes blazing and her tail twitching, then rushes toward the male with an arm lifted as though ready to tear him to bits, only to soften her blow at the last second into an affectionate pat on the cheek. If the male balks at such mock aggression, the mating may not progress. Throughout the courtship, the tigress is more often the initiator, rubbing her flanks against the male's body, rolling over on her back in a playful invitation, nuzzling her face into his.

Tiger copulation is a raucous affair. "Conceive a chorus got up by a hundred pairs of cats," wrote one hunter, "multiply copiously, and even then you will fail to realize the awful sounds." After the tigress has presented herself to the male, he mounts her and quickly grabs the nape of her neck with his teeth. The male lets out a deafening roar as he climaxes, then

The affectionate play of mating tigers helps the pair establish trust before copulating.

ducks to avoid the female's paw as she pivots, roars, and takes a swipe at his face. Her gesture might be in response to the pain caused by the male's barbed penis as he withdraws. Tigers are induced ovulators, and the rough projections of skin on the penis probably serve to stimulate ovulation. Afterward, the pair lie about together, perhaps sharing a kill. The interludes of quiet are of necessity short: probably to ensure conception, tigers copulate very frequently, as much as twenty times a day, before the female's estrus is over and the pair go their separate ways again.

The tiger's prodigious capacity for sex—twenty copulations or more per day between a consorting pair—may contribute, ironically, to the progress of the animal's extinction. Because of the tiger's reputation for virility, the Chinese believe a tiger penis is an even more powerful aphrodisiac than rhinoceros horn. Folklore holds that much of the rest of the tiger can be made into potent medicine for human ailments. Tiger tail ground up and mixed with soap is applied as a salve for skin disease. Sitting on a tiger-skin rug is a sure way to rid a person of fevers caused by ghosts. A mixture of tiger brain and oil cures laziness and acne. Eat the tiger's heart for strength and courage, carry the tail tip to ward off evil, roll the eyeballs into pills to calm convulsions. If one is plagued by centipedes, dispatch them easily by burning a little tiger hair in the vicinity.

Tigers are not threatened by large-scale slaughter-for-profit operations as are rhinos and elephants, but the practice does occur. Taiwan has become notorious in recent years for its trade in tiger parts. In 1985 the meat of one large male sold for $15 a pound, and its bones at seven times that price. Bottles of tiger blood were going at $50 apiece. The gall bladder fetched $125; the liver, $50; while the tiger's penis fetched $1,500, outsold only by the skin.

If the mating has been successful, the tigress will give birth some fifteen weeks later. She finds a secluded spot in her territory to deliver her young—a deep cleft in a rock, perhaps, or a pocket of hidden thicket in the grass. The kittens are blind and helpless at birth. As might be expected from so short a gestation period, they are tiny when born, weighing at the most four pounds. Within a month the cubs triple their weight, but they will still be shortsighted and entirely dependent on their mother.

Newborn tigers do not enjoy the safe intimacy of a hibernating den. If there is the least suspicion of danger, however, the tigress will move the litter to a safer location, carrying them one at a time in her mouth. But she must often leave them unattended while she hunts. A lactating tigress has higher nutritional requirements than normal, and after a couple of months, the cubs too will begin to eat a little meat, even as they continue to suckle. Until they are six months old, the cubs show little inclination to leave their mother's side. When she lies down for a rest they climb over her, stroking her head or gently chewing a convenient ear. Like most young, the cubs play among themselves too, mock-biting and pouncing on each other, much like domestic kittens. They continue to nurse for up to six months, their long, tawny bodies stretched out perpendicular from their mother while she lounges in the dust.

Within the tapestry of tigers one has to look closely to find the figures of a tigress and her cubs. The mother is cautious and reclusive, well aware that the cubs are incapable of defending themselves against fire, human beings, and other predators. Though she may bear a litter of up to seven young, only half are likely to survive, even in the hospitable confines of Chitwan Park. In harsher habitats, even fewer will live through the year-and-a-half to two years of dependency.

As the cubs grow, the pressure on the mother increases to find them enough food to eat. For the first few months she makes her kills close to the den site, then calls her cubs to the feed with a soft roar. Even when they are old enough to accompany her on the hunt, she confines her range to familiar, closed terrain, often making long detours around broken country in order to avoid any possible confrontation with other tigers. The ones most to be feared are strange males, who may try to kill any cubs they come across. If the tigress encounters a passing male, she will most likely attack, even if he is twice her size. Usually the male will withdraw rather than risk his skin. The safest strategy for the tigress, however, is to avoid places where other tigers are likely to be prowling.

Male tigers who kill cubs are not driven by hunger or by some dark trait in their nature. So long as a female tiger has dependent cubs in tow, she will not come into heat, which effectively eliminates her as a potential mate for as much as two-and-a-half years. An unrelated male can hasten her estrus by eliminating her cubs, an act that removes the hormonal brake on her reproductive cycle. Obviously, there is no advantage in a tiger murdering his own cubs. But a strange male who kills a tigress's cubs creates a vacancy which he can quickly fill with his own offspring and, at the same time, remove potential competitors for the area's resources. Of course this scenario is not consciously plotted out by the tiger. The decision to kill is made on a genetic level: If infanticidal tendencies in a male lead to more of his own offspring being born, tigers in future generations are more likely to carry the same predisposition in their genes, and the habit persists.

Infanticide is practiced by many mammal species, including lions, bears, prairie dogs, and many primates. The silver-haired Hunaman langur, a long-tailed, black-faced monkey common on the Indian sub-continent, is one of the better-studied examples. Langur troops, from six to seventy individuals, are composed of related females and their offspring, together with, normally, only one breeding male. The infants

Hunaman langurs are extremely solicitous toward their young, but the infants may be killed when new males take over the troop and establish a dominance over succeeding generations.

in a troop are much fussed over; they are freely passed from hand to hand, with each female getting her chance to stroke and groom the baby. If the infant is female herself, she will eventually be incorporated into the troop. Adolescent males, however, leave home and form what amount to teenage gangs: bachelor bands that roam about, attacking the stable breeding troops on their borders.

Their belligerence is understandable: Unless a young male is aggressive, he will remain a bachelor until he dies. Even if he succeeds in establishing himself as the virile breeder in a troop, he will probably hold on to his breeding rights for no more than two years before being ousted by a more dominant male.

A border battle of langurs is usually fought with a great deal more screaming, chasing, and hand-grappling than actual violence. Normally, the resident male, backed up by his harem, succeeds in repulsing the attack of bachelors. But if the bachelors manage to chase away the resident male, they may snatch the infants away from their mothers and aunts and destroy them. If the initial attempt at infanticide is unsuccessful, a newly ensconced male will keep his eye on the infants afterward, looking for an opportunity to erase his predecessor's lineage.

Lacking brute strength, a pregnant female may resort to an elegant form of deceit to save her unborn young. By behaving as if she is experiencing estrus, she tricks the usurping male into responding to her sexual advances and mating with her. When her infant is born, the new lord of the troop believes the child is his own, and allows it to live.

Besides protecting her cubs from present danger, the tigress also bears the responsibility of preparing them for the future. Tigers are not born with the ability to kill. Untrained tiger cubs attack incoherently, snatching at the prey's legs, belly and rump. They learn the proper technique in training sessions conducted by their mother, who captures live langurs and other prey and brings them back to use as instructional tools.

George Schaller once observed such a training session at a tethered buffalo bait site in Kanha Park. For two hours one morning, he watched a

Two young tigers bring down a tethered buffalo. In order to get a close look at tiger feeding habits, researchers offer sick and dying buffalos as tiger bait.

group of cubs try futilely to bring the buffalo down. When their mother arrived, she grabbed one of the animal's hindlegs with her teeth and knocked the other leg out from under the buffalo with a swipe of her paw. The buffalo fell virtually unharmed, and the tigress dragged it farther back by the leg. As the cubs rushed in, she let go of the buffalo and stepped away, clearly giving them a chance to practice on the prey. They fell upon it in a clawing heap, each cub tearing and biting wherever it could get a hold. The buffalo rose up and whirled, shaking off the cubs and charging at the tigress herself.

It required another training session in the early afternoon to finally subdue the buffalo (the tigress held him down while her cubs bit and tore at its hump, belly, hindquarters—anything). The cubs began to feed while the animal was still alive. One even grabbed the buffalo's nose and was nearly gored. A month and a half later Schaller watched the same four cubs make another stab at a killing, once again arranged for them by their mother. Already over a year old, they still made a mess of the business. Three more months passed before Schaller witnessed the male of the litter make an efficient kill on a buffalo. By this time he was almost as large as his mother, and his sisters were not much smaller.

Gradually, the cubs begin to drift apart from the mother and make their own kills. Typically, the male leaves first. Females abide longer with their mother, and when they do become independent they stay closer to home. If there is room on the fringes of the mother's territory, they may eventually carve out a range of their own there, sometimes appropriating some of their mother's domain. Mel Sundquist, for several years a researcher with the Smithsonian Institution's tiger project in Chitwan, recorded one case of a tigress who was separated from her normal territory by the annual burning of grass. When she returned six weeks later, she found that her independent daughter from a previous litter had laid down her scents and claimed 90 percent of the territory for herself. The dispossessed older tigress was forced to wander in marginal areas. Such allocation of territory only happens between parent and offspring. The mother would never have tolerated a stranger preempting so much of her claim.

Male cubs, less cautious from the beginning, wander farther from the natal range. According to David Smith, who studied the dispersal of tigers in Chitwan from 1977 to 1980, the males may take four or even five years before they establish territories of their own. In the meantime, their exuberance only leads to trouble. Without the prey-rich abundance of a personal territory, young males may have to make do with domestic livestock on the periphery of a park or reserve. If this marauding becomes a habit, the villagers will organize and end the killing spree by setting out poisoned bait. These subadult males are also the most likely to be injured or killed in territorial battles with bigger tigers. Their vulnerability is echoed in the statistics: In a park such as Chitwan, the females reaching adulthood outnumber the males by as much as four to one.

The animals that survive their vulnerable early years will eventually find their own place among the tigers in Chitwan. In time, they may grow strong enough to drive a resident tiger from its territory. Or perhaps a vacancy will occur without violence, as when a tiger dies because he is too old to hunt effectively anymore, or perhaps because he is brought down by parasites. His scent marks fade, his scrapes are obscured by wind and the traffic of animals. Soon there is no trace of the old one, save for the scratch marks he may have left behind on some favorite trees.

All around, there are other tigers waiting for just such an opportunity for enfranchisement. Quickly they sense his absence. Within a matter of days, some enterprising young male has moved in, or perhaps several carve up the dead one's territory. One huge male, weighing over six hundred pounds, maintained an expanse of land in Chitwan embracing the territories of seven different females. His death in 1979 triggered a period of violent disputes over who should occupy which part of his formerly peaceful domain. Infanticide rose dramatically. Reproduction fell off. Before the dust settled several years later, three tigers had died in fights over territories and access to females. In less pressured circumstances, however, tigers are quite capable of tolerating and even enjoying each other's company, at least for a time.

A good place to find a gathering of tigers is at a feeding site; best of all are the bait sites established by researchers, where the tigers know they are likely to find an easy kill. When tigers congregate at feeding sites, a surprisingly distinct etiquette emerges to keep aggressive behavior in check. Rule number one: When approaching another tiger at the feed, do so slowly and completely out in the open. Any sudden or stealthy movement might make the feeding tiger feel threatened. Rule number two: Whoever has made the kill eats first, no matter how much bigger or fiercer are those waiting their turn. Rule number three: Respect each other's space. Adult tigers do not all feed at once. One will take its fill while the others sit about in the grass a discreet distance away, patient, stretched out on their flanks or resting with heads on forearms. Tiger table manners, ironically, are much better than those of their relatives, the lions. The most sociable of all cats, lions lose all trace of propriety as soon as food is at stake. Feeding lions snarl and snap and fight for the juiciest bits. Sometimes the cubs are left with nothing at all. By comparison, a group of tigers around a carcass resembles a social tea.

A temporary association of a handful of tigers is not evidence of some dormant disposition to be more social. Nevertheless, there is something deeply revealing about such a gathering. Tigers are solitary by nature, and each one lying in the grass represents a furnace of potential fury. Yet the distance from each to each traces the lines of an invisible net that holds them suspended in a strangely quiescent harmony. By mutually determining that the tiger who has made the kill eats first, the animals in effect exhibit a social hierarchy that departs from the simplest principle of Might Makes Right. If a bigger tiger is very hungry, perhaps he will usurp the killer's privilege; but even in this case the takeover is often achieved by a simple change of expression—a flick of white-tipped ears, a subtle flaring of pupil—rather than a snarling attack.

If you stand high on a ridge top above Chitwan, you can look across the green valley and hills to the snow-capped Himalayas rising in the distance. In the valley, the tapestry of tigers reweaves itself, moment by moment, its pattern measured in scent marks and matings and the gradual drift of young animals from the scene of their birth. Somewhere in the forest a great tigress, gripped by her estrus, roars out for attention. Still swathed in mud from a cool lie-down in a river, the resident male rises, roars in answer, and moves toward her through the grass. At the far fringe of his domain a younger male grimaces at a scent mark left a day or two before and walks on, quickening his pace. A few miles away, tucked in a hidden ravine, a mother moans anxiously to her cubs, who leave off chasing

A tiger disturbed at its feed confronts an intruder with a typical feline expression of threat—ears pulled back and lips retracted to reveal two-inch canine teeth.

a hare and run to her side. Where the ravine flattens out below into marsh-land, two young males, littermates, prowl together. One kills a muntjac, and both lie down to feed on the small deer. At the edge of the park, an old, half-lame tiger limps along a road, hoping to cadge a meal from some hidden carcass before its owner returns to chase him off. Time and seasons work their changes. The figures slowly revolve around water hole, scent mark, and the movement of deer. Boundaries blur and overlap, adjusting to changes in the habits of prey, the alterations in the land, the personalities of the tigers within.

Only one boundary is absolute. India is a land of some eight hundred million people, and the population continues to grow. No tiger can survive or even travel in open land, and a collar of rice paddies or other cultivation around a park is in effect an impenetrable barrier, isolating that tiger pop-ulation from all others. The slow dance of tiger life and interaction, the hunting and breeding and raising of young all takes place in a confined space. The fragmentation of the forests puts the tiger in severe danger from what are called stochastic events—random catastrophes. A bad flood, for instance, can wipe out a small but significant percentage of the world's remaining tigers, as could a sudden disease in a species of grass that brings starvation to the tiger's natural prey. For an animal scattered in isolated populations, the question of extinction becomes a local, lonely battle, fought independently in each of the tigers' habitats.

With each population reduced in numbers, the tiger also faces the threat of inbreeding. The farther a young male can roam, the greater is the possibility that he will breed safely with an unrelated female. But if crops and grass burning keep him close to his natal territory, the chances are greater that he will mate with his sisters and daughters. This is not an unusual or harmful event in itself, but if the pattern persists through generations, it could be disastrous. A recessive gene for some detrimental characteristic might eventually become a feature of the whole population. If all the male tigers in an area suffered from a lowered sperm count, for instance, the number of cubs conceived each year might fall below that needed for the population to survive.

With its breeding population hovering near the minimum of fifty needed to sustain itself over time, the tigers of Chitwan Park are by no means assured of survival. If there is a future for them, it will be found in the context of what is called the "metapopulation": the whole structure of tiger populations viewed in relation to the geography of the land. In this larger, grander tapestry, Chitwan and the Sunderbans and all the other forested terrain appear as patches of hope amid the great expanses of desert, mountain, and cultivated land that make up the Indian subcontinent.

Such a view can only be obtained from space. Investigators have recently begun to use satellite images to take stock of the distribution of forests, and their areas and positions relative to one another. Since the tiger can be relied on to be territorial, there will be a limit to how many can live in any given forest area. Thus by measuring the size of the forests, one can come up with a rough estimate of how many tigers exist in each parcel of habitat. The satellite images can also determine where forest "corridors" might be planted to connect two isolated tiger habitats and provide the animals with a bridge to roam across and extend their breeding opportunities. In Nepal, a tiger reserve called Suhla Fanta, merely one hundred kilometers in extent, has already been connected to the next patch of woods by relocating the human population between and returning the cultivated fields to forest.

On a large scale, re-creating forest bridges across cultivated land may prove too expensive, both economically and politically. At the very least, though, the satellite pictures will provide a better idea of the tigers' numbers and distribution. Having shared the planet for so long with these magnificent earthlings, it is encouraging that our extraterrestrial technology can help us find out where they really are.

Taking to the Trees

There was a time, within living memory, when an earthling could have set off from the southeastern corner of Nepal and traveled to the very tip of the Malay Peninsula, without ever touching the ground. The trip could be navigated through the forest canopy, a continuous billowing blanket of rain-speckled leaves, exotic flowers, hanging vines, mosses plunging down like emerald cascades. Through what is now Bangladesh, across Burma, Thailand, and Malaysia, the forest touched tree to tree to tree for two thousand miles. If one can imagine some strategically placed rafts of vegetation to ferry the aerial traveler across water, the trip could continue another two thousand miles aloft, through the thickly forested islands of Sumatra, Borneo, and New Guinea, all the way to the northern coast of Australia. To make the expedition, a creature would have to be appropriately outfitted. A prehensile tail, for example, would be useful for grasping onto branches, as would hooked paws or clawed digits. An upward-facing shoulder socket is needed to brachiate, gibbonlike, from tree limb to tree limb. Alternatively, one might vault across space on sails of stretched skin. Arboreal snakes scuttle over rough bark aided by belly scales stiffened into keels. Tree frogs, geckos and tree hyraxes use suction pads on their feet to cling tightly to trunks and branches.

The tropical rain forest straddles the equator through Southeast Asia, the Amazon Basin in South America, and western Africa. Though it covers only 2 percent of the earth's surface, the forest harbors over half the world's species of animals and plants. On the island of Madagascar alone there are five times the number of tree species than on the entire North American continent. Mount Makiliang, a volcanic peak in the Philippines, has more woody plants clinging to its slopes than can be found in all of the United States. According to a 1981 report by the National Academy of Sciences, a typical, four-square-mile patch of rain forest contains 1,500 species of flowering plants, 750 different trees, over 100 kinds of mammals, 400 birds, 100 reptiles, 60 amphibians, 150 butterflies, and—merely the roughest of estimates—*42,000* species of insect.

Like an aging matriarch, the rain forest remains strong and implacable if left unmolested, but collapses when forced to follow new ways. Its fantastic crowd of dependents grow abundantly, not through wealth, but through thrift, time, and mutual support. In some areas, when human beings level the forest for crops, their harvests prove surprisingly meager. The yields diminish year by year, and soon the farmers are forced to destroy more of the forest. The land developers don't understand that the potency of the rain forest rests not in its soil, but in its age. The organisms have reproduced unceasingly through millions of years of heat and moisture, competing and conspiring so thoroughly that they can hardly be perceived as having life independent from each other. The great, high-crowned trees of the rain forest, for instance, rest their survival on lowly fungi, which weave a fabric of tentacles among the tree roots, pulling nutrients from the impoverished soil.

Pluck a single element out from this tangle of interactions and see how it fares. One developer tried to raise Brazil nuts on a plantation, rather than depend on Indians and peasants to collect the nuts from the forest. His trees were sterile. For pollination, the Brazil nut relies on a particular species of bee, whose mating ritual, in turn, depends on stimulation from a chemical found only in a few kinds of orchid. The Brazil nuts also rely on a rabbitlike rodent, the agouti, to break open the hard outer casing and disperse their seeds. To make his plantation work, the developer would have been forced to turn it back into rain forest.

Around the globe, slash-and-burn agriculture and logging interests are leveling the tropical forest at an incredible pace. The damage is vast, complete, and irrevocable. Every three seconds, somewhere in the world, an area of rain forest the size of a football field falls to human development. A journey by tree through Southeast Asia is not even imaginable anymore: Bangladesh has no primary forest left, and in the other countries scarcely 25 percent remains. According to current predictions, in eighty-five years there will be no rain forest left on earth, and the life-forms it supports will vanish from existence.

Most people think of the jungle as a dense clutter of leaves and vines, but visitors to old, primary forest can leave their machetes behind. At ground level, there is very little growth to hack through. The forest floor is covered by only a tin layer of leaf litter. Decomposition is quick in the forest; dead things are quickly detected, consumed, and returned to life. The profusion of greenery is above, thickest of all in the sun-drenched canopy some one hundred feet overhead where leaves of canopy trees are positioned so as to soak up the utmost amount of sun possible. Some even swivel on their stalks, keeping their broadest face trained on the sun as it arcs across the sky each day. Beneath the canopy, the vaults of space are broken by thinner layers of branches, all laced together with climbing vines called *lianas*, anchored in soil, and various epiphytes—orchids, bromeliads, and ferns— that hang down from higher limbs and trunks.

Most of these air-bound plants do not harm the trees on which they grow, and in fact help the host tree suck nutrients from the air and water. A few, however, begin the relationship innocuously as epiphytes, only to strangle their host later. Mostly members of the fig family, these stranglers germinate in the highest branches of a tree, slowly growing earthward until they reach the ground and secure roots. In the canopy, the fig's leaves reap the benefits of the extra nutrients from the soil. They grow richly, en-croaching on the host tree's allotment of sun. The strangler's roots gradually starve the host's, and slowly insinuate themselves around the tree trunk. Eventually—perhaps a century after the fig seed first sprouted—the host tree dies. Its trunk decays, leaving a hollow, gnarled cylinder of fig roots standing strong.

Compared to the swelling diversity of other life-forms, mammals are only modestly represented in the rain forest. Most are nocturnal and elusive. Primates—and their cousins the lemurs, bush babies, and other prosimi-ans—are more often heard than seen. The forest is also home to arboreal cats and arboreal mice, forest genets and palm civets, tree shrews and tree kangaroos, flying squirrels, flying lemurs, and even flying foxes. These last are actually huge bats, with wing spans reaching six feet. Some species of flying fox congregate in roosts of a million or more, hanging upside down in the trees, their wings wrapped around their bodies like cloaks against the night chill or spread open to catch the warming sun.

Like many of the mammals in the forest, the flying foxes are fruit-eaters. Frugivores are essential to the forest. When a monkey or bat or bird ingests a piece of fruit, it also swallows the seeds, which pass through the animal's gut and are dispersed in its dung. The fruit itself, created at considerable expense of energy to the tree, is nothing more than a colorful lure to tempt the animals. The frugivores have in turn evolved adaptations for spotting the fruit: color vision and eyes positioned forward in their heads, the better to see a speck of luscious red hanging in the green distance. The business of fruit-eating, meanwhile, is made easier by sharp incisors, probing digits, and heavy jaw muscles to break through casings.

The fruit of the fig tree is eaten by more animal species than any other tree genus on earth. A single tree of *Ficus sumatrana* in Malaysia, for example, was found to shelter thirty-two species of birds and mammals at

The tree kangaroo of Australia hops along hori-zontal branches, aided by muscular forelimbs and squat, broad feet.

A flying fox—actually a gigantic bat native to sub-tropical and temperate rain forests—prepares to spread its six-foot wingspan for flight. Recent re-search suggests that the species may be a flying rel-ative of the primates.

one time. The fig is a spectacularly successful earthling. Over nine hundred species grow throughout the tropics, many of them coexisting in the same areas. One might think that such an extravagant number of variations would be reduced through time by neighboring species cross-pollinating and blurring the distinctions between them. Each fig species, however, has evolved in tandem with its own species of fig wasp. These insect predators lay their eggs in the tree's seeds, and in the process pick up pollen, carrying it to the next tree they visit, always one of the same species. The fig and the wasp have achieved a neatly balanced interdependence: The tree sacrifices half its seeds to the wasp so that the other half will grow to be fertilized by the wasp.

The fig tree may have played an intriguing role in the evolution of increased social behavior in mammals, especially among our ancestral primates. Some frugivores can eat green, bitter fruit, but others, like the spider monkey of South America and the chimpanzee of Africa, can only digest ripe fruits. In some fig species, the trees do not bear fruit simultaneously. But when a tree comes into season, all of its fruit bursts into ripeness at once. A fruit-eating monkey is thus provided with an abundant but finite supply of food that lasts only a limited time before another tree must be scouted out. Under such circumstances, it would profit the fruit-eater to bond into cooperative social groups that could move together through the forest. When an individual found a newly ripened fig tree, it could call its companions to the feed with whoops and howls. There would be plenty for all for a time, but soon a new tree would need to be located.

While the plants depend on the animals for seed dispersal and pollination, they must also evolve ways of defending themselves against animal predators. Some plants have erected physical barriers—sharp spines on their branches and tough bark and seed casings. Another effective kind of defense is chemical warfare. The plants in the rain forest have developed a huge arsenal of toxins produced solely for the purpose of destroying or discouraging animal herbivores. The parts most valuable to the plant itself—the leaves, seeds, and circulatory systems just beneath the bark—are those best defended. As is the case with any biological process, the plant must balance its production of toxins—an expensive business—against its other metabolic needs. Many plant poisons are lethal only to specific predators, while others are generally distasteful. The oil of the basil plant, smelling so delightfully fragrant to us when crushed between thumb and finger, is repulsive to many insects. Other plants seem as grotesquely overdefended as a medieval knight in full armor. The sandbox tree covers its trunk in hoary spikes, and its sap can blind a human. Not surprisingly, it does not depend on animals to disperse its seeds. When warmed by the sun, the fruit of the sandbox tree simply explodes, showering poisonous seeds sixty feet away.

Herbivores must either avoid the toxic plants or become extremely picky eaters, always on the brink of poisoning themselves. As a result, a surprisingly small portion of the canopy's tenants feed directly on the plant life—the rest eat either decomposing matter or each other. Leaf-eaters require not only mechanisms to circumvent the plant's toxins, but digestive apparatus able to extract nutrients from the protein-poor green parts of the plant. To save energy, leaf-eaters are often large in body and slow in habit.

Every adaptation has its extreme adherents. For sheer sluggishness, no earthling outperforms the leaf-eating sloths, the cumbersome, long-armed tree-dwellers of South and Central America. Sloths eschew haste. Three-toed sloths (who actually have two toes, but three fingers) rarely travel more than forty yards in a day. Their cousins the two-toed sloths (two fingers, two toes) are larger and even less compelled toward movement once they've found a warm branch to hang from in the sun. With a metabolic rate and muscle tissue less than half that expected for their body weight, sloths cannot afford exuberance. They seem to aspire to the lifestyle of plants; even their fur bears a greenish tint. The color is actually produced by a species of algae that has taken up residence in grooves in the sloth's hair. The algae serves the sloth well, providing effective camouflage against predators in the canopy.

Inside the sloth, digestion proceeds at a very comfortable pace, aided by massive, chambered stomachs and cellulose-devouring bacteria. Leaves swallowed by the sloth in the beginning of March will not pass through till early April. A sloth's bowel movements are both solemnly predictable and deeply mysterious. Once a week, the sloth slowly descends from the branches to the ground, digs a hole with its tail, and deposits a pile of small, pellet-like feces. It then returns up the tree trunk, not to descend again for another week. Given the enormous metabolic expense of such an excursion, it is baffling that the sloth would endure it for such a terribly pedestrian purpose. Why not simply defecate from on high, and let the feces fall? The ground, moreover, is alive with predators, while the tree tops are relatively safe.

No one really understands the hidden purpose of the sloth's journey earthward, but it may have something to do with a long-term alliance to the tree itself. With its range restricted by its sluggish lifestyle, a sloth tends to spend most of its time feeding in only a handful of trees. By depositing its feces directly below its host, the sloth could be contributing to the new growth of leaves on which it depends. To bury a mound of droppings below one's tree might provide only a tiny bit more fertilizer than that of droppings filtering down through the leaves. Through its ancient association with the forest, nevertheless, the sloth may have learned that it is worth the trip.

Whether or not the sloth's weekly commute services the tree, it un-doubtedly benefits an unobtrusive third party. In the fur of the three-toed sloth lives a species of moth found nowhere else in the world. The moths accompany the sloth on its descent to the ground, and when the mammal defecates, the females fly out and deposit their eggs on the fresh excrement. There is little mystery in the moths' behavior: Hatched directly upon their food supply, their progeny will enjoy an obvious advantage over the count-less other dung-eaters in the forest. When the caterpillars metamorphose into adult moths three weeks later, they take to the trees in search of sloths.

The sloth is by no means the only tree-dwelling, leaf-eating earthling with a penchant for staying put. The koala of Australia spends almost all its life in the silvery foliage of eucaplyptus trees, climbing down a trunk only when enticed by the hope of a more promising tree or a mate. The creature is yawningly phlegmatic in its habits. Recently two biologists from California studied the daily activities of koalas in the Australian state of Victoria. The bravery of the biologists in the face of immense tedium is as awe-inspiring, in its way, as the exploits of researchers tracking polar bears through the Arctic or trailing the tiger in the mangrove swamps of the Sunderbans. In a twenty-four-hour period, the koalas spent an average of 14.8 hours sleeping, 4.8 hours resting while awake, 4.7 hours eating, and four *minutes* "traveling." Not a bad model for a stuffed animal.

Koalas feed almost exclusively on eucalyptus leaves, which are highly poisonous to most other mammals. They are understandably careful eaters, never touching some species of eucalyptus unless they are on the brink of starvation, sampling others only in certain months of the year, or tasting only the leaves on certain trees. If the koala uses its sensitive nose to stay clear of the really dangerous leaves—especially the young, more nutritious growth, which is rich in toxins—the animal can live ten years or more in the wild on its narrow diet. Over the long term, however, a price may have to be paid for a diet of poison. In a recent study, brains of adult koalas were found to be slowly shrinking within their skulls, year by year. The diminishing brain could be a result of the toxic compounds slowly working away at the animal's nervous tissue.

The sloth and the koala form a good example of what is called evolutionary convergence: two species in widely separated habitats who have arrived at the same solution to an ecological problem. In this case, the problem is how best to live on a diet of leaves. An adult koala weighing some 30 pounds eats about two pounds of leaves a day. Like the sloth, the koala has evolved a massive digestive organ to cope with the fiber-heavy diet.

The similarity is all the more remarkable because the sloth and koala are about as remotely related as two mammals can be. The koala is a marsupial, an order of pouch-bearing animals that branched away from the mammalian mainstream some hundred million years ago. For centuries, the marsupials of Australia and South America were thought to be primitive mammals, ill-suited to the struggle for survival on earth. Only recently have biologists begun to look deeper into the marsupial's pouch, and pulled out a bounty of revelations.

CHAPTER THREE

Diversions Down Under

I

On a moonlit night in June of 1770, the bark *Endeavor*, carrying an expedition of British scientists, was proceeding serenely through deep water off the northeast coast of Australia. Captain James Cook and his company had made landfall on the continent some weeks before, farther down the coast. The naturalists on board the vessel had been so thrilled by the profusion of new plants found there that they had persuaded Cook to name the place Botany Bay. Their encounter with the animal life had not been so fruitful, amounting to little more than examinations of dung and "a bad sight of a small Animal some thing like a rabbit." The *Endeavor* left Botany Bay in early May, and the voyage up

111

the coast had been uneventful, "one continuous safe harbour," according to Cook's journal.

Cook was an exceptionally skillful navigator. Since leaving England two years before, he had guided the *Endeavor* flawlessly through thousands of miles of uncharted sea. But shortly before 11:00 P.M. on June 11, his vessel struck a submerged nipple of coral and stuck fast. The crew tossed some of the heavier cargo, including the cannon, overboard, and managed to pull her free. Cook steered the damaged ship into a protected harbor. It was estimated that repairs would take about seven weeks—enough time for a leisurely exploration of the countryside.

On June 23, one of the men spotted a strange sort of animal, moving very fast, that looked something like a greyhound. The next day Cook himself encountered one of the creatures:

> *I saw myself this morning a little way from the ship one of the Animals . . . it was of a light Mouse colour and the full size of a grey hound and shaped in every respect like one, with a long tail which it carried like a grey hound, in short I should have taken it for a wild dog but for its walking or runing [sic] in which it jumped like a Hare or a dear [sic]. . . .*

What Captain Cook saw that day was most certainly some sort of macropod, a member of the kangaroo family. It may have been a grey kangaroo, a wallaroo, or perhaps a whip-tailed wallaby. Whatever the species, the serendipitous collision with a coral reef had brought those on board the *Endeavor* into contact with a great order of animals unlike greyhounds or anything else within their experience.

"Nothing certainly that I have seen at all resembles him," the naturalist Joseph Banks wrote of the macropod. His reaction would have been the same to any number of species inhabiting the continent: animals that glide aloft through the trees on furry wings; wolfish creatures with the stripes of tigers; tiny mammals that suck nectar from flowers in the manner of honeybees, or others living upon termites, tree sap, or poisonous leaves. Nearly all the females of these species are endowed with curious folds of skin in which they harbor their young—a trait that earned them the name of *marsupial*, from the Latin word for *purse*.

The evolutionary voyage of the Australian mammals began forty-five million years ago, in the huge supercontinent of Gondwanaland, a landmass three times the size of Africa which at one time cupped the bottom of the globe. A hundred million years earlier, convection currents just beneath the planet's surface had begun to chip away at the cup. First a fragment destined to become the Indian subcontinent broke free and inched slowly northward, eventually to meet with Asia in a collision so powerful that it lifted the Himalayas into the sky. Over millennia Africa, Madagascar, and New Zealand also separated from Gondwanaland. Australia,

Antarctica, and South America stayed attached for about fifty million years, and then they too broke apart and began to edge toward their current locations.

Since its isolation from the other landmasses, Australia has lain in the sun for many millions of years, flat and unchanging. Vast stretches of rock two billion years old cover much of the continent or lie just beneath its surface. Recently some chips of zircon from a mountain in western Australia were discovered to be over four billion years old, formed not long after the earth itself coalesced out of a mist of particles circling the sun. Bacterialike fossils from northwestern Australia are believed to be almost as old, the first traces yet discovered of the earliest life on the planet.

During the passing of eons, erosion and weather have softened the texture of the land, smoothed its mountains down to stony hills, created deep canyons. The Great Dividing Range, the continental backbone running through Queensland and New South Wales in the east (with a coccyx bending into the southwestern state of Victoria and the island of Tasmania off the coast), provides the highest peaks and the most beautiful scenery. Even here, however, elevations seldom exceed five thousand feet.

When Charles Darwin arrived on the Australian continent aboard H.M.S. *Beagle*, he traveled inland from Sydney and described the scene:

The extreme uniformity of the vegetation is the most remarkable feature in the landscape of the greater part of New South Wales. Everywhere we have an open woodland, the ground being partially covered with a very thin pasture, with little appearance of verdure. The trees nearly all belong to one family, and mostly have their leaves placed in a vertical, instead of, as in Europe, in a nearly horizontal position: the foliage is scanty, and of a peculiar pale green tint, without any gloss. Hence the woods appear light and shadowless: this, although a loss of comfort to the traveller under the scorching rays of summer, is of importance to the farmer, as it allows grass to grow where it otherwise would not. The leaves are not shed periodically . . .

the greater number of trees, with the exception of some of the Blue-gums, do not attain a large size; but they grow tall and tolerably straight, and stand well apart. The bark of some . . . falls annually, or hangs dead in long shreds which swing about with the wind, and give to the woods a desolate and untidy appearance. . . .

Darwin's trees were all members of the great family of eucalyptus, also known as gum trees. Highly adaptable, the eucalypts are found in the rain forests of the north and the sandy plains of the interior. River red gums dot the landscape of the Outback, interspersed with ghost gums, whose bark-stripped limbs and trunks shine brilliantly white in the sun. Snow gums in the southeast grow at altitudes of more than four thousand feet, their twisted limbs covered with mottled bark in shades of reds, browns, and whites. While most of the gum trees are not particularly tall, the giant species—the tingle-tingles, karris, and especially the mountain ash of Victoria and Tasmania—can reach fantastic heights, exceeded only by the giant redwoods of California.

As Darwin noted, the eucalypts retain their leaves year-round, and are thus continually prepared to take advantage of favorable conditions brought on by the unpredictable climate. By hanging vertically, the leaves receive the sun's rays at an angle, which helps to keep them cool. Other adaptations to the environment are less obvious. The leaves of some eucalypts have a sharply pungent fragrance, betraying the presence of toxic oils evolved as a defense against herbivores. The oils also serve the tree against another enemy: The terrible brush fires that sweep through parts of Australia in summer. When a spark from a distant fire arrives on the wind, the parched foliage of a tree explodes into flame. But the fire, though intense, lasts only a short time. The quick-burning oils protect the tree itself from catastrophic damage. When the winds carry the fire away, the tree is charred and denuded of leaves, but still alive. Beneath the blackened bark, dormant leaf buds quickly shoot forth and restore the vital process of photosynthesis.

Without extensive mountain ranges to coax clouds to form, the climate of Australia is exceedingly dry. Unornamented pebbled plains called *gibbers*, sand-ridged deserts, and low grassy plateaus form a rough patchwork through the interior. With so little slope to the land, much of the rain that does fall is lost to evaporation. All of Australia's rivers combined carry less water to the sea in a year than any one of fifteen major rivers in the world; the Murray River, the continent's longest, takes a year to discharge the volume of water that the Mississippi delivers to the ocean in nine days.

The coastal fringe of the continent is less parched than the interior. Mangrove swamps skirt the northern border, and along the north and northeast, patches of rain forest have developed, especially in the eastern slopes of the Great Dividing Range. For the most part, however, the plants and animals of Australia have adapted themselves to life without an abundant or consistent supply of water. (In a place in western Australia aptly named Whim Creek, only 0.16 inches of rain fell in 1924, but in another year 30 inches fell in a single day.) Dominating the landscape are the eucalypts, a magnificently resourceful family of trees. In spite of the harsh conditions and a plethora of parasites, the eucaplypts have managed to spread and diversify into some six hundred species.

When Australia began its journey northward, the continent was probably inhabited by insect-eating marsupials similar to the conical-snouted, mouselike dasyurids found there today. Over the centuries this marsupial stock gave rise to a variety of tree-dwellers, burrowers, flesh-eaters, sap-suckers, and leaf-munchers, ranging in size from the one-ounce ningaui of central and northwestern Australia to the extinct kangaroo *Procoptodon*, a browser as tall as an elephant. Today almost two hundred marsupial species

The tiny honey possum is found only in the heathlands of western Australia. It draws nectar and pollen from flowers with a long tongue tipped with a dense cluster of bristles. Weighing only half an ounce, the honey possum can cling to all but the slenderest of twigs.

share the continent, along with two species of egg-laying mammals, the platypus and the echidna, called *monotremes* (meaning "one-holed") because they route all their reproductive and excretory traffic through a single channel. In addition, Australia hosts a handful of "true" mammals, or eutherians: bats and rodents who probably arrived from Asia on floating mats of vegetation within the last million years; wild dogs called *dingoes*, descended from domestic animals introduced by the aborigines; as well as the domestic stock, foxes and cats-gone-wild brought by European settlers.

One might wonder what it is about the marsupials that has convinced us to see them as less than true mammals. Ever since marsupials were brought to the attention of European scientists, they have been viewed as inherently primitive, and by implication, less fit for survival than their pouchless counterparts. The marsupial's reputation for primitiveness seems to have arisen because of their unusual mode of reproduction. Not all marsupials have pouches, but every one bears its young in an embryonic state: tiny, hairless, half-formed newcomers, their hindlimbs mere buds. On the average, these infants weigh less than a thousandth of their adult body weight. Not even bears, birthed in hibernation, come close to showing such a discrepancy between what they are at birth and what they will become. The newborn grizzly or polar bear cub, moreover, falls immediately into the protective embrace of its mother. Marsupials have a much more arduous introduction into the world. Without any assistance from their seemingly uncaring mother, they begin life by pulling themselves, hair by hair, from the birth canal to the safety of their mother's pouch, where, unaided, they must find a teat on which to feed.

This natal trek—a few centimeters across the abdomen of a koala, a few inches for a kangaroo—is one of the most incredible journeys undertaken by an earthling. But to the scientists trying to find a place for these creatures in their scheme of life, the struggling marsupial newborn was taken as an emblem of a deep and disturbing flaw.

The hollow logs of wandoo and jarrah trees provide shelter for the numbat, one of the most unusual of Australia's marsupials. Although it is sometimes called the banded ant-eater, the numbat rarely eats ants on purpose, feeding almost exclusively on termites. It shares many of the peculiarites of ant and termite eaters around the world, including a long snout, a darting tongue nearly half the length of its body, and large salivary glands that keep the tongue lubricated with a sticky fluid.

Formerly distributed in a crescent-shaped band across the entire southern portion of the continent, the numbat is now restricted to the southwest corner. It is a delicately proportioned creature about the size of a housecat. The numbat's head tapers aristocratically toward a jet-black nose, the profile accented by prominent stripes of dark fur, bordered in white, that extends from the nose to each ear. The forward half of the animal's body is covered with reddish-brown fur, but at its midriff faint black-and-white vertical stripes

The numbat—another carnivorous marsupial—was once common across much of southern Australia. Today it is an endangered species, confined to rare and scattered populations in dry eucalyptus forests.

emerge, widening and acquiring sharp definition toward the rear. Unlike most marsupials, the numbat feeds in daylight; perhaps the lateral stripes help disguise it in the brush. The stripes end with the flourish of a long and bushy tail.

The numbat's dependence on hollow logs for shelter has engendered some remarkable adaptations to log life. Consider for a moment one of the great hazards of living in such confining quarters: Though it is easy enough to enter a log head-first, how can one safely exit, with a blind and most vulnerable part of one's anatomy leading the way? Numbats cannot depend on finding only open-ended logs on the forest floor. Instead they have evolved a flattened, flexible rump, which takes up very little room even when the animal is negotiating a flip-turn inside a log scarcely wider than itself. If a numbat ever *wants* to be stuck—for instance, when someone or something is trying to pull it free of its hiding place—it can puff up its chest and mid-body enough to hold tight to the inner surface of the log. The extinction of numbats in their former eastern range, in fact, may have been hastened by their reliance there on burrows for shelter rather than hollow logs. The excavations could readily be dug out by the enterprising red fox, a species first introduced in Australia in the 1860s for the purposes of sport.

Marsupials vary widely in appearance and behavior, and each species has its own reproductive idiosyncrasies. Consider a newborn male of the species *Macropus rufus*—a red kangaroo. He shares his place in the kangaroo family with some fifty other species, including wallabies and wallaroos, potoroos, pademelons, and quokkas. There are kangaroos that live on wooded plains or open grassland, kangaroos fit for hopping over rocky slopes or for browsing in trees. The red kangaroo, largest of the family, inhabits shrubland and grassy plains and even the arid regions of the interior. The species can be found in good abundance across a swath of the continent extending from the west coast clear to the edge of the Great Dividing Range in the east.

At the moment of birth, the male red kangaroo weighs less than three hundredths of an ounce, or about as much as a single kidney bean. By the time he reaches sexual maturity, he may weigh as much as several bushel baskets full of beans. When he stretches his heavy-shouldered form up in the grass, (startled perhaps by a strange footstep), he stands almost seven feet tall. Most likely he will be covered with a dense, rust-colored fur. His drooping eyelids and heavy jowls give him a somber, pugnacious look, like a boxer sizing up his opponent. His typical response to danger is flight, covering twenty feet or more with each hopping stride. If cornered, however, the red can fight back, balancing his weight on his strong tail to deliver a kick of the hindfoot powerful enough to eviscerate a dog.

The male kangaroo's social life is only loosely defined, but he is rarely completely alone. Usually he grazes with two or three other kangaroos, in small fluid and changeable groups which are part of an amorphous collection of individuals called a "mob." When not busy foraging or resting out the heat of the day, he may pay random visits to the females scattered about, sometimes called "blue-fliers" for their speed and the tint of their fur. He sniffs at their genital areas, checking for signs of estrus: Red kangaroos come into heat not in a regular cycle of seasons, but whenever conditions are good. The red will have to be strong if he intends to mate. In any gathering, only the largest males breed, the issue decided in ritualized boxing-and-shoving matches. Should he triumph and copulate with a female, his fifteen minutes of thrusting will still be frequently disturbed by other males attempting to intervene. If the mating is successful, the female red kangaroo will give birth in one month. The mammalian record for shortest gestation period—twelve days—belongs to another Australian marsupial, the short-nosed bandicoot.

To the first European settlers in Australia, accustomed to the long gestation and final commotion of most mammal birth, the sudden appearance of an embryonic kangaroo dangling from its mother's nipple was a great mystery. Colonists in early America were similarly mystified by birth in the marsupial opossum. Relying on their observation that male opossums have two-pronged penises, and female opossums stick their snouts into their pouches just before giving birth, the observers concluded that the species copulates through the nostrils; the female later blows her nose into her pouch, and presto, out comes a new opossum.

In Australia, meanwhile, they arrived at an equally imaginative explanation for the origin of the newborn: Kangaroos and other marsupials do not give birth, but *grow* their young, like animal buds sprouting from the mother's teat. As one naturalist wrote in 1832, the newborn kangaroo "neither differs in size or form from the fetus of another quadruped at a similar period of progression; save that the umbilical cord is here attached to the lips; in such a manner that the lungs cannot be inflated previous to its rupture. It is therefore most likely that the nipple, during the first stage, constitutes the mouth of a fallopian tube."

To be fair to these early interpreters, a female red kangaroo or any other marsupial gives almost no indication that she is carrying a fetus until the last few hours of her pregnancy. The kangaroo's only unusual behavior occurs about a day before birth, when she leans forward and begins to clean out her pouch, which is lined with brownish scales. Her housekeeping intensifies as birth approaches, and she may grow increasingly restless. Birth itself is a transitory event, easily overlooked. The mother assumes a characteristic posture, with her hind legs extended straight in front and her tail passed forward between them. ("Rather like someone slumping down in an office chair," according to Pamela Parker, an authority on marsupial reproduction at the Brookfield Zoo in Chicago.) In this position the distance from the birth canal to the pouch is significantly shortened. It is the only assistance that the mother gives to her newborn, for when it emerges from the canal she is much too preoccupied with licking herself clean to notice that she has just delivered an offspring.

The marsupial's reproductive road in fact diverges from the straight and narrow well before birth. In the great majority of other mammals, the fertilized egg divides a few times and then implants itself on the mother's uterus. This bundle of cells is called a blastocyst. The blastocyst is genetically derived half from its mother and half from its father; in other words it is a bit of foreign matter, not entirely of the mother, and thereby vulnerable to attack by antibodies produced by her immune system. Before the immune system can mobilize to destroy it, however, the blastocyst secretes protein-dissolving enzymes and proceeds to sink slowly into the uterine wall. The outer membrane of the embryo (analogous to the thin skin beneath the shell of a hen's egg) sprouts a covering of tiny projections called *villi*, which will later become part of the mediating organ called the placenta. The villi protrude into the maternal tissue, which degenerates into a nourishing broth.

The enormous quantity of villi (thirty miles of them in a human placenta) allows the passage of nutrients from the mother to the fetus. At the same time, and in ways no one completely understands, the placenta prevents maternal antibodies from attacking the fetus. Throughout the long period of gestation, this eutherian fetus develops in an intimate, continuous bond with its mother's body, living off its nutrients, orchestrating its hormonal balance, all the time safely buffered until birth from the mother's immune response.

For a marsupial, prenatal life is much different. The European anatomists who first examined specimens arriving from South America and Australia were amazed to find that the internal workings of the marsupials' reproduction system appeared suspiciously reptilian. The female's uterus and vagina are double-horned, and in many species the male sports a double-pronged penis to match. The unfertilized marsupial egg is large, sometimes yolkier than a typical mammalian egg, and surrounded by a shell membrane like a reptilian ovum. After fertilization, the blastocyst takes up residence in a uterus hemmed in on either side by excretory ducts from the kidneys. This bit of anatomical architecture would seem to limit the expansion of the uterus, and hence the size of the fetus. There is relatively little connection with the mother: The prenatal marsupial finds its nutritional needs in secretions from the uterine walls, and to a certain extent from its internal store of yolklike protein.

Among the tenants of the eucaplytus trees are the marsupial gliders. These shy creatures are primarily nocturnal in their habits, and their moist, protuberant eyes gives them a characteristically wistful expression. When a glider decides to abandon one tree for another, it leaps from a branch and unfolds a thin, furred membrane stretched between its fore- and hind-limbs, a hidden sail that holds it aloft in arcing descents. Larger gliders, vaguely resembling flying monkeys, drop rather precipitiously after a few yards. But the sugar glider and some other small

Like its membraned relatives, the sugar glider is nocturnal and rarely seen, its presence betrayed only by its yapping alarm call and the soft "plop" sometimes heard as it lands on a tree trunk.

on a cherry blossom. Slow-motion films, however, reveal that the glider's flight actually terminates in a high-speed collision with a branch, the glider bouncing back on impact, scrambling with specially enlarged claws to keep from falling from the tree.

Some gliders (as well as their cousins the ring-tailed and pygmy possums) rely on the eucaplypts for nourishment as well as shelter. The greater glider of eastern Australia has managed to adapt itself to feeding on the oil- and phenol-rich leaves of swamp gum, common peppermint, and long-leaved box trees. Other gliders feed on the eucalyptus sap and gum. The yellow-bellied glider, also native to eastern Australia, is particularly voracious in its quest for sap, carving V-shaped gouges in the bark with its incisor teeth and licking up the sweet, carbohydrate-rich ooze. Only certain trees come in for this sort of abuse, suggesting that they exude a specially palatable sap. Such feeding sites are precious resources for a glider, ferociously defended from interlopers.

species can draw their flights out for the length of a football field or more, banking around trees, swallowing distance. The sugar gliders grace their descents with a sudden upward swoop just before landing, a maneuver that appears to be carried off with all the finesse of a butterfly alighting

---

For one to four weeks the marsupial fetus develops in what is called a yolk-sac placenta, isolated from the physiological climate around it. Through most of that time its shell membrane protects the fetus from the maternal immune system. The mother also profits from this separation; unlike the placental mother, whose entire hormonal system is hijacked by the requirements of her fetus, the marsupial female's reproductive cycle proceeds on course, little affected by the growing embryo. According to Pamela Parker, there is little difference between a pregnant and a nonpregnant marsupial female.

During the last few days of gestation, the fetus emerges from its shell and begins to travel down a birth canal formed for its benefit between the two lateral vaginas. At this point in its journey, the fetal marsupial may be vulnerable to assault from its mother's antibodies. But before her immune

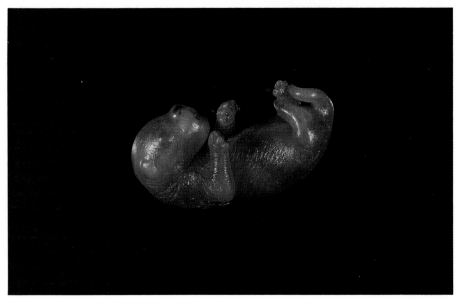

Few animals seem so unprepared to cope with existence as this newborn kangaroo, born without eyes, lungs, or developed hind legs. It will absorb oxygen through its skin, but its mother will give her newborn very little help in its struggle toward her pouch.

system can mobilize an attack against it, the fetus—tiny, translucent, glistening like a drop of dew—wriggles out of the birth canal and sets off on its journey to the pouch. Its hindquarters are mere suggestions, tucked under in the characteristic lima-bean shape of embryos. Its lungs have not developed enough to bring in air, and its kidneys have yet to mature. The animal is not only blind, but *eyeless*. Its skin is thin and free of pigment, the internal organs peeping through a filigree of blood vessels. Altogether the newborn seems an ephemeral, otherworldly creature, scarcely ready for existence. And it is in this condition that it must struggle through its mother's fur and find a teat to fasten upon.

Given such shaky beginnings, especially with their lizardly overtones, it is not surprising that many scientists consider the marsupials poorly constructed for survival. It seems as if something has gone astray in marsupial evolution, forever stunting the order's ability to produce full-fledged infants. The discovery of their oddly formed reproductive biology has cast the marsupials down from the mammalian heights of the animal hierarchy. In a sort of taxonomic snub, Thomas Huxley formalized their status in 1880, defining the marsupials as "metatherians," or quasi-mammals, one step above the egg-laying platypus and echidna. These even lowlier creatures were thenceforth rated as "prototherians," or premammals.

Paleontologists, meanwhile, soon found more incriminating evidence of marsupial inferiority in the fossil record. About the same time that Australia separated from Antarctica, the continent of South America followed suit and began to drift northward. The landmass carried with it a menagerie of marsupial species, including some large and impressive carnivores. Among these were *Thylacosmilus*, a jaguar-sized killer with canines long as a saber-toothed tiger's; and the *Borhyaenids*, huge, hyenalike predators. Like their Australian counterparts, the South American marsupials flourished in isolation. But when the Isthmus of Panama rose two or three million years ago, connecting North and South America, they were quite suddenly confronted with some new and formidable competition. The two New World landmasses swapped some species, armadillos and some marsupial species heading north, while various eutherian carnivores and ungulates crossed over the isthmus into the southern regions.

All told, the southern native species suffered much the worse from the mingling. Among the southern fauna, two whole families of marsupials were driven to extinction, including all of the carnivores. They were replaced in their ecological niche by jaguars and other predatory cats—all placental mammals, of course. It seemed as though pouched mammals could manage nicely on their own, but their natural inferiority would doom then when challenged by "real" mammals with placentas and long gestation periods. Some scientists even argue that much the same is happening in Australia today: The European carnivores introduced within the last couple of centuries, especially the fox and feral cat, are making a disproportionate dent in the populations of the native marsupials.

Charles Darwin was not impressed by the marsupials' evolutionary attainments. Though the H.M.S. Beagle *stopped for two months in Sydney Cove, Darwin's journal barely mentions the region's animal life, except to point out how badly it seemed to be faring against the English greyhounds imported for hunting. "It may be long before these animals are exterminated," Darwin wrote, "but their doom is fixed." Above, a kangaroo hunting scene painted in 1880.*

The trouble with this argument is that it begins with its own conclusion as a premise: that marsupials are inherently inferior. True, the great meat-eating marsupials of South America were not able to meet the challenge of the invaders from the north, but did their defeat have anything to do with their pouches, or giving birth to embryonic young? Over seventy opossum and other marsupial species survived the competition intact, some even moving across the isthmus and thriving in the north. On the other side of the coin, just as many southern placental mammals as marsupials were driven to extinction by the northern interlopers.

What was it, then, that gave the competitive edge to the northerners? Citing the work of Robert Bakker, Stephen Jay Gould has argued that the southern natives may have been lulled into vulnerability by undisturbed centuries of mild environmental conditions. In contrast, the mammals of the north had undergone two periods of mass extinction during the Tertiary period, a convulsive circumstance that may have led to more diverse, better-adapted mammal groups. According to another point of view, the northern mammals were no better, just luckier. As Bryan Patterson and Rosendo Pascual have pointed out, the jaguars and other species from the north were given a boost by a coinciding shift in the climate of South America. The rise of the Andes mountain system changed the uniformly mild environment into a harsher, less predictable place, exactly the sort of habitat that the northern animals were already accustomed to in their native regions.

This embryonic red kangaroo has completed the arduous journey to its mother's pouch and has attached itself to a teat. From now on, life will be easier.

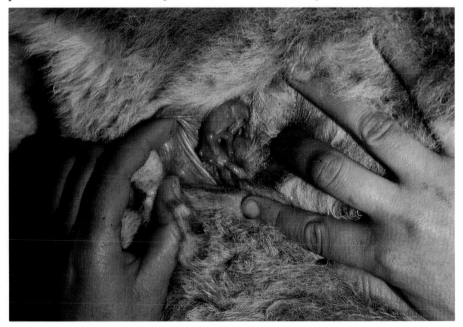

Neither viewpoint has anything to do with some inherent flaw in the marsupial approach to birth. The case against modern marsupials in Australia is equally unconvincing. It is true that nine species of Australian marsupial have recently become extinct, and more hover on the brink. But the plight of native Australian rodents—placental mammals—is equally drastic. According to Pamela Parker, the extinctions may have less to do with some competitive disadvantage than with radical alteration of the Australian habitat brought about by massive agricultural development.

Consider again the blind, hairless kangaroo a moment old, struggling through its mother's fur. Its critics have regarded it as a little more than a perpetual preemie, chased out of the womb by maternal antibodies long before it is ready to cope with the trials of early life. But a closer examination of the newborn reveals that it might not be so ill-prepared for its journey after all. It has no eyes yet, but wide, scent-hungry nostrils crowd its tiny face, the better to find its way to the pouch. The embryo lacks lungs, but can absorb oxygen and other gases through its skin. Its hindquarters may be nothing more than budlike protrusions, but its forelimbs and shoulders are well-formed and muscled. Each finger is tipped by a tiny claw—a startlingly precocious development, belying the notion of the newborn as half-baked and primitive.

With respectable speed, the newborn kangaroo grabs hold of its mother's fur and begins to clamber upward. After a few steps the umbilical cord breaks. The infant is on its own. Its mother continues to lick up blood and amniotic fluids, but seems oblivious to the baby on her belly. The newborn moves along with a curious back-and-forth swing of the head, aided in this action by other specially developed muscles in the neck and shoulders. Its progress is sure and direct, an incredible feat, if one considers that this ordeal is orchestrated by the merest wisp of a brain. Here, in a living, functioning mammal that will literally fit in a nutshell, one can find life expressed in its simplest splendor: a tiny dollop of flesh endowed with only enough muscle and sense to keep it struggling forward, and nothing more.

With one last heave of its shoulders and head, the newborn "joey" reaches the rim of the pouch and topples in. A little groping and he quickly finds a nipple; the journey is complete. Relying only on his own resources, he has made the trip in the impressive time of three minutes, and he now makes use of precociously developed sucking muscles to earn his reward.

Stimulated by her offspring's powerful sucking, the female kangaroo's nipple quickly swells, locking tight the connection between them. The joey is now safely fastened to his food supply, a connection that will not be broken for two months. Up to this point, at least, the newly arrived kangaroo has not seemed to suffer much from his "premature" birth, in spite of the fact that he has just undergone a test of strength and adaptability unlike anything facing a newborn eutherian. So long as his mother is not disturbed during his travels pouchward, his chances of making it alive appear to be good.

The vividly spotted native cat—a marsupial carnivore—gives birth to young weighing about as much as the salt one would sprinkle on an egg. To reach its mother's nipple, the newborn props itself up on a bladderlike swelling on its chest, a built-in cushion that keeps its head at right angles to the teat.

The koala is a creature of contradictions. A shy, nocturnal animal living in a remote part of the globe, the koala became the prototype for the teddy bear, and thus the nightly companion of millions of children all over the world. In fact the koala is not a bear at all, but merely suggests one—a bear divested of danger, smaller, cuter, altogether a more predictable fellow. It has the slanted, beady eyes of a fearsome martinet, but they are rendered comical by bushy ears sprouting up like two enormous cowlicks. The koala's mouth is a tight and stubborn slit, but its severity is wholly undone by what appears to be a black rubber nose. The complete effect suggests an attempt at an authoritative demeanor that has turned out rather less than one had hoped—a dour schoolteacher proceeding through the geography lesson, unaware that his toupee is all askew.

Through most of the year, koalas live slow and solitary lives. In the breeding season in summer, the males rouse themselves into territorial piques, bellowing through the night to warn other males away. They mark the trees in their territory with secretions from a scent gland in their chests. Female koalas give birth to a single offspring once a year. Like other marsupial newborns it is extremely undeveloped in most respects, weighing in at less than two hundredths of an ounce. After five months of nursing in the pouch, the young koala is weaned on a pablum composed of half-digested eucaplyptus leaves. The mother eats the leaves and passes them faster than usual through her massive digestive tract, where they collect the microbes that her young will need to digest eucalyptus leaves when it matures. The mother's pouch is upside down, an arrangement that seems odd for an animal that spends most of its time upright in trees. But when the mother voids the eucalyptus paste out of her anus, her young in her topsy-turvy pouch is in an excellent position to lick it up.

In spite of the koala's inferior pelt and unpalatable meat, white settlers in Australia hunted the animal close to the brink of extinction. Since the 1940s, koala populations have been better managed, and are now quite common in the eucalyptus forests east of the Great Dividing Range.

Pamela Parker and her colleagues, Virginia Hayssen and Robert Lacy, believe there may even be some distinct advantages to bringing forth newborns the marsupial way. The Parker–Hayssen–Lacy theories concern what is called the "reproductive value" of the female marsupial—the number of offspring she can potentially contribute to the population for the rest of her lifetime.

Every living thing is driven by a need to perpetuate itself and do what it can to ensure the survival of its genes into the next generation. In most mammals, this drive is expressed in the protective care of the mother for her offspring. (Since males invest relatively little energy in the production of their young, it is in their interest to mate with as many females as possible, and in most species males share less of the burden of parenting.) It does not follow, however, that *each* offspring should be protected at all costs. In some species, a mother gives birth to a large litter of young, a strategy of reproduction that will accommodate the death of many, so long as some survive. Other species produce few offspring, but invest enormous time and energy in ensuring their survival. In the end, what matters most is how successful the female will be in reproducing over the course of her whole lifetime: how many new pangolins, feather-tailed opossum, or Siberian tigers she can set on their way before she herself is killed or loses the capacity to reproduce.

With this in mind, it doesn't make sense, in terms of survival, for a mother to continue to nurture and protect an offspring doomed to die anyway. (It is important to remember that such a decision is not a conscious act; it simply means that the mother possesses the genes that make such a choice possible in the first place.) If disaster threatens, there comes a point where it is better to bail out of a current attempt at reproducing and save one's energy for a later try. Some rodents and rabbits can cancel a reproductive attempt early on by absorbing the embryo into the uterine wall. The triumph of an infanticidal male over one's mate can cause pregnant lionesses or horses to spontaneously abort their fetuses. When one's mate has been killed, why finish a pregnancy only to deliver the newborn into the jaws of a hostile stepfather?

Spontaneous abortion, however, takes a terrific toll on the placental mother's energy supplies, not to mention the investment she has wasted in carrying the fetus along. It should be kept in mind that it is the fetus, via the placenta, that is in charge of the pregnancy. It will do what it can to stay alive, diverting the mother's hormonal system to its own ends. If drought should come and the mother is no longer able to find enough food to nourish herself and her fetus, her unborn infant will begin to feed on her internal reserves of protein and minerals. In contrast, the marsupial mother hops or scampers or scurries along relatively unaffected by her own pregnancy. After a fairly breezy period of gestation she gives birth, usually to one joey in the case of the kangaroo, although other marsupials give birth to larger litters. But even the litters of prolific species—the American opossums, for instance—represent, at birth, an investment that is only a tiny fraction of their mother's body weight.

Marsupial young catch up to their placental counterparts while attached to the teat. Nursing lasts longer among the marsupials. Lactation is an "expensive" proposition for any mammal, perhaps as costly as nourishing a fetus in the womb. But according to Parker, Hayssen, and Lacy, it is a much easier enterprise to abandon. If a prolonged drought makes it unlikely

Virginia opossums typically live through only two breeding seasons, but they make the most of the opportunities given them, giving birth to as many as fifteen young in each litter.

that the young will survive, the marsupial mother can quit the risk of reproducing simply by shutting off her supply of milk. In contrast, the placental mother, having invested most of her energy in gestation, shares this option for only a short time. All other factors being equal, the marsupial mother would be able to produce more young in her lifetime than a comparable eutherian female, since she would waste less energy in doomed attempts.

It should not be inferred that the nurturing faculties of the kangaroo, koala, or other marsupial are less developed than those of a mountain goat or a tree shrew. When the newborn is small and hairless the mother continues to appear indifferent to its existence, but every day the bond between them grows stronger, with the mother frequently licking her joey clean and keeping the pouch in impeccable shape. When the joey begins to make its first tentative explorations beyond the pouch, its mother keeps a close eye on it, calling out if it should temporarily stray from her sight. The joey too wails mournfully when lost, which summons not only its mother but whatever other female kangaroos happen to be within earshot. Once the joey is found, its mother obligingly spreads her hindlegs and bends down, and her infant climbs back into the security of the pouch. He will spend about 235 days there, and with every day of his dependence, her investment in him grows higher. Eventually, however, there will come a time when she no longer allows him back in the pouch, holding him away with her fore-paws or simply avoiding his company.

The more one looks into the much-maligned accoutrements of mar-supial reproduction, the more they seem to harbor secret advantages. Con-sider, for example, the double-tracked reproductive canal of marsupials. Since pregnancy does little to alter a female's reproductive cycle, she will continue to mate even as her young gestates in her womb. Virginia Hayssen says this poses something of a conflict between present and future embryos. What is good for the growing fetus is a disaster for the male's spermatozoa, which require a very special chemical environment in the uterus in order to become capacitated—able to fertilize the egg. But two reproductive tracts neatly dispense with the problem; the sperm swim up the lateral ducts, while the fetus descends through the birth canal between. Theoretically, a kangaroo could be giving birth to one young and conceiving a second at the same time. (Usually two days elapse between the birth of a joey and another copulation.)

The one-way routing of embryo and sperm lends support to another macropodal miracle, a sort of reproductive insurance policy called *embry-onic diapause*. Kangaroos have no specific breeding season. They can, and do, come into estrus in a seemingly random pattern, and will mate whether they are nursing a joey or not. The fertilized egg goes through a few cell divisions, but much like the ovum of the polar bear, it will suddenly suspend its development at the blastocyst stage. The bear's blastocyst implants itself on the uterus and resumes growth according to a fixed schedule. In the case of the kangaroo, however, the blastocyst will hang dormant as long as the joey in the pouch continues to suckle. The sucking action of the joey stimulates the release of prolactin, a hormone which holds the blastocyst in check. When the joey slackens its nursing, the prolactin "brake" on the suspended embryo's development is released, and once again its cells begin to divide and differentiate. In a good environment a female kangaroo may have a joey "at heel," another sucking in the pouch, and an embryo in storage just in case. Although it takes twenty months for a red joey to become independent, its mother needn't wait that long before bringing another infant along. She can deliver a new kangaroo to the world about once every eight months.

Diapause proves most beneficial during difficult times. If a drought lasts for months, the mother's milk will not be adequate to keep her pouch joey alive. As soon as it dies it releases the hormonal brake on its sibling embryo, which rapidly completes its gestation period, emerges from the birth canal, and completes its trip to the pouch. Meanwhile, its mother mates again. The tiny newborn makes very few demands on the mother's

The wombat, a hairy, heavy-bodied relative of the koala, lives a warren life on the ground in stable social groups. Like that of other burrowing marsupials, the wombat's pouch opens to the rear. Wombat excavations are so expansive that they show up clearly on LANDSAT satellite images.

nutritional supply, but should the drought continue, it will go the way of its dead sibling. Still the mother has not lost much of an investment. Furthermore, waiting its turn is yet another blastocyst from the most recent conception, and so it goes on, several times over. When the rains finally come, the mother, having expended very little reproductive energy in the meantime, is now in a perfect position to take advantage of the improved conditions with whatever blastocyst is stored in diapause.

Rather than develop their young internally, the marsupials have simply opted for a longer, stronger reliance on milk. Lactation, the very essence of all that is mammalian, achieves its highest expression among these supposedly second-class citizens of the mammalian world. Instead of producing one steady grade of milk, the concentrations of fat and protein in marsupial milk rise and fall according to the growing infant's nutritional needs and their ability to digest more complex molecules.

Our red kangaroo, along with some macropod cousins, has devised an even more ingenious lactational stratagem. A mother kangaroo often has to feed both a well-developed joey at heel and a bean-sized baby in the pouch, but milk too rich for the newborn's digestive tract will kill it, while the joey hopping around in the grass would starve on the watery brew fit for its tiny sibling. How then can the female satisfy both babies at once? The kangaroo's solution is a hormonal *tour de force*—two grades of milk simultaneously from the same mammary apparatus. From one teat, the joey on the ground suckles a "whole" milk, rich in fat but poor in protein. Meanwhile a low-fat, high-protein "skim" milk flows from the nipple suckled by the embryonic young. Such elaborate artifice demonstrates a very high level of evolution. If milk is the surest measure of mammalian development, there is no truer mammal on earth than the kangaroo.

It seems we habitually judge the worth of other earthlings according to how closely their evolutionary course has followed our own. We rate the tiger as a higher work of nature than the tiger shark; the shark above the tiger lily, and so on. Long ago, the marsupials set off on their own course, and we have judged them harshly for it. But who knows? Except for the vicissitudes of continental drift, human females might be wearing pouches too, and birthing thumb-sized babies with the painless poise of kangaroos.

Several years ago an airplane enticed us to Australia by advertisements featuring the cuddly koala. They probably would not have sold many tickets if they had based their campaign on the Tasmanian devil, an unsociable nocturnal prowler now found only on the island of Tasmania. Devils are about as repulsive as koalas are cute. They are smelly, drooling, tar-black, beady-eyed carnivores about three feet long, counting their stiff, tapering tails. Their heads seem too big for their bodies, and their mouths too large for their heads. The devils first got their name from the unholy cries they issue in the night, which one writer has described as combinations of "a bobcat's screech, a large dog being strangled, and the cry of a man who has smashed his thumb with a hammer."

Such a ruckus from the bush means that two devils are engaged in combat, probably disputing the ownership of some piece of food. Usually these battles are confined to ritualized intimidations, the combatants gaping and lurching at each other, constantly licking spittle from their lips, their ears flushed crimson with blood. The same awful display faces anything that corners a devil. Its gape, however, is far worse than its bite; while the devil is working itself up to a full rage, a dog can easily move in and kill it.

The huge, hinged jaws and sharp molars of the Tasmanian devil are well-suited to bolting down meat. Being somewhat slow-footed and slow-witted, they prefer their prey sick, young, disabled, distracted, entangled, unlucky, or best of all, dead. The carcasses of sheep and kangaroos form the bulk of their diet. When nothing else is available, devils will eat beetles, grubs, old boots, and cartridge cases. They dabble in cannibalism too. They rarely pass up a chance to feed. One farmer heard his sick cow bellowing in the night, and arrived to find her lying on her side, a devil munching on her udder. A sheep farmer in Tasmania once brought his herd into a shearing shed with a slatted floor, unaware that there were devils underneath. Sheep whose feet slipped through the cracks had them bitten off.

For all its apparent iniquity, the devil really causes little damage to

The carnivorous Tasmanian devil is a clumsy killer, but an extremely efficient eater.

sheep farming or other human enterprises. The million or so devils on Tasmania may actually do some good, devouring the carcasses of dead sheep before blowflies have a chance to establish a breeding site on the carrion. According to one farmer, if a sheep dies in the night, "by morning there'll be nothing left but the fleece and the plastic ear tags."

Whether or not they serve human interests, the devils deserve some respect for being such wonderfully efficient opportunists.

II

Australia is home to another unusual order of mammals believed to lie even farther down the evolutionary scale than the marsupials. These are the egg-laying monotremes, limited now to the bizarrely fashioned platypus and two species of echidnas, the spiny anteaters of Australia and New Guinea. Though monotremes are shy and unobtrusive mammals living in a remote part of the world, no other mammals on earth have provoked such uproar and debate in the scientific community.

When the first, dried specimen of a platypus reached Europe in 1798, it was immediately denounced as a preposterous fraud. How could there be a furbearer with a beak? A mammal *sans* mammaries, delivered of an egg? Under the best of circumstances, the platypus was bound to raise some eyebrows. The scientists' unwillingness to believe had been further stiffened by the recent arrival of "genuine" mermaid specimens from Chinese waters.

These turned out to be nothing more than monkeys' heads artfully sewn onto the bodies of fish. Having once been so easily duped, the men of learning were not likely to be fooled by a beady-eyed quadruped so crudely fitted with the bill of a duck!

Closer examination of the creature, however, failed to turn up any stitches or glue. When the scientists found that its upper jawbones extended into the bill, they were forced to acknowledge that they were burdened with an animal even more troublesome to classify than the marsupials. In 1798, evolution was seldom discussed. The natural world was largely viewed as a sort of enormous chest of drawers, each drawer divided and subdivided into fixed compartments. If the platypus was not a mammal, then what drawer could it be fit into?

The animal's posterior, meanwhile, was a taxonomist's nightmare. Unlike other furred animals, the platypus and echidna made use of a single channel called a *cloaca* for urination, defecation, copulation, and birth. The platypus's bill might be explained away as a natural curiosity, but the cloaca was known to be a feature of reptiles and birds. Quickly, the nature-labelers came up with the name *Montremata*, to cover the platypus, the echidna, and their own confusion.

For the next one hundred years an argument over the paradox of the

The duck-billed platypus is an extremely capable swimmer, using its wide, webbed forelimbs for thrust. Long guard hairs and a thick blanket of underfur keep it warm even in freezing water. The bill of the platypus is even more eccentric than it appears: it has special nerve sensors that guide the platypus, swimming with its eyes closed, to home in on the tiny electrical currents generated by shrimp and other platypus prey.

platypus occupied the attention of some of the greatest scientists of Europe, including the celebrated German anatomist Johann Meckel and the French evolutionist Jean Baptiste de Lamarck. As evidence of the animal's mammalian nature, there was its fur—extremely thick fur, and, like the polar bears', composed of a layer of sleek guard hairs protecting a perpetually dry blanket of shorter hair beneath. The platypus also boasted a skeletal hallmark of mammalhood: one bone, the dentary, in its lower jaw, and three—the hammer, anvil, and stirrup—in its middle ear. Reptiles possess several jawbones but only a single bone in the ear.

But the evidence of the bones also showed some unambiguously reptilian traits. In its shoulder girdle the platypus had an interclavicle bone, a feature found in reptiles but not mammals. And there were other anomalies, suspiciously primitive. Someone discovered, perhaps painfully, that the male platypus boasted venomous spurs on its hindfeet, capable of causing excruciating pain in a human and killing a dog. While certain species of shrew were known to be venomous, toxic fangs and stingers were much more characteristic of lower orders, such as snakes, spiders, and insects. The echidna too displayed at least vestiges of these spurs. Less circumstantial was the apparent evidence that the platypus was unable to control its body temperature, a defining trait of mammalhood. It was believed that the animal had to paddle back to its burrow periodically to warm up. This notion persisted until 1973, when it was shown that, like any other mammal, the platypus is fully capable of precise thermal regulation, although its body temperature does hover a few degrees lower than most.

As described in an essay by Stephen Jay Gould in *Natural History* magazine, the taxonomic talents of the nineteenth century were severely strained by the platypus's organs of reproduction. Clearly the female possessed two ovaries, but only the left one produced eggs. In this the platypus was decidedly birdlike. Two oviducts proceeded downward, to meet in the cloaca; there was no trace of a uterus, no room for a placenta to form. This suggested the impossible: oviparity, or young hatched from eggs. The animal also lacked teats, and by inference, mammary glands and the ability to produce milk. In 1824 Meckel discovered glands beneath the platypus's skin which he claimed to be mammary. But others were not convinced, suggesting that the glands secreted not milk but sweat, or perhaps some sexual scent. Even when Meckel managed to coax a whitish substance from the glands, one of his rivals declared the liquid to be not milk at all, but a sort of mucus that thickens into food when mixed with water.

While these European scientists were scrutinizing their several preserved specimens of platypi in the laboratories of Paris, Oxford, and Halle, the living platypi on the east coast of Australia were swimming out their lives, free of self-doubt and wholly unaware that they had suddenly become a paradox of modern science. There seems to be little in the natural life of a platypus to cause it unease. It is a water-dweller, equally at home in the rocky streams of Tasmania and the green, shrouded pools of the rain forests of northern Queensland. Without serious natural predators, the platypus lives a long life in the wild, especially since the turn of the century, when hunting them became illegal and the trade in platypus rugs collapsed. Its life is made all the more easy by the security of its ecological niche—a place in the larger design of its ecosystem—apparently free of competition from other species. It eats mostly shrimp, insect larvae, and other invertebrates, feeding ten hours a day, consuming half its body weight.

Among the tiny marsupial insectivores is the brown antechinus, a mouselike creature found in the heathlands of southeastern Australia. The species is short-lived and breeds once a year, timing its mating season so that the young can take advantage of the seasonal abundance of insects when they are weaned in the spring. Faced with only a single chance to reproduce in its lifetime, the male makes a frantic, Cassanovian effort to breed with as many females as possible in the few days allowed it. Immediately afterward the males collapse and die *en masse*, mostly from stomach ulcers and other stress-related diseases. Within ten days, all the males are dead.

For the Brown Antechinus, mating season brings a burst of feverish activity, with pairs copulating for up to twelve hours at a time. After two weeks of effort, all the males of the species suddenly and mysteriously die.

It was formerly thought that the male die-off of the antechinus was due to exhaustion from the flurry of matings. Researchers now believe that the stress actually works to the advantage of the males, allowing them to go without food during the breeding season. Animals under stress are able to use body proteins for energy instead of relying on the protein obtained from food.

Ironically, the platypus's accomplishment as a feeder depends greatly on the very feature of its anatomy that first caused all the hoopla. When a platypus dives down to the bottom of a pool, it closes its eyes, ears, and nostrils. How then can it locate its food so efficiently? In 1802, the anatomist Everard Home dissected a platypus bill and discovered a pair of enormous nerves connecting the face to the brain:

"We should be led from this circumstance to believe," Home wrote, "that the sensibility of the different parts of the bill is very great, and therefore it answers to the purpose of a hand, and is capable of nice discrimination in its feeling."

For years after Home's discovery, neurophysiologists focused their attention on the bill's sensitivity to subtle movements in the water that might be betraying the location of prey. Touch is indeed important to the platypus, but it now appears that its bill houses a stranger sense as well. In 1985, Australian researchers discovered that the platypus detects tiny electrical fields generated by the nerve and muscle action of shrimp and other prey. Lining the ducts of certain glands in the bill are electrical receptors, derived from fibers that join to form Home's "big nerves" and carry information to the brain. Some species of fish and amphibians are known to have electrosensory powers, but the platypus's receptors are unlike anything else, suggesting that it evolved its electric sense independently. Certainly there is nothing like it in any other mammal discovered so far.

When it is not feeding, the platypus spends its time grooming its fur, sleeping, or lazily swimming about. (By some accounts, the platypus even swims in its dreams.) While it does not seem to be strictly territorial, it may have some sense of spatial relationship to its fellows. Direct evidence is rare, but it appears that the males may compete fiercely for breeding rights during the mating season. The venom gland supplying the lethal hind spur swells during the season, and numerous individuals have been found with suspicious puncture wounds. The initiative for courting among platypi belongs to the female. She solicits the males' attention with a repertoire of

Though monotremes have been much maligned for their reputed stupidity, the echidna, or spiny anteater, actually possesses a relatively large brain, and scores very respectably on tests of mammalian intelligence.

approaches—diving under and around him, rubbing flanks as she passes, or simply lolling about within reach. Perhaps the most unusual enticement is a muddy cloud of vomit issued by the female; the male swims through the cloud and signals his eagerness by grasping her tail. The female then tows him around for a while before they mate.

During the breeding season the females excavate deep and impenetrable burrows in the banks, often running sixty feet or more in length, ending in a chamber filled with damp leaves. With the young delivered in such seclusion, and echidnas similarly uncooperative, it was many years before the overwhelming question of monotreme birth—eggs or live young?—could be answered. In 1884, a young English biologist named William Caldwell solved the riddle, announcing it to the world in one of the most famous telegrams in scientific history. The economy of scientific language kept Caldwell's telegraph charges to a minimum. Sent from Australia to the annual meeting of the British Association in Montreal, the telegram read "Monotremes oviparous, ovum meroblastic." To put it more expensively, this means that the platypus and echidna do lay eggs; the eggs are yolky like those of reptiles and birds, and when the cell begins to divide after fertilization, the initial cleavages do not penetrate the yolky part—another reptilian characteristic.

Caldwell's discovery put to rest the question of egg-birth versus live birth, but the announcement only further contributed to the platypus's status in limbo. While egg-laying is decidedly unmammalian, it later turned out that the monotreme's eggs failed to develop according to the reptilian model. At the time of fertilization, the platypus's eggs are about the size of garden peas. Reptilian and avian eggs never increase in size, but the monotreme's eggs begin to grow as they descend down the oviduct, absorbing nutrients from the uterine environment much like other mammals. This is accomplished through a structure called the *corpus luteum*, which *is* found in mammals, but rarely in reptiles or birds.

A week after the female platypus lays her eggs, usually two at a time, they hatch into tiny, hairless earthlings about as sophisticated as a newborn marsupial. The female echidna, meanwhile, lays her single egg on the ground, then stoops down and picks it up in her pouch. When it hatches ten days later, it too will have a great deal more developing to do before it becomes recognizably echidnian. In spite of their lack of nipples, both the platypus and the echidna depend greatly on lactation after birth to nourish their young. In the platypus, which has no pouch, the milk flows from glands under the skin on its stomach. The young coax the milk out with their soft "milk bills." Newly hatched echidna, meanwhile, struggle around in the pouch until they find one of two patches of milk-exuding skin. The echidna infant will stay pouchbound until its spines begin to grow. When they are sharp enough to annoy the mother, she drops her young in a shallow burrow and returns to nurse it every day or two.

An Eastern gray kangaroo absentmindedly grooms her nine-week-old joey.

A southern opossum from Brazil ranks as the first marsupial ever entertained at a royal court. In 1500 the explorer Vincente Pinzón presented an opossum to King Ferdinand and Queen Isabella. Their majesties politely fingered the animal's pouch and expressed wonder at "the incredible mother." The opossum's public image has steadily declined since then. It is generally thought of as ill-tempered, dim-witted, and foul-smelling.

The opossum answers its critics with a startling record of success in its habitats, aided by its opportunistic feeding habits. Seventy-five species are distributed throughout South, Central, and North America. The Virginia, or common opossum, has extended over two million square kilometers north and west in the last fifty years alone, and is now common through much of the eastern United States.

Like many opossums, the Virginia species is fantastically prolific, giving birth to as many as fifty-six young at one time. But by no means will all of these survive. The female typically has only thirteen teats, and some of these do not produce milk. The newborn who cannot find a teat fall off and die. The mother pays no attention to these early casualties, responding to the distress calls of her young only after they have left the pouch some seventy days later. Normal litter sizes at weaning are about seven. Curiously, if only one newborn attaches to a teat, it too will perish, its sucking stimulus too weak to trigger the release of milk.

It is hard to imagine that human earthlings, who position themselves on the very summit of mammalian evolution, could have much in common with an egg-laying ball of spines that roots about in the dust looking for termites. People tend to see in another earthling whatever they need to make their point. Undoubtedly, the monotremes parted ways with the other mammals very long ago—the most recent fossil evidence suggests about 150 million years. It would be a mistake, however, to confuse an early divergence from the mainstream with a permanently primitive condition, a point that Gould has eloquently argued on behalf of the monotremes. When the platypus and echidna set off on their own evolutionary journey, they preserved some traits of reptiles, and discarded others. But like their neighbors, the marsupials, only their reputations have suffered in the process.

Milky
Ways

At the mid-point of our journey, we meet gaudy deviants like the platypus and echidna, and discover them much more like ourselves than we thought. It really makes no difference whether the echidna delivers its milk through a nipple, in a patch of pouch skin, or for that matter, in a tin cup. It's all in the family, or at least in the class. Evolution's greatest gift to mammals is lactation. Sharks have placentas, some snakes and other reptiles also give birth to live young, and most mammalian males have rudimentary mammary glands. But, with some rare exceptions, only the mammalian female has evolved the ability to concoct a nutritious, digestible beverage expressly to sustain her young through the most vulnerable period of life. Not only does milk provide nutrition, it also contains vital maternal antibodies that the infant will need to combat disease. The milk is secreted by specialized skin tissues called mammary glands. In most species, the glands come in pairs— from two, as in human beings and goats; to eighteen, as in pigs. The absolute record in this category goes to an oddball, the pale-bellied mouse opossum, who bucks the trend with nineteen.

The words *mammal* and *mammary* are derived from the Latin for breast. Not all mammals, however, wear their mammae on the breast as humans do, nor are they usually so prominent. In whales the glands are positioned on the stomach, and in various rodents, rabbits, and canids they run the whole length of the chest and underbelly. The mammary glands of the coypu, a hefty, aquatic rodent native to Argentina, poke up from its back, the better to nurse its offspring as it swims. No matter what their external shape and position, the mammary glands in all species contain tiny, saclike structures called *alveoli*, whose walls consist of a single layer of milk-secreting cells. The alveoli are connected through a system of ducts and sinuses, leading to larger channels that open to the skin.

The composition of the fluid secreted by the alveoli varies greatly among the species, each adjusted to the particular needs of its young. In Arctic species like the polar bear, the milk contains over 30 percent fat, the better to build the cub's protection against the cold. Marine mammals such as seals have even richer milk. With those exceptions aside, the milk of most other mammals conforms to a curious pattern. Mothers that carry their young about with them or otherwise keep them physically close, such as monkeys and marsupials, provide a relatively watery milk. The infants suckle often, but in a leisurely sort of way. Mammals such as rabbits and rodents, who leave their young behind in "caches," produce a richer, frothier concoction, and the young greedily gulp it down whenever their mother comes within reach. The tree shrews of Southeast Asia take the caching mode to an extreme, the mother visiting her babies only once every forty-eight hours. When she finally arrives and offers a teat, the little shrews drink till their bellies bloat.

One other exception to the "cache or carry" distinction is the human

Here, a trio of eight-week-old oppossums suckle in their mother's pouch.

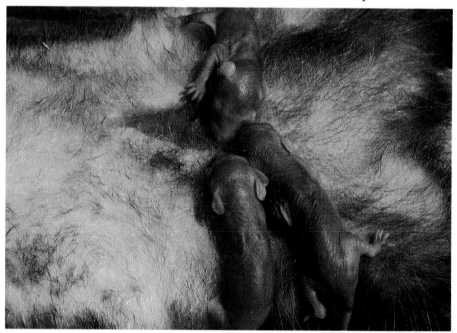

female in developed societies. Like other higher primates, she produces a thin milk (about 5 percent fat), but she suckles her baby only once every several hours, leaving the baby for the rest of the time in a cache-like contrivance called a crib. Among some hunter-gatherer tribes, such as the !Kung San of Botswana, nursing habits conform more to the predicted norm. According to Melvin Konner of Emory University, !Kung women nurse through a good part of their waking lives, and even while they sleep. Their children follow them everywhere, and routinely nurse until they are four years old or more.

Milk, of course, is not the only distinguishing feature of mammals. The earliest mammals lived in the shadow of the dinosaurs, and for many millions of years the only mammals were scuttling nocturnal creatures the size of mice. The mammals managed to hang on, barely, and their survival might have depended on the innovation of endothermy: the ability to precisely control body temperature from within. This innovation required the development of hair to provide insulation. Endothermy and body hair may have enabled the early mammals to side-step an ecological confrontation with the dinosaurs by enabling them to feed at night, when the cooler temperatures lulled the great reptiles into lethargy. Liberated in their movements and able to forage more efficiently, the early mammals could grow faster than the dinosaurs, and to breed more prolifically.

Endothermy undoubtedly contributed to the cynodont's ascendency, but in the catastrophe that swept the dinosaurs away, the mammals were also buoyed up by mother's milk. Much like modern crocodiles and other reptiles, infant dinosaurs came into the world as miniature versions of their parents. While the adult dinosaurs may have provided some care and protection, the young reptile was largely dependent on its own foraging ability to survive. Obviously a creature only a fraction of the size of its mother could not feed immediately on her sort of diet. The young dinosaur had to eat a series of different foods as it continued to grow. (To give a modern example, a newly hatched crocodile feeds first on insects, turns to crabs and crayfish as it develops, and eventually feeds on the same vertebrate prey as its parents.) In each of these food niches, the dinosaur would suffer from all the disadvantages of a stranger passing through a country already crowded with natives far more familiar with the terrain, including, of course, the dinosaurs who preceded it on the road to maturity. Much energy would be spent foraging, and growth would be slow and perilous.

In contrast, consider the young mammal granted what amounts to a luxurious detachment from its environment by the gift of milk. If food becomes scarce, the brunt of the hardship falls on the mother, who must continue to supply food to her young by sacrificing her own bodily proteins and minerals to keep the milk flowing. While the reptile struggles through unfamiliar niches, the young mammal stays close to the teat, saving its energy for growth. If we could bring together a newborn polar bear and a hatchling dinosaur, they would both weigh in at approximately 1 to 2 percent of their

The protein and fat content of kangaroo milk changes according to the needs of the growing joey.

mother's weight. In five years, however, the polar bear will be full grown, sharing the environmental niche of its parents, while the dinosaur will still be struggling in immaturity, dependent on a succession of different foods and constantly competing with larger members of its own species.

With nothing more taxing to ingest than a warm liquid, the infant mammal enjoys another long-term advantage over its reptilian ancestor. Nursing postpones the need for teeth, giving the jaws time to grow and make room for the more complex teeth and precise occlusion that enables mammals to chew more foods with better efficiency. The jaws and teeth of a jaguar, more powerful than even a lion's or tiger's, can reduce the leg bone of a deer to ingestible shards with a few bites. The crocodile, on the other hand, feeds at a rotten, half-submerged carcass by clamping down hard with its jaws and rotating its whole body until a morsel twists free.

In many mammal species, nursing also serves as a built-in method of population control. After birth, a mother's nipples become very sensitive. When stimulated by the infant's suckling, the nipple releases the hormone oxytocin, which triggers the discharge of milk and the release of another hormone, prolactin. One function of prolactin is to suppress the release of two other hormones that govern the mother's reproductive cycle. With some exceptions (for instance, the kangaroos with their embryonic dia-pause), the act of nursing tends to prevent ovulation, giving the nursing infant a chance to develop through its dependence without having to con-tinually compete with subsequent newborns. Should the suckling infant die, the prolactin brake on ovulation is released, and the female comes into estrus and is ready to mate.

If milk is so extraordinarily important, how did we mammals come by it in the first place? The origins of lactation have thoroughly perplexed evolutionary biologists since Darwin. Presumably the mammary gland did not tumble down from space, but developed through a series of modifi-cations upon some preexisting bit of anatomy in the ancestral reptilelike creatures. Today's reptiles, however, show no inkling of a structure that could evolve in the direction of such a gland.

Whatever confounds the evolutionists can be counted on to delight their opponents. In 1871, the British anti-evolutionist anatomist St. George Mivart summed up the milk dilemma this way:

> *Is it conceivable that the young of any animal was ever saved from destruction by accidentally sucking a drop of scarcely nutritious fluid from an accidentally [enlarged skin gland] of its mother? And even if one was so, what chance was there for the perpetuation of such a variation?*

Darwin answered Mivart's skepticism himself by proposing a marsu-piallike ancestor who nurtured its young in a pouch. According to Darwin, secretions from skin glands in the pouch—either sweat glands or oil-se-creting sebaceous glands—might have been licked up by the young. Through generations, Darwin reasoned, this habit would lead to selection for females who secreted more nutritious fluids from localized regions of the pouch. From that point on, it was simply a matter of fine-tuning before full-fledged mammary glands emerged to boost the mammals to their privileged po-sition on earth.

Darwin's theory was ingenious, but it failed to hold up against some subsequent discoveries. The first we have already witnessed: Caldwell's announcement that the milk-bearing monotremes laid eggs like reptiles. Assuming that the monotremes did not dally with live birth for part of their history and then revert to their egg-laying habits, Caldwell's discovery would suggest that lactation was a part of mammalian life even before there were live infants crawling around in pouches. The second objection to Darwin also concerned a matter of timing. By most indications, lactation also pre-ceded the evolution of pouches, leaving one to wonder what urge would lead the infant to gravitate toward a particular patch of glandular skin.

Evolutionists have since approached the riddle of lactation from a different angle. Rather than begin, as Darwin did, with an existing mammal and work backwards, why not call upon the reptiles themselves to suggest a milk-bearing descendent? In the early twentieth century, the theories of Ernst Bresslau and William Gregory focused on the reptiles' habit of incubating their eggs. Noting that some birds possess a warm, veiny area of skin called an incubation patch, Bresslau envisioned ancestral reptiles with a similar structure. The rich blood supply to the region might have led to the development of glands that secreted a fluid meant to bolster the temperature of the eggs. Gregory enlarged upon this idea by proposing that the secretion was a gluey ooze that kept the eggs stuck to the incubation patch. In both cases, the fluid in question would be licked up by the young as they hatched. If the secretions turned out to be nutritious as well, then the evolution of milk was well under way.

Unfortunately, the incubation theories stumble into the same quagmire that plagues much evolutionary thought: With no current evidence available either to prove or refute them, the theories cannot break out of the realm of speculation. What is the inherent advantage to an egg in being glued to its mother? How valid is the assumption that a bath of maternal fluid would warm an egg? Couldn't the egg just as likely be cooled by the evaporation of the fluid, much as sweat cools an overheated horse or human? Later theories—that lactation developed from thirsty hatchlings licking water from their parent's fur, or from sweet-smelling secretions designed to bond the infant to its mother—are similarly untestable.

Recently, Virginia Hayssen of Smith College and David Blackburn of Vanderbilt University found a possible clue to the mysterious origins of lactation. Their approach was to look at the composition of milk itself. Among the many ingredients of milk is an enzyme called *lysozyme*, also found in most other bodily secretions and in the whites of many bird eggs. Lysozyme is an antibacterial agent that destroys bacteria by dissolving their cell walls. Another component of milk, one much more central to lactation itself, is a protein called *alpha-lactalbumin*. Working in conjunction with another substance, alpha-lactalbumin triggers the synthesis of the sugar lactose, the basic carboyhdrate of most mammal milk.

Lysozyme and alpha-lactalbumin perform very different functions—the one acting as a defense against bacteria, the other essential to milk production—but the two substances are nevertheless remarkably similar in genetic structure, which strongly suggests that they may have a common evolutionary past. In view of these molecular similarities, Hayssen and Blackburn suggest that lactation may have evolved from some fluid originally meant to protect the female reptile's egg from bacterial infection. Lysozyme secreted by a gland of the premammalian mother either coated the eggshell or mixed with the egg albumen, in either case erecting a barrier against microbial invasion. With only slight mutations, the lysozyme could have given rise to alpha-lactalbumin, a substance that could have contributed to the production of a nutritional beverage—mother's milk.

This version of the origin of lactation also rests substantially on untestable grounds. But at least Hayssen and Blackburn can point to clear evidence in the molecular record of life. Curiously, the spiny echidna waddles in here to lend support to their theory further. It seems that the lysozyme found in echidna milk may be able to juggle both functions at once—defending against bacteria and stimulating the production of lactose. From this angle, at least, the echidnas seem frozen in time, caught in a telling transition two hundred million years old.

However milk evolved, it gave to the mammals their precious, prolonged reprieve between birth and naked independence. In addition to all its other advantages, milk keeps the infant physically close to its parent— a good place to be in a world full of predators. The mammals are not the only earthlings to have evolved the notion of parental care, but they extended the concept in new and richer directions. The bond between mother and infant, thickened with milk, developed into a cohesive period of apprenticeship, wherein the infant could learn from its parent by paying close attention to her behavior. In some species—the bear and tiger, for instance—the early relationship an animal enjoys with its mother is the only lasting attachment it will ever know. But for other mammals, the nursing knot is just the first stitch in a splendidly intricate fabric of society.

CHAPTER FOUR

The Gregarious Giant

I

There is an animal called an elephant . . . no larger animals can be found. They possess vast intelligence and memory. And they copulate back to back. Elephants remain pregnant for two years, nor do they have babies more than once, nor do they have several at a time, but only one. They live three hundred years.

This natural history of the elephant is excerpted from a twelfth-century Latin bestiary. Considering its age the report is remarkably accurate. While the account goes astray in some important respects, the errors tend toward exaggeration rather than sheer nonsense. Elephants do not live three hundred years, for instance, but they do live a very long time, longer than most humans in the

149

twelfth century. Gestation does indeed last close to two years, and twins are very uncommon.

For all its strangeness of form—the ever-startling mass, the great dangling nose, the tarpaulin ears, and reaching tusks—the elephant is an old familiar to humankind. Drawings of elephants, mastodons, and mammoths are found among the earliest examples of cave art. The Asian elephant figures in the lore and religion of India, Pakistan, and Sri Lanka as far back as 3000 B.C. and still holds immense ceremonial importance in festivals. Egyptian paintings dating from 1500 B.C. clearly show tiny pachyderms the size of dogs. Aristotle correctly reported the elephant's twenty-two-month gestation period and knew as well that the testes of the male were internal, resting high up in the abdominal cavity.

In ancient times the elephants were used, somewhat problematically, as engines of war. One hundred years before Hannibal crossed the Alps mounted on an elephant, King Porus of India faced Alexander the Great with an army bolstered by two hundred mighty elephants in the vanguard. The tactic backfired when the animals panicked, killing as many Indians as Macedonians before they were finally slaughtered themselves. The Romans had a great fascination for elephants, and set them in their arenas against other animals, including men. The iconography of later European civilization fairly bristles with trunks and tusks—elephants carrying castles on their backs, conquering lions, stomping on snakes and dragons. In nearly all Western art, the elephant is shown as a force for purity and good.

Much of our modern understanding of elephant behavior rests on the work of Scottish biologist Iain Douglas-Hamilton, who in the late 1960s undertook the first thorough study of a free-living elephant population. Charged with determining whether the elephants in Tanzania's Lake Manyara National Park were endangering the park's acacia trees—the favorite hangouts of local lions, the park's most popular tourist attractions—Douglas-Hamilton extended his study to include an examination of the elephant's social habits and organization. He identified and named some 450 individual elephants, keeping track of their seasonal movements for four and a half years. In 1975, Douglas-Hamilton and his wife, Oria, published a popular account of their work, *Among the Elephants*. Since then they have conducted census and management studies of elephants throughout Africa, while other investigators have continued studying the animal's behavior in the wild. Most recently, Cynthia Moss, Joyce Poole, and other investigators in the Elephant Research Project in Kenya's Amboseli National Park have greatly enhanced our understanding of the elephant's reproductive habits and social patterns.

Every schoolchild knows that the elephant is the largest animal on land. An African elephant bull weighs as much as six tons and stands as much as twelve feet tall. It is not the animal's enormous dimensions that so overwhelm us, but rather the magnitude of life held within such a frame. The elephant is among the longest-living of mammals, greatest in appetite, largest of heart and mind, deepest in memory, and most unshakable in the

For thousands of years man has employed the elephant in war, commerce, transportation, and ceremony. In this eighteenth-century painting a British officer, surrounded by native attendants, is transported in regal style aboard a large, bejewelled elephant.

strength of its attachments to others of its kind. At zoos, one can always find a gathering of people, young and old, suspended in a murmuring trance around the elephant enclosure, watching enraptured as the great creatures do nothing more than graze. The females are considerably smaller than the males, but even an elephant cow of three tons, approaching across a zoo enclosure, quickly shrinks one's sense of self-importance. Her skin, cracked and gnarled like oak bark, is dyed the color of dust by the powderings she applies with her trunk. When she raises her head and spreads her ears, it seems as if a great, heart-shaped piece of the earth were lifted up and thrown against the sky. From above, her weathered forehead falls in a cascade of narrowing rings, and the heavy trunk combs the air, seeking one's scent. Satisfied that the scent signals no danger, she lumbers away with an easy, swaying gait, leaving behind a musky odor and a strangely restful throbbing in the air, as if one had been visited by a ethereal spirit manifest in a profound quantity of flesh.

Next to its great size, nothing so distinguishes the elephant from other animals as its trunk. To some eyes, this deeply furrowed, tapering appendage appears grotesquely primitive, a feature more at home on the face of some atavistic mammal which should have relinquished the planet long ago to more refined species. The elephant's trunk is an ancient instrument, evolved thirty million years ago as an attenuation of nose and upper lip. It is the proboscidean's solution to the problem of how a large, plant-eating animal is to reach its food. The elephant's heavy head, which supports the ponderous tusks, ruled out the option, taken by the giraffe family, of extending the neck. The elephant's ancestors chose a different evolutionary ploy: If you can't bring your mouth to the food, then find some way of bringing the food to your mouth. Individuals with more extended snouts were better able to forage, grew healthier, bred more successfully, and passed on their longer snouts to the next generation. Over the millennia the trunk gathered new agility and, simultaneously, new functions—a situation which would continue to favor individuals with the most agile, developed trunks.

For sheer versatility, the elephant's trunk matches the arms, legs, and tails of any flat-faced creature on the planet. It serves as a hand to pull up grass by the roots, strip the bark from trees, lift a younger brother out of the mud, or grab hold of a twig to scratch between one's shoulder blades. Its "fingers" on the tip can pluck a berry off a bush or pick up a pebble. Lifted high, the trunk's sensitive olfactory tissues warn of danger hundreds of yards away. Entwined in greeting or placed in the mouth of another, it welcomes familiars and identifies strangers. The trunk stores up to two gallons of water for pouring down a thirsty throat or showering across a sun-scorched back. It is a scoop to pick sand from one's toes, a trumpet to signal danger or to declare one's lustiness, an arm to caress a newborn calf, a snorkel, back-duster, missile launcher, shower nozzle, branch-stripper, and battering ram. Composed of thousands of muscles uninhibited by bone, the trunk's dexterity is limited only by the elephant's ability to master it.

The tip of the trunk distinguishes the two species of elephant remaining on earth. The African elephant, *Loxodonta africana*, has two fleshy projections on the end of its trunk, while the Asian elephant, *Elephas maximus*, has only one. African elephants are also slightly larger than their Asian relatives. *Loxodonta*'s imposing ears are shaped roughly like a map of Africa, while its smaller cousin has smaller ears, coincidentally shaped like a map of India. *Elepha*'s back is convex, *Loxodonta*'s slightly concave. The tusks of the African elephant, found on both male and female, are more developed than those of the Asian species. Female Asians almost never grow tusks, and tuskless males, known as *makhnas*, make up a good part of the population. The Asian elephant has come under the yoke of humankind far more than its comparatively high-strung relative, and now exists throughout Southeast Asia both completely wild and fully domesticated. (One has to resist the temptation to attribute its wizened, long-suffering countenance to this human association.) In their behavior and social organization in the wild, the two species are very similar.

In Roman times, the African elephant roamed freely from the Cape of Good Hope to Syria and the shores of the Mediterranean. The animal is highly adaptable, and only the Sahara and other desert regions were beyond its reach. Their enormous requirements for food, however, have brought elephants into direct and tragic conflict with the spread of human agriculture. Today, the remaining one to two million elephants either live in areas too full of tsetse flies and other hazards to attract human habitation, or else congregate in the great African national parks. There the elephants so beleaguer the vegetation—tearing grass up by the roots, stripping bark, knocking down whole trees—that they threaten the entire park ecosystem. Especially vulnerable to the elephants are the flat-topped acacia trees, as much a symbol of African wildlife as the elephants and giraffe that feed on them and the leopards who loll in their branches. Once the woody vegetation in a park is removed by the elephants, the surviving grassland becomes even more vulnerable to fire.

The "elephant problem" in the parks cannot be attributed completely to the animal's feeding habits. Over the last twenty years, ivory hunters have pursued the elephant with increasing determination and effect, employing automatic weapons and increasingly sophisticated equipment to stay one step ahead of anti-poaching ranger patrols. Elephants are very intelligent animals who quickly learn to seek refuge within park boundaries. The more hunters threaten the elephants outside the park, the more they congregate within its borders, further exacerbating the overcrowded conditions within. In Serengeti Naitonal Park in Tanzania and Tsavo National Park in Kenya, the elephants and seasonal fires have converted hundreds of square miles of woodland into open grasslands. Fortunately, the damage is not irrevocable; given time and good management, the woody vegetation may return.

In 1985, Iain Douglas-Hamilton surveyed the elephant population in part of the Central African Republic. He counted 11,000 elephants: 4,000 living animals, and 7,000 carcasses, their tusks torn out and the corpses left to rot. This gruesome statistic is not in the least unusual. Some 50,000 elephants a year are illegally slaughtered for their tusks throughout Africa. Until recently, an elephant living inside a preserve had a good chance of surviving. During the past decade, as tusked elephants outside the parks have been decimated, widescale poaching has violated park boundaries.

What accounts for the human relish for ivory? Elephant tusks, like those of the hippo, narwhal, and walrus, are composed of dentine, which is easily carved into intricate artifacts.

Naturalist Wolfgang Bayer captured this sad evidence of the widespread illegal poaching that continues across Africa. Butchered where it fell, this elephant may have been mourned for days by its extended family.

Elephant ivory is unfortunately endowed with a distinctive diamond-shaped pattern in cross section that imparts a much-coveted warm luster. The ivory proves remarkably durable when used for the handle of a knife, sliced thin for piano keys, or rounded into the smooth shape of a billiard ball.

Such utilitarian purposes, however, have long been served by synthetic substitutes. Today, the high value of ivory can be attributed to the whimsy of commodity economics: ivory, like gold, is valuable because we *think* it is valuable. In the 1970s, the price of ivory suddenly began to climb, going from about $3 a pound in the late sixties to $45 a pound in the late seventies. This surge caused a virtual elephant holocaust, with most of the ivory funneling into the hands of a small group of investors. More recently the price has stabilized at about $29 a pound, though the concept of price stabilization suffers somewhat in the context of such widespread slaughter.

Elephants are supreme dietary generalists. On the savannah they feed mainly on grass, surrounding a tuft with their trunks and pulling it up by the roots. A few slaps against a foreleg dislodge most of the dirt and stones, and a graceful curling motion of the trunk delivers it mouthward. Sometimes the elephant prepares the morsel with a little more care, coiling it up and down the trunk until it tightens into a roll—much the way a baker kneads dough between his palms. In the dry season elephants spice up their diet with a selection of desert dates, wild celery, black plums, butternut, fig, wild raspberries, and coffee berries. Fruits and seeds of the wild ginger tree must be especially delectable; one study in Uganda's Murchison Falls National Park found that they comprised 8 percent of the elephant's diet, in spite of being hard to reach. In addition to the leaves of the acacia, dry-season menus include the leafy parts of tamarind and sausage trees. Forest elephants, a slightly smaller subspecies of *Loxodonta*, depend less on grass. Their diet usually consists of woody material and fruit. Like other large herbivores, the elephants require great amounts of sodium and other minerals in their diet, and will go to great lengths to obtain them.

High on Mount Elgon along the Kenya-Uganda border, forest elephants climb a centuries-old path to Kitum Cave, a cavern extending hundreds of yards into the mountain. Arriving at dusk, the elephants feel with their trunks in the gloom, gingerly skirting deep crevasses—graves for less dexterous waterbuck, buffalo, and elephant. They seek deposits of salt to help digest their vegetarian diet. Deep inside the cave they search for exposed veins of sodium sulfate. In utter darkness the Mount Elgon elephants mine the cave walls, leaving polished gouges known as "tuskings." Revealed to us through infrared photography, Kitum is a Dantesque tableau of looming, shadowy shapes and light-startled eyes, while above, the fruit bats rustle in their roosts.

When the loose pebbles and rock debris left by periodic rockfalls have been harvested off the cave floor, the mineral-starved elephants are forced to use their tusks as grinding tools. Infrared light was used to photograph a trio of Mount Elgon forest elephants mining the mineral-rich walls and ceiling in pitch-black Kitum Cave.

The African elephant uses both its trunk and its tusks to gather food. Tusks evolved as elongated incisor teeth about thirty-five million years ago, to help the elephant's earlier ancestors root up low-lying forage. The *deinothere*, an elephant look-alike that flourished until two or three million years ago, had downward-curving tusks which could rake through submerged swamp vegetation, while the animal's short trunk was held topside like a snorkel. Various *gomphotherids*,—the shovel-tuskers—which emerged in the Miocene period twenty-five million years ago, had flat, bony extensions to their lower jaws and incisors and literally shoveled plant life into their mouths. The great woolly mammoth, which roamed the forests of Siberia until as late as ten thousand years ago (and according to some authorities may still exist), possessed magnificent spiraling tusks up to sixteen feet in length. Their crossed tusks would have been well-suited for use as snowplows to uncover buried vegetation, and to sweep aside brushes and vines, exposing the succulent greenery they so relished. The sheer bulk and length of the tusks of bull elephants suggest that they also may have evolved through competition between males over breeding privileges.

An elephant spends over three-quarters of its day feeding. During its sixty-five-year life, a truly fantastic quantity of plant life passes through it, some four thousand tons of grass, leaf, twig, and shrub. In spite of these prodigious requirements, the species has survived through drought after drought, virtually unaltered for seven million years. Elephants have an uncanny sense that guides them toward rain and, if dry weather persists, leads them to dig for underground reservoirs—a practice that incidentally brings drinking water within the reach of other, tuskless species.

Acacia trees are almost as ubiquitous and diverse in Africa as the eucalyptus in Australia. Several hundred species thrive on the savannah. Most common are the umbrella tree, *Acacia tortilis*, the yellow-barked fever tree, *Acacia xanthophloea*, the smaller whistling thorn, *Acacia drepanolobium*, and *Acacia mellifera*, which smells like honey. While the eucalyptus family relies primarily on chemical defense against herbivores, the acacia arms itself with thorns. One of its chief predators is the giraffe, who has evolved an eighteen-inch tongue, an extremely agile upper lip, and horny plates in its mouth to cope with the acacia's formidable spikes.

The whistling thorn uses symbiosis to foil the giraffe's attack. The tree harbors a species of stinging ant in thousands of galls the size of golf balls in its branches. When a giraffe feeds, the ants attack its face, driving it off to browse on another tree. The acacia repays the ant with a sweet nectar from each leaf stem, manu-

Giraffes are efficient browsers, able to pick their way around the acacia's thorns. But the tree has another line of defense: a symbiotic species of stinging ant that swarms out from the black galls the ants build on the acacia's branches.

factured solely to provide sustenance for its insect defenders.

The real secret to the elephant's evolutionary success is hidden in the caverns and channels of the animal's alimentary system. If one wants to fully understand this magnificent earthling, look at it from the inside out, following the path of a bit of elephant food, a branch of acacia torn from

a tree by an elephant's trunk. The mouth awaiting the woody morsel is a soft, slippery cavern, "a mucosa blancmange," as elephant specialist Harvey Croze describes it. The tissues of the elephant's mouth are much more vulnerable to the prick of acacia thorns than are, for instance, the hardened layers inside the mouth of a giraffe. Elephants consequently shy away from the low-lying acacia bushes, which are better fortified with thorns than the mature trees. There are exceptions; according to Croze, some elephants in the Serengeti flatten the thorns by pulling the branch through a loop they form with their trunk.

In contrast to the elephant's delicate mouth, its teeth easily cope with the bark and thorns of the acacia branch. A newborn elephant calf comes into the world with only eight teeth, two in each quadrant of the jaw. Within a year, four more teeth push forward to join the eight natal teeth. Soon after, the front four molars drop out, establishing a pattern that the elephant shares only with its distant, water-dwelling relative, the manatee, and, curiously, the kangaroolike rock wallaby of Australia. Over the elephant's lifetime, it grows only six pairs of teeth in each jaw, each pushing forward as the older teeth are ground down by the backward and forward working of the jaws. The last set of molars—grinders about the size of small bricks—emerges when the elephant is about thirty years old.

While the elephant patiently chews upon a sprig of acacia, let us ruminate for a minute on its dental design. Teeth form an accurate record of an animal's evolutionary past, each tooth a rune inscribed with a tale of survival in a changing environment. The elephant's ancestors—the gomphotherids, deinotheres, mastodons, and their relations—chewed their food with low-crowned, relatively smooth teeth, grinding tufts of greenery with a side-to-side rotation, much like antelopes and zebras. The teeth of the African and Asian elephant living today (as well as the woolly mammoth, so lately extinct) are high-crowned and heavily ridged. According to biologist S. K. Eltringham, the difference is so distinct and essential that elephants are considered an entirely different family in the proboscidean order, despite the similar appearance of their extinct ancestors.

The true elephants emerged in Africa toward the end of the Pliocene period, at a time of lower rainfall and expanding grassland. Their hightopped molars met the challenge of the tough diet of grass. The parallel ridges on the chewing surface break up rough stalks, the ridges of each upper tooth meeting those of the complementary lower molar at a slight angle, so that each pair of ridges shears through the wads of grass and bark.

After reducing the acacia branch to a spongy ball, the elephant swallows. Like all mammals, it cannot digest large amounts of cellulose, a carbohydrate found in grass, leaves, wood pulp, and bark. Even this largest of land animals depends upon millions of microscopic bacteria and protozoa in its gut to manufacture the enzymes that break down cellulose. These microbial tenants, and not the elephant itself, set to work digesting the

The elephant plays an enormous, sometimes destructive, role within the fragile savannah ecosystem. Here a persistent elephant stretches for a morsel of acacia.

acacia. In return, the great beast provides them with a steady source of food.

Herbivorean digestion is a kind of fermentation process. In ruminant species—animals that chew their cud like cows—the fermentation takes place in an organ, located in front of the stomach, called the *rumen*. Ruminants extract protein from food relatively efficiently. The same cannot be said of the elephant who, like the horse and rhinoceros, lacks a rumen. These species are called hindgut fermenters. The acacia twig slides down the elephant's gullet directly into its stomach, where it joins as much as 400 pounds of undigested plant matter. The stomach is just a storage chamber; the real business of digestion takes place in a bulbous swelling of the intestine called the *cecum*. Here the microbes convert the mass of vegetation into usable proteins.

The elephant's digestion process is much less nutritionally efficient than that of the cud-chewers. However, hindgut fermenters enjoy an important advantage over the ruminants, who must break down their food into tiny particles that pass through small openings between their several stomachs. Food processing for ruminants is time-consuming, so each mouthful must be full of nutrients. In the dry season, when green matter is scarce, ruminants have a more difficult time getting enough to eat. The non-ruminants like the elephant, on the other hand, can simply increase their intake of less wholesome food—the woody parts of trees and bushes, for instance. So long as the elephant has enough room to satisfy its large but unchoosy appetite, it will not directly compete with ruminant species like the antelope and giraffe.

But what of its fellow hindgut fermenters, the zebras and rhinos? When the proboscideans first emerged, their ecological niche was already crowded with primitive horses and other hindgut fermenters who fed on coarser vegetation. In spite of this competition, the proboscideans not only held onto their habitat, but managed to thrive over most of the globe. Their success may be attributed to the elephant's sheer bulk. The larger an animal is, the slower its metabolic rate becomes in proportion to body size. And the slower its metabolic rate, the easier it is for an animal to subsist on less nutritional plant parts. Up to a point, natural selection favored an ever-larger proboscidean, who could not only reach virtually inaccessible plant parts, but could survive on the woody parts unpalatable even to the horses and other nonruminants.

Another common browser found in the acacia's foliage is the bush hyrax, a furry creature that looks like a rodent, walks on hooves like an antelope, and smells very distinc-tively like a hyrax. This ancient animal's closest relative turns out to be the elephant itself, and while the two parted ways some sixty million years ago, their kinship is unmistakably re-

Ancient relative of the elephant, the bush hyrax is another African mammal that lives among the thorns of the acacia.

vealed by similarities in their blood chemistry and in certain features of limb construction. Both are hindgut fermenters. They also have in common pronounced incisor teeth; in elephants these have become tusks, and in the hyrax, sharp, fanglike teeth used for defense. Elephants and hyraxes lack scrotums; their testicles are lodged high up in their abdomens, and during the mating season, the hyrax's testicles swell up to twenty-two times their normal size.

Reproduction in the hyrax is marked by fierce competition on the part of the males, who advertise their claim to a group of females with a harsh territorial screech. The bush hyrax's penis is an extravagant affair nearly half the length of his body, the shaft fitted with a cuplike glans from which arises another slender appendage. Bush hyraxes mate in a dusty commotion lasting only a few seconds; the male is tethered to the female by his penis alone, while the rest of him flails above. The earthbound female puts an end to the mating by simply walking forward a few paces and letting him fall.

For all the competition that goes on between male hyraxes of the same species, there yet exists a curious harmony between two hyrax relatives: the gray-brown Bruce's yellow-spotted hyrax (a bush variety); and the larger, darker brown Johnston's hyrax (a species of rock hyrax). These two species inhabit the outcrops of rock known as kopjes, which rise from the plains of East Africa like hump-backed islands. In an interspecies intimacy rarely found in the mammalian world, the Bruce's and Johnston's hyraxes share the same sleeping holes, hug close together for warmth on chilly mornings, and even make use of common "latrines." Newborns are welcomed with equal celebrations of sniffing and greeting by both species, and their young romp about together in communal playgroups.

No two species that were competing for food or territory could possibly cohabit so peacefully. The key to their harmony rests in their differences, rather than in their similarities. The lack of a match in penis anatomy rules out any potentially disruptive interbreeding, and their territorial calls are unalike—imperatives declared in different languages. Most importantly, bush hyraxes browse on leaves, and rock hyraxes dine only on grass.

Over the long run, this digestive strategy helps the elephant to endure long droughts that kill many smaller beasts. The cost of this privilege, however, is a life bound to hunger. The elephant's digestion is grossly inefficient; in its seventeen hours of daily feeding, the animal eats much more food than it actually digests. The sprig of acacia, chewed up and swallowed, stands about a 60 percent chance of emerging, mangled but intact. Each day an elephant defecates roughly 250 pounds of dung, which draws a swarm of insects, who themselves attract guinea fowl and mongooses. One species of dung beetle takes full advantage of the elephant's less-than-careful digestion. The beetle disguises itself as a bit of twig, lying motionless in the dung even when the pile is disturbed. This camouflage shields the beetle from the sharp eyes of birds such as the francolin, who close in on each mound of elephant droppings.

There are even more exquisite wonders hidden in the elephant's dung. Lying in the pile of droppings, among the remnants of the branch we've followed on its digestive journey, are some acacia seeds. Like many plant-eaters, the elephant is a seed disperser, helping the plant by softening the seeds and providing an ideal medium for germination. But the elephant does more for the acacia than simply sow its seed. Acacias are members of the pea family, which hides its seeds contained in tough pods. Some acacias are besieged by a pod-drilling, parasitic beetle called a *bruchid*, which uses the acacia's pods as nesting sites, laying its eggs in the pods while they are still ripening on the tree. When the larvae hatch, they eat their way into the seeds themselves, where they ensconce themselves, a beetle in each seed, and enter their pupal stage. Approximately 95 percent of the acacia's seeds are beetle-infested and will never grow.

If there were no natural means of controlling the beetles, their host acacias would soon die out. Ironically, it is the elephant, destroyer of trees, who helps to save the acacia from extinction. If the infected pods are eaten by elephants or other browsers before the beetle larvae have a chance to attack the seed, the elephant's digestive juices penetrate the pods to soften the seeds for germination, killing the resident bruchid beetles. Sequestered in the pile of dung, the healthy acacia seeds are discovered by dung beetles, carted off, and buried. Eventually, from a seedpod that has been parasitized, torn from a tree, swallowed, and dispersed, a new acacia sprouts forth.

II

Elephants need other elephants, a fact as firmly entrenched in their nature as their need for food and water. Elephant society is a fluid complex of kin relations, friendships, acquaintances made and long remembered, grand gatherings, gradual dispersals. The core of the society is the family unit: a group of from two individuals to a couple of dozen closely related elephants who feed and travel together throughout most of their lifetimes. Beyond the family unit, elephants' social organization expands like the

A family of elephants rests in the cool shade of an acacia on the Serengeti Plain in Tanzania.

ripples from a stone thrown into a pool, each level encompassing a larger segment of the population.

Until about twenty-five years ago, people believed that elephant groups were led by a dominant bull, lording it over a harem of females and sheltering them from danger. This view of elephant society was conceived by hunters, most often male themselves, and it expresses the bias of our own society. Elephant gender is difficult to guess at a distance, since their genitals are obscured by a drapery of convoluted flesh. We now know that the dominant elephant in each family unit is invariably a large, older female, known as the matriarch. Males either leave on their own when they reach puberty, or are chased out of the family when they become randy, rambunctious, and generally unpleasant to have around. Thereafter the bulls either live alone or in loose, temporary associations with other bulls.

The matriarch is often forty years old or more, sometimes past breeding age and perhaps no longer the strongest member of the group. Her authority, which is absolute, rests entirely on the consent of those she leads. She rarely bullies or threatens, because she is seldom challenged. She leads with her wisdom. It is the matriarch who decides when the time has come for the group to march to the stand of acacia clumped on the horizon or to follow her down to the river for a mud bath. The geography of the family's home range is written in her memory; she learned it as a young calf following her own mother and grandmother, and she will pass it on to her offspring, along with the knowledge gathered during her lifetime. The favorite stands of woodland, the grassy swamps, the paths up an es-

Elephants are among the most social of species, confirming lifelong loyalties with frequent body contact. Here a herd encircles its young to protect them.

carpment that bypass human settlement to fine woody browse—the whole book of elephant lore rests inside her massive brain. A traumatic event such as a flood or an attack by poachers will be remembered for the rest of her life. Whatever change in behavior she undergoes because of it—such as an intensified hostility toward humankind—will be passed to her descendents. When she dies, her place will be assumed by the next oldest cow, the various sisters, nieces, and cousins falling into place below the new matriarch.

The matriarch's signals are subtle and little understood by researchers. Her leadership is noticeable most when her group is in danger. A scent of man will prompt the elephants to cluster around her flanks, their trunks bristling up, probing the air. The calves fall in behind. If she chooses to retreat, the matriarch signals the others to withdraw, covering their rear. Often, the matriarch is the first to make a charge at an intruder, screeching, her tusks arching skyward and her gigantic, time-tattered ears slapping like battle flags against her sides. Though she may look like some creature of the apocalypse, the spectacle is usually a loud and terrible bluff. In most cases, the elephant pulls up short and withdraws, venting her anger on a nearby bush or fallen log. Bull elephants stage even more ferocious threat displays, and are even less likely to actually attack. The elephant to fear most is the one who approaches without bravado, head down, silent, eyes fixed on its target. Iain Douglas-Hamilton barely survived an attack in Lake Manyara Park by four implacably violent females he called the Torone

Sisters, named after a shrill queen in Greek mythology. They charged without warning, burying their tusks in his Land Rover and hoisting it up like so much cargo on a forklift.

An animal as well-defended as the elephant has little to fear from any predator other than man. Only a very desperate or foolish lion would challenge an adult elephant. The calves, however, are fair game for lions, and a lone female with a calf will treat the cat accordingly, keeping her young close by her side when lions may be lurking. Full-grown lions can easily escape an elephant's aggression, but there are other ways to encourage their respect. In his book, *The Serengeti Lion*, George Schaller tells of a lioness who killed an elephant calf and suffered bitterly for it. When the elephants discovered the loss of the calf, they deliberately sought out the lioness's cub where it hid in the grass and trampled it to death. Any lion cub discovered by chance will be treated similarly. Douglas-Hamilton once saw an elephant family give chase to an entire pride, "the elephants

Every elephant should be considered dangerous, especially stampeding bulls in season and cows with young. According to one zoo director, elephants are responsible for more human deaths and injuries every year than all other zoo animals combined.

Elephants and rhinos normally get along quite peaceably, though the proboscidean furiously defends her calf against any hint of aggression. Once a baby elephant at a water hole near Tree Tops Lodge, in Kenya's Abedare National Park, playfully approached a rhino. The rhino charged, sending the calf squealing back to its mother, and then sauntered off. The mother elephant was so enraged that she turned and attacked another rhino drinking nearby, sending a tusk into its chest. While tourists watched from the lodge's terrace, the elephant then held the innocent rhino underwater with her forefeet until it drowned.

shrieking and bellowing while the lions ran low to the ground giving vent to furious growls." The lions finally found safety in a tree.

Elephant calves enjoy a long childhood, and the care accorded them is one of the primary socializing forces in the species. The matriarch might be the largest and strongest in an elephant group, but herd life revolves around its smallest members. Nurturing the calves is a collective responsibility. A lactating female will occasionally share her milk with a calf belonging to a sister or aunt. "Babysitters"—subadult females of nine years or more—play a crucial role in the family long before they have calves of their own. The juveniles keep an eye on the calves and make sure that they do not stray from the group, where they might meet with an accident or fall prey to lions.

If a calf is accidentally left behind when the family trudges off to new ground, its squeals of distress will be answered as likely by a babysitter as by its true mother. The young female returns to give the calf a reassuring touch with her trunk and a helpful nudge along. As elephants must feed almost constantly, such surrogate mothering is more than a luxury; it gives the parent freedom to forage undisturbed. The young females gain useful experience in child-rearing, and improve their chances of having their generosity reciprocated when they have young of their own.

Surrogate mothering is a example of behavior motivated by kin selection, a genetic predisposition to protect one's brothers and sisters and other close relatives. According to sociobiological theory, the social behavior of an animal is determined at least partly by its genes, which have been shaped by natural selection to benefit their own chances of survival. The surest way to perpetuate one's genes, of course, is to reproduce oneself. Since an animal has half of its genes in common with any brother or sister, the next best course of action is to nurture and protect relatives, so that the shared genes can survive and spread throughout the population. The closer their relation, the more genes two animals have in common and the stronger the bond between them. ("I would lay down my life for two brothers or eight cousins," the biologist J. B. S. Haldane wryly remarked.) The genetic investment represented by an animal's offspring combined with those of its relatives is known as its "inclusive fitness." Naturally, the young elephant who reassures a bawling yearling or pulls a struggling nephew up a steep bank is unaware of any genetic motive for her solicitude. Nevertheless, her behavior gives expression to the very genes that will ensure their own survival.

Babysitting an infant elephant is no easy task. Much like human children, elephant calves are mentally precocious, their reach far exceeding their grasp. The elephant calf shares with the human baby a brain that weighs far less at birth than when fully grown—35 percent of adult weight in the elephant newborn and 26 percent in the human being. Other mammals are born with an average of 90 percent of their brain already developed. A growing brain is, above all, a brain that can *learn*, and during the calf's long years of immaturity it soaks up a wealth of specific information and subtle impressions. At the same time, it must learn to master basic functions as well. For instance, a newborn elephant will find its trunk a terrible nuisance, always underfoot and in the way. When the young calf drinks, it holds its trunk to one side and tries to slurp the water in through its mouth. It will take a year or more of watching and experimenting before the calf learns to suck up water in its trunk and pour the drink into its mouth.

Much of what a calf knows is learned through play. Practically from birth the young elephant takes a joyful interest in its brothers and sisters and anything else that moves. Egrets are fun to chase, as are baby antelope, snakes, or even stray feathers. If nothing else is handy the calf may charge its own shadow. Even before they are a year old the male calves take sport in shoving matches and mock sexual mountings, something the females rarely do. As they begin to wander farther and farther from the group, the calves will get themselves into trouble—falling down slopes, stepping in mud too soft to step out of, or perhaps running amiss of a ratel, a bold and unamiable badger known to sink its teeth into elephants' trunks. A calf's shrill squeal quickly brings its mother or somebody else to the rescue.

The ratel, or honey badger, is native to much of Africa and large stretches of Southeast Asia. A vicious fighter, it wears the colors of a skunk, boasts an equally revolting scent, and emits an awful, grating snarl when disturbed. The ratel's deep love of honey accounts for the thick, rubbery quality of its hide, which is practically invulnerable to bee stings. It scurries quickly, low to the ground. Legend has it that the ratel will attack men while they sleep, grabbing their genitals in its powerful jaws.

For all its belligerence, the ratel maintains a close relationship with a black-throated bird called the honey guide. This little bird also has a taste for honey, but can't break open the hives to reach its favorite meal. By flapping its wings and chattering, the honey guide alerts a ratel and leads it to the hive. The badger breaks open the hive, and together they feed on its contents. Human foragers, too, sometimes follow the bird's flutterings to honey. It is said in Africa that if a man leaves no honey behind for the bird, next time it will lead him to a lion or a snake.

While his sisters develop an interest in nurturing, a male calf grows increasingly obstreperous as he approaches puberty, around the age of twelve. If he does not leave on his own initiative, the older members of the group force him out, the point driven home by increasingly irritable pokes, shoves, and stabs in the backside. For several years a teenage male may linger on the periphery of his family, but eventually he wanders away.

If left alone by poachers, the core of females that make up the family unit live peacefully, enjoying long lives with little fear or disruption. Like all intelligent animals, they are at times emotional and moody. Each female harbors her own set of attitudes about the others in her group. In the family led by a matriarch he called Boadicea, Douglas-Hamilton noticed that two elephants he dubbed Virgo and Right Hook spent much of their time browsing together, as did two other young cows, Diana and Calypso. Boadicea herself seemed to have a special fondness for a cow named Giselle, often resting nearer to her than to the others.

No one in the group seemed to care much for a cow called Isabelle. Along with her three calves, Isabelle grazed apart from the others. Douglas-Hamilton witnessed a jabbing she endured from Giselle, and on another occasion a shove in the ribs from Right Hook. Boadicea held no great love for her, and once the investigator saw the older elephant bully Isabelle into dropping a particularly appetizing branch. The matriarch promptly retrieved the meal and ate it.

After the birth of a calf named Bottlebrush to one of Isabelle's daughters, Douglas-Hamilton became especially interested in Isabelle's story. Through the dry season, Isabelle and her offspring increasingly distanced themselves from the rest of the Boadicea family group, and after the birth of the new calf they drifted even farther apart. One day when her group was foraging in some woodlands, Boadicea gave the signal to move toward a swampy area. Isabelle and her family stayed behind, quietly eating, un-harassed by the others. Though Isabelle eventually rejoined them, over time she lost her immediate attachment to Boadicea's group and became the matriarch of a new family unit.

The departure of Isabelle and her children reveals the next level of society, what elephant researcher Cynthia Moss calls the "bond group." Through some thirteen years of elephant watching in Kenya's Amboseli National Park, Moss confirmed that certain family units spend far more time traveling and feeding near each other than to other groups, and that relationships between the members of these bond groups are especially strong. More than half the times that Moss sighted a family unit led by a matriarch named Echo, its members were mingling with those of another family, led by Estella. When a member of Echo's band encountered one of Estella's followers, the two elephants would greet each other with an effusive out-pouring of gestures and vocalizations. In this display, which Moss calls the "greeting ceremony," both animals rush toward each other, heads raised

A bull elephant in Amboseli National Park gives himself a dustbath to keep cool. Elephants take on the color of the soil where they reside.

and ears flung wide. Suddenly they stop, turn, and back into each other, both cows urinating and defecating, their apparent delight accompanied by a duet of trumpets, deep rumblings, and high screams. Such displays of affection are only seen within family units or between members of the same bond group.

Families within a bond group often wander miles from each other, especially in the dry season, though they somehow maintain contact, as proven by their ability to quickly regroup. Investigators in the wild have long been baffled by this strange cohesion in elephant group movements. Whole herds of elephants, spread out over a mile and hidden from each other by tall grass, simply pick up and leave, as if they were all listening to the same silent command. In 1984 Katy Payne, a researcher from Cornell University who has spent most of her career studying whale communication, began to examine elephant vocalizations as well. Her curiosity was piqued by the strange throbbing in the air one sometimes feels around elephants, rather like the sensation produced by the lowest notes of a church organ. Payne wondered if this throbbing might be some form of communication, and made recordings of Asian elephants in captivity. She later joined Joyce Poole to tape African elephants in the wild, and they confirmed that the animals were transmitting robust but extremely low-frequency sounds.

At fourteen to twenty-four hertz, these vocalizations are well below the range of human hearing. The finback whale is the only other animal known to emit infrasonic pulses. Above water, the only other natural sources of such sounds are storms, waves, and earthquakes. Payne noticed that the elephants' rumbles are accompanied by a fluttering in a spot on their foreheads, which might indicate that air was traveling through the nasal passages. When she and her colleagues played the tapes at ten times normal speed, they were amazed to hear what sounded like distinct, fully formed "dialogues" taking place between elephants—one calling, the other answering, and back again, with other voices joining in.

Coming from an earthling who seems so focused and deliberate in its actions, it seems likely that these well-defined vocalizations bear some message. But if the elephants are communicating with infrasound, what are they saying? Low-frequency sound waves travel much farther than higher-pitched bursts. Payne has suggested that perhaps the silent sounds explain the mysterious cohesion between separated groups of elephants. The soft rumblings often heard by researchers in the field might be the audible, harmonic overtones of louder sounds much lower in pitch, used by the animals to reach out to each other as easily as a human mother calls her child from a different floor in a house. It may be that elephants miles apart are conversing, unheard by tourist, tribesman, or poacher, in the ghostly voices of earthquakes and far-off thunder.

Beyond the bond group, the social organization of elephants becomes more a matter of water than of blood. Elephants that share the same home range in the dry season—usually swampy areas near rivers or woodland

Burnished with the red dust of Tsavo West National Park, a group of elephants gathers by a water hole. Their movements may be coordinated by vocalizations below the level of human hearing.

browse—comprise what Douglas-Hamilton and Moss both call a "clan." Members of the clan know each other, and will often feed together and move *en masse* from one feeding area to another. When they meet, however, they do not greet each other with the same effusion shown to a family or bond group member. Elephants on less intimate terms simply place their trunks in each other's mouths, a routine gesture within families. In the context of the clan, perhaps this gesture is a means of recognizing an old acquaintance or discovering more about a stranger.

In Amboseli, Moss defined two subpopulations beyond the level of the clan: a loose conglomerate of four clans that use swampy areas during the dry season, and another collection of two or three peripheral clans that tend to gravitate toward the bushland surrounding the park. Finally, there is the population itself—over 600 elephants in Moss's study area, including 160 independent bulls.

Even after the layered complexity of elephant family life was revealed, bulls were still believed to have only the most rudimentary social organization, joining up with other bulls only briefly, and never staying close for long. In 1976, Joyce Poole joined Cynthia Moss in Amboseli and turned her attention to male social life. After monitoring the bulls' movements over months, Poole concluded that they were not nearly so anarchic in their social habits as had been thought. Rather than wandering aimlessly through their entire range, Poole found that the Amboseli bulls congregate in four "bull retirement areas." Here the sexually inactive bulls, especially the older ones, abide in a loose but harmonious association, occasionally sparring with each other and wrestling trunks. If it comes to a question of who is to have first crack at a tender bush, or which bull is to proceed first down a path to a cool river, the smaller, lower-ranking bull defers. The bulls even forage close together in groups like the females, but the resemblance is superficial. When attacked, the bull groups are less likely than female groups to clump together into a defensive phalanx, and sometimes even scatter. Their behavior jibes with the theory of kin selection; since the bulls are not so closely bound by blood, they are less inclined to come to each other's aid.

When the bulls depart the retirement areas to search for mates, they leave their cozy indifference behind. Females advertise their estrus by scent, and when several males follow their trunks to the source of the odor, there may be trouble. The most volatile meetings involve bulls of comparable size and strength. The bulls approach each other with a great deal of bravado, their heads held high and ears tensed, glaring at each other over raised tusks. These spectacles give the rivals a fairly accurate impression of each other's strength and condition. A characteristic wave of the ear closest to the opponent drives the point home, wafting over to him an identifying odor that emanates from the temporal gland on the elephant's cheek, especially strong when the bull is in a heightened, sexual condition. These bulls plow their tusks into the ground or even pick up logs and other objects and hurl them about. The bluster gives an obviously weaker male a chance to avoid a certain defeat.

If neither bull backs down, both collide with a great clashing of tusks. The weaker animal still has a chance to withdraw, and if he does so, the victor triumphantly chases him off. Joyce Poole witnessed a six-hour-long battle, which ended only when one elephant nearly succeeded in wrestling the other to the ground with his tusks. The vulnerable animal chose to flee rather than fall and be impaled. In some cases, the battles can be fatal; there is good evidence that two males in Amboseli have died from wounds received in fights. In Lake Manyara Park, Douglas-Hamilton once came across the corpse of a bull who had apparently been tusked through the brain. Following the drought in Tsavo National Park in 1970–71, British filmmaker Simon Trevor discovered six bulls that had been tusked to death. By killing off so many elephants, the drought had apparently confused the bull's hierarchy, leading to many more battles.

Temporary shifts in the male hierarchy also result from the strange physiological phenomenon known as *musth*. Derived from the Hindi word

"A bull elephant in musth doesn't like anybody or anything," says Toby Styles of the Metropolitan Toronto Zoo. "He doesn't even like himself."

for intoxication, musth refers to a regularly occurring period of heightened excitement, long recognized—and dreaded—in the Asian elephant. A bull in musth is dangerously aggressive and unpredictable. He secretes copious amounts of a sticky, powerfully scented fluid from his temporal glands, and continually dribbles urine over his legs. Domesticated bulls in musth are unmanageable and are quickly chained up. In 1974 U. T. Gale, working with elephants in the timber industry in Burma, reported one bull "who suddenly went on full musth and at the height of his madness . . . stood on his head, his tusks in the ground and his hind legs kicking the air." While musth is seldom so dramatic, there is no mistaking the change in an elephant's demeanor.

Joyce Poole's study of the Amboseli bulls sheds some light on this perplexing change of personality. Together with Cynthia Moss, Poole proved for the first time that African elephants also undergo musth. The presence of musth in *Loxodonta* was obscured because both male and female African elephants secrete from the temporal gland (visitors to zoos should check for a dark, spreading stain down the cheeks). In 1981, Poole and Moss noticed that many of the bulls in Amboseli had penises with a greenish tinge. The two researchers first thought that the elephants were affected by some disease, and named the condition GP, or "green penis syndrome." Later they realized that the condition was caused by the constant dribble of urine of a bull in musth.

Males come into musth at different times throughout the year, though the musth of the highest-ranking males tends to fall in the months when most of the females are sexually receptive. Only bulls over twenty-five years old come into musth, and while some bulls will stay in the state for months at a time, others trip in and out every few days. Bulls mate even when not in musth, though they have a harder time competing for the cow of their choice against musth-emboldened rivals. The females, moreover, greatly prefer the hot-tempered, urine-stained males in musth. The condition thus grants an enormous reproductive advantage to a male in musth.

Poole has shown that the timing and duration of musth influence an individual's rank in the bull hierarchy. A bull is given "super powers" as long as he stays in musth. He can challenge and vanquish bulls much larger than himself (so long as they are not in musth themselves), and by doing so, sometimes "leaps" far up in the ranks to dominate the very largest animals. But the length of time that lower-ranking bulls stay in musth— and whether they ever enter the state at all—seems to depend on whether larger bulls in the area are in musth at the same time. Somehow, probably through a hormonal mechanism, the more dominant males reinforce their competitive edge by suppressing musth in their inferiors. Poole actually witnessed several confrontations between competing bulls in musth in which the vanquished elephant immediately stopped dribbling urine, and his temporal glands dried up as well.

Back in the peaceful retirement areas, Poole made some fascinating discoveries. Elephants who retreat to the same retirement areas appear to stagger their musths, so that they are less likely to come into direct competition with each other. Poole also noticed that these fellow browsers bore some resemblance to each other. Perhaps the retirement areas are inhabited by more closely related bulls than had previously been thought. By avoiding conflict with each other, the bulls might be boosting each other's breeding opportunities and indirectly helping their own inclusive fitness.

III

Through its natural lifetime, an elephant will come to know and recognize virtually every other member in its population. Elephants socialize most frequently in the wet season. When the rains come to Amboseli in November and December, and through the heavier rains between March and May, the elephants gradually gather into huge herds. Families join their bond groups, bond groups mass into clans, until the herd numbers as many as 550 individuals, including bulls. Relieved of the competitive pressure for food, the elephants enjoy each other's company and reestablish relationships suspended during the dry season. Prepubescent male calves find new playmates to spar with, and in their frolicking help establish the hierarchy of the future.

The great herds also provide the best opportunities for mating. It behooves the elephants to conceive during the wet season, since this will provide the new calf, born approximately two years later, with an adequate supply of food during its infancy. Thus many of the females come into estrus when the herds reach their peak. Similarly, the dominant males tend to come into musth during the wet season, giving them an even greater competitive edge against the lower-ranking males.

A bull will approach a group of cows to test them for estrus, touching their genitals with his trunk and then slipping his trunk into his mouth. Very likely the male elephant has on the roof of his mouth a "Jacobson's organ," the gland which in many species is used to detect sex hormones in the female's secretions. The cows greet the bull by placing their trunks in his mouth, perhaps signaling with the gesture their acknowledgment of his superior strength. This is by no means an invitation to copulate, at least not immediately. Cynthia Moss says that a female in estrus usually avoids the probing trunk of a bull, walking away and looking back over her shoulder every once in a while to keep him in sight. Her backward glance lends to her gait a characteristic twisting motion that Moss calls an *estrus walk*. The bull strides along behind, his progress occasionally impeded by the four-foot erection he drags along the ground.

The elephant's penis is a curious appendage. Weighing up to a hundred pounds in a mature bull, the penis assumes a decided S-curve when erect to reach the female's vulva, which is tucked up in an unusual position. The elephant's enormous penis is shaped to cope with the odd location and

length of the female's reproductive tract. Joyce Poole speculates that once mounted, a male with a large penis can release his sperm farther up the female's long vaginal canal, where it will be less likely to seep out. If the cow has been mated by several bulls during her estrus, sperm of the well-endowed bull will consequently have a head start in the race to fertilize the female's single egg. There would come a point where this evolutionary strategy would trip over its own excesses. Any sort of growth borrows energy from other physiological processes that might pay more direct dividends in survival. Furthermore, the advantages of a large penis are meaningless to a bull if the organ keeps him from catching the cow. According to Joyce Poole, even a semi-erection in a large bull may force him to walk clumsily, with his hind legs spread apart.

Most of the time this scene evolves into a full-blown chase, the cow running at full-speed with the bull in pursuit, sometimes joined by as many as five or six other bulls. In their wake, excited cows flap their ears and trumpet while the startled calves race about. The pursued female flees in an arc that takes her half a mile from her family. If the bull can touch her with his trunk, she usually concedes the game. Then the male, after placing his trunk alongside her back, props his tusks up on her backside, rears up on his hindlegs, and mounts her, hooking his curved penis into her vagina. Mating takes less than a minute, with the cow showing little excitement, perhaps even continuing to feed at the same time. The bull also remains unusually still, while the muscles in his penis do the work. When he withdraws, either or both of the mating pair give voice to a tumult of rumbles, screams, and bellowing, and the surrounding elephants freely join the chorus.

In the dance of elephant sex it is the calf, yet to be conceived, who calls the steps. The elephant's twenty-two-month gestation period, longest of any mammal, puts tremendous pressure on both male and female to make the most of every mating opportunity. Even before birth, the cow has invested tremendous resources in the single fetus she carries. An interval of three or four years will elapse before she can give birth again and she must try to ensure that each calf is sired by a strong, healthy bull. The male elephant's strategy is to breed with as many females as will tolerate his advances. A cow is receptive for only three to six days in each estrus cycle, and if impregnated by some other male, she drops out of the pool of available mates for several years. The bull must be as assertive as the cow is perspicacious.

Given what is at stake, one would think that the successful male would be the bull who rushed in to a family group and tackled the first cow in estrus he came upon. This is precisely the tactic used by the younger bulls. But the race is not always to the swift. The younger bull's aggressive invitations are not favored by the females, especially the older ones. Moss and Poole discovered that these experienced cows steer clear of adolescent ardor, greatly preferring larger males, especially those in musth. A mature male has proved his ability to survive, making him the surer bet. Males in musth, moreover, show greatly increased levels of the male hormone testosterone, a reliable sign of fertility. By selecting the big bulls in musth, the cow simply tilts the odds in favor of mating with a fertile male and conceiving a healthy calf.

Mature bulls rarely betray the same impatience to mate as small fry weighing only three or four tons. The big bulls bide their time. There may well be a method in their coolness: Perhaps ovulation does not occur until the cow is several days into her cycle, and therefore the frantic chases of the younger animals, even when successful, go for nothing. After a mature male mates, he stays close to his partner, fighting off other males and protecting the exclusivity of his sperm. It is an arrangement apparently preferred by the female as well. She will move with her mate for the remaining days of her estrus, and when the group is stationary, she will inch closer to him, rubbing up against his side. Protected against the younger male's persistent intrusions, the female can continue to graze in peace.

The pairing of males and females in an elephant herd rarely works out to everyone's satisfaction. In February of 1978, Cynthia Moss was ob-

A young female stares out from her family group. Elephant cows take an active role in selecting their mates.

serving a herd of two hundred elephants when she noticed a cow named Wart Ear casting what might be called suggestive glances in the direction of a large adult male. This bull, labeled M22 by the researcher, showed little inclination toward Wart Ear, being preoccupied himself with Jeanette, a larger female in her prime. For two hours Wart Ear followed M22 while he trailed Jeanette. Twice the bull presumed to test Jeanette's genitals with his trunk, but proceeded no farther. Meanwhile, Wart Ear was distracted long enough from M22 to mate with a different bull. Darkness put an end to Moss's observations for the day.

The next morning she found Wart Ear fixed again on her first devotion, tagging after M22 while he steadfastly shadowed Jeanette. But now a young bull designated M5 joined the intrigue, traipsing after Wart Ear with obvious intent. Wart Ear greeted his approaches with cold disdain. With Jeanette shunning M22, who meanwhile avoided Wart Ear, who herself turned up her trunk at M5's fervid advances, the scene was set for some new character to break the deadlock. Enter a huge bull named M80, who looked up from his meal in a swamp just in time to see Wart Ear running by, M5 in quick pursuit. M80 abandoned his browse and followed the pair into some thick brush.

Five minutes later Wart Ear emerged from the thicket, trailed closely behind by her new admirer. While M5 stood by and watched, his head hung low in a subdominant's despair, Wart Ear backed into M80 and allowed him to mount her. When the bull dismounted a minute later, Wart Ear reached around with her trunk and touched his penis seven times, then turned and backed closer still, rubbing her head against him. The pair stood together quietly for almost an hour, surrounded by a scattering of younger bulls. Twenty-two months later, Wart Ear gave birth to a calf.

The birth of a new elephant calf is a family event, accompanied by much rumbling, trumpeting, and general commotion even among elephants not directly involved. Biologists Walter and Barbara Leuthold witnessed such a birth in the wild. Having come upon a group of twelve elephants in the Samburu Game Reserve in Kenya, the Leutholds noticed one cow acting strangely, walking backwards and attempting to squat down on her hind legs. Suddenly a great uproar erupted from the group, and before them in the grass the Leutholds beheld a baby elephant, still wrapped in its fetal sac. Researchers at the Metropolitan Toronto Zoo who witnessed a birth there confirm the suddenness of the event. For a full day the investigators had closely monitored the behavior of a cow they suspected was about to give birth. The actual event was so explosive, however, that they were not able to tell whether the calf emerged head first or rear first.

According to Iain Douglas-Hamilton, a mother elephant is often too exhausted after giving birth even to approach her new calf. The other females gather around to greet the new addition to the family unit, their trunks dancing in excitement. Despite its appearance, elephant skin is extremely sensitive, and they fondle the baby with their trunks. When the mother has recovered a little of her strength, she helps remove the fetal sac with her trunk and gently nudges the calf onto its feet. Once it has succeeded in standing, the mother turns her attention to the afterbirth, eating a bit or waving it about in her trunk.

The calf's overwhelming need is to find a source of milk as quickly as possible and start to suckle. In most cases, the other females in the family treat the newborn's gropings with utmost tolerance. Douglas-Hamilton, however, witnessed one case in which the calf's craving brought him to the wrong cow, who sent him sprawling with a kick. The new mother—barely thirteen herself—was too exhausted to notice the attack, much less defend her infant. Luckily a nine-year-old female calf, who had been engrossed in the whole scene, came forward to rescue the newborn, tucking him under her forelegs and sheltering him while the young mother regained her strength.

With the height of the wet season soon approaching, it is a good time to be an infant elephant. Food is plentiful, and milk flows abundantly. (Calves suckle with their mouths, not with their trunks.) Elephants from distant ranges mingle in great numbers, greeting each other with throaty rumbles, trunks outstretched, entwining. Rivers overflow their banks, and the mud is cool and deep for wallowing. There are other newborns around to play with, birds and lizards to chase, impala dancing in the distance. If the calf wanders off to investigate the shimmering shapes or gets lost among the forest of legs in the herd, a sister or aunt is soon by its side, urging it back.

Baby elephants, like this calf in Namibia's Etosha National Park, are born with a covering of silky hair and a highly sensitive, deeply wrinkled skin.

Elephants share their water holes and pastures with a host of ungulates, none so conspicuous as the plains zebra. Its crisp stripes of black and white standing out against the earthy tones of the elephant and the tawny shades of gazelle and kob, the zebra parades like a guest at a barbecue dressed in a tux.

Various explanations have been offered for the zebra's bold attire: that it helps regulate body temperature, ward off harmful insects, or bedazzle an attacking lion. None of these theories measure up well against the evidence. Zebras live in several different habitats, for instance, but their stripe pattern shows little variation with climate. Insects, meanwhile, pose no great danger over most of the zebra's range. And dazzled or not, lions stalk zebras with impressive success.

Another accounting for the zebra's stripes depends more on observations of the animal's social behavior. Zebras are affectionate animals, their social bonds articulated with both real and ritualized gestures of grooming. They are also naturally attracted to striped patterns. It may be that the zebra's coat has evolved, not as protection or disguise, but as a means of staying in touch, of reinforcing with a strong visual signal the tactile alliance with other zebras.

The core of zebra society is composed of very stable family groups, from one to six mares and their foals sharing the leadership of a single stallion. Relationships within a zebra "harem" are built on strong personal bonds—one might say friendships—between the mares that last for life. If the stallion should die, the mares still stay together, moving collectively into the harem of another stallion. Male zebras without harems assemble into bachelor groups, less permanent than the families, but also marked by unusually friendly and peaceable interactions among the members. Even the stallions possessed of harems seek out each other's company. When they meet, they give themselves over to an elaborate greeting ceremony. They stretch their necks forward and sniff each other's muzzles, assuming a facial expression called "the greeting face"—ears tipped forward, lips retracted, chewing on air. After rubbing flanks and sniffing genitals the stallions take their leave with a "farewell jump" onto the hindlegs. Often this ritualized departure is abbreviated into a simple kick of a forefoot—a tip of the hat rather than a formal bow.

Zebra stallions are far less amiable when they clearly have something to lose. When a female foal is just over a year old, she comes into estrus for the first time, advertising her condition with a provocative stance, legs apart, tail lifted up. For her father, her maturation inflicts a terrible load of anxiety. Zebras obtain their mates by theft. The young mare's estrus stance draws every stallion in the area to her side, all of them bent on abducting her from the family group. The father vigorously drives them off, chasing one suitor away only to return and find a dozen more sidling up to his daughter. If challenged, he will fight,

Bright against the morning sun, the zebra's stripes may have evolved, not as a means of protection or defense, but as a means of staying in touch, of reinforcing with a strong visual signal the tactile alliance with other zebras.

biting his opponent or kicking out with his hooves. But no matter how powerful he is, the father eventually grows exhausted with the battle. The gang of suitors succeeds in isolating the mare from her group, and one of them leads her away.

At first, the successful stallion gains little from his triumph but a host of worries. The young mare spurns her abductor's advances, refusing to allow him to mount her. During her estrus—about one week—she may be abducted several more times before settling down with a stallion. If he already possesses a harem of other mares, he must defend his new mate against their initial aggressions against her. Every time she comes into estrus, her frankly suggestive posture and estrous secretions bring other males galloping over, and she may be stolen again.

If the stallion manages to keep the young mare, he will eventually copulate with her, but he may have to wait as long as six months. Nevertheless, she will not be fertile for at least a year. By that time, the mare will have become a stable member of the family group. Her delayed fertility serves to ensure that only mature, established stallions are likely to sire new foals. The next generation grows to maturity, and a new clutch of suitors arrives to abduct the abductor's daughter. Violent as it is, the mating system of zebras thus discourages inbreeding within highly stable family groups.

As the rains taper off, the herds fall away again into smaller groups, clans returning to their home ranges and dispersing into bond groups. When food is scarce, it is better to forage in old familiar areas. The ranges of the elephants shrink in the dry season, and the animals stay close to where they will find deeply rooted vegetation that can tap the water below. At the same time, each elephant requires a larger foraging area in which to feed, so the bond groups fan out across the plains. The families are once again on their own. Under the harshest conditions—such as the crippling drought that killed some six thousand elephants in Tsavo National Park in 1970-71—even the family units disintegrate temporarily, each cow accompanied by only her own calves. In every elephant, however, the memory of the others persists through the long months of drought, waiting for the rains to once again bring them back together.

If drought can drive the elephant groups apart, another form of hardship bunches them closer in mutual defense. When Douglas-Hamilton returned to Lake Manyara Park after a two-year absence, he was shocked to find that several of the mature cows in the group led by Boadicea had disappeared. Isabelle was gone, and her daughter Laila now cared for both her own and her mother's calves. Another family had lost both its matriarch Leonora and her daughter Slender Tusks. The fate of the group was in the hands of a distraught and overtaxed teenager named Two Holes, who was clearly unable to cope. She moved about aimlessly, trumpeting in alarm at the slightest disturbance.

It is almost certain that Isabelle, Giselle, Leonora, and the other missing elephants in the Manyara population had been the victim of poachers. Matriarchs such as Leonora are prized for their ivory, but the poacher who brings down a matriarch steals more than her tusks. If she is killed before she has time to pass on what she knows, the younger animals, like Two Holes, will be left without the benefit of her accumulated knowledge, not to mention her leadership in defense and foraging. The survivors of a decimated family have no recourse but to reestablish connections with more stable family units. Wisely, Two Holes attached her group of orphans and siblings to Boadicea herself, so that they too could take shelter behind the aged matriarch's threat charges. Reduced by death, a bond group was tightening up into a closer, more familial relationship.

The death of a companion deeply grieves an elephant, and they seem loath to accept the notion of its permanence. One female, groaning in distress, was seen carrying the decomposing corpse of her newborn calf in her tusks for three days. As might be expected, the death of a matriarch causes the greatest amount of anguish. Harvey Croze, working in the Serengeti National Park in Tanzania, witnessed such a demise. For several hours he watched an obviously sick old cow lagging behind her family. When she finally collapsed, her companions rushed back to her, rumbling and trumpeting, and strained to pull her back on her feet. A bull who had been sojourning with the group tried several times to lift her up with his tusks, and when that failed he stuffed vegetation into her mouth in what seemed like an attempt to revive her. Finally, he tried to mount her sexually. The others stood by, tracing the outline of her corpse with their trunks.

When the group eventually moved away, one female, perhaps a close companion of the matriarch, stayed behind in the gathering dusk, facing away from the dead cow and touching her occasionally with her hindfoot. Only reluctantly did she heed the calls of the group, walking slowly away up the hill. Sometimes a whole group of cows clusters like this around a fallen member of the family, defending the corpse for days against intruders. Even independent bulls sometimes keep watch over wounded companions. Against human predation, such loyalty proves as disastrous to elephants as it does to the musk oxen in the north. To secure the tusks of one well-endowed elephant, poachers may be forced to eliminate the entire group, calves included.

For some mysterious reason, the tusks and bones of their deceased hold a deep fascination for elephants. A group that comes across a decomposing corpse of even an unrelated elephant gathers about the deceased and gives it a thorough examination with their trunks. The living worry the bones of the dead with their forefeet and carry them about. Tusks elicit even more attention; they are pulled out and passed from trunk to trunk among the group. These remains may be carried off and dropped miles away. There are even reports of elephants smashing the tusks of their dead against rocks. It has even been suggested that they are aware of the special value accorded the tusks by their chief enemy, and destroy them to keep the ivory out of human hands.

Equally inexplicable is the elephant's habit of burying the dead—their own and that of other species. One famous case involved a Turkana woman who lost her way in the bush after nightfall and fell asleep. She awoke several hours later to find a group of elephants standing over her, sniffing with their trunks. As the woman lay frozen with fear, they proceeded to break off branches from nearby trees and place them on top of her. She was rescued the next morning when a passing herder responded to her cries. A tourist killed by a charging bull in Lake Albert National Park in Zaire in 1936 was later found similarly covered in plants.

One persistent belief about elephants concerns the so-called elephant graveyard, a place where old and infirm elephants go when they know death is near. The belief stems from the fact that elephant bones tend to be found in drainage areas near rivers. It may be that seasonal rains and floods wash the scattered remains there after the dead animal has decomposed. Another explanation for the phenomenon can be deciphered in the last set of molars the elephant brings into use around the age of thirty. In time, these too wear down. No longer able to chew rough grasses and woody feed, the aging elephant gravitates toward swamps and riverbanks, where it finds softer, fleshier plants to eat. It goes there not to die, but to stay alive. Eventually, around the age of sixty or sixty-five, the final four

molars fall out altogether. No longer able to chew even the softer leaves into palatable form, the elephant starves or dies of disease. For all its longevity, an elephant's life is thus circumscribed, its end ineluctable. There is something almost heroic about this, in a quiet, herbivorean way. After a life devoted to eating, the elephant simply runs out of teeth.

The Familiar Stranger

A short distance from the plains of East Africa, in the mountain forest only a few hundred miles away, lives one of our closest relatives, a far more recent acquaintance than the elephant. Though rumors of its existence go back hundreds of years, the gorilla was not officially introduced to Western civilization until 1847. In that year an American medical missionary named Thomas Savage emerged from the forest of west-central Africa with reports of a "monkey-like animal, remarkable for its size, ferocity and habits." Savage backed up his claim by producing four skulls that confirmed the identity of the new ape as distinct from the chimpanzee.

For almost twenty years thereafter the public fervor for knowledge about the "ape-man" had only skeletal remains to feed upon, along with a few specimens shipped from Africa preserved in rum. Live gorillas transported to Europe died either from stress en route or soon after their arrival. The first living specimen to make it to England, in 1855, became the property of a showman named George Wombell, who ironically mistook its identity and exhibited it as a chimpanzee. The gorilla died within a few days. Meanwhile, the public's hunger for gorilla news was nourished by horrifying accounts of the animal's exploits. Most popular of all were the writings of Paul du Chaillu, an American explorer who in 1861 published a highly colorful account of his travels in West Africa. The gorilla, according to du Chaillu, was "an impossible piece of hideousness . . . some hellish dream creature. . . . One blow of that huge paw, with its bony claws, and the poor hunter's entrails are torn out, his breast bone broken or his skull crushed."

Soon after came information on the gorilla from an ostensibly more reliable source. In 1865, the renowned British anatomist Richard Owen published his *Memoir of a Gorilla*, the first scientific evaluation of the animal. Included in Owen's monograph was this intriguing description of gorilla–elephant relations:

> *If the old male [gorilla] be seen alone, or when in quest of food, he is usually armed with a stout stick, which the negroes aver to be the weapon with which he attacks his chief enemy, the elephant. When therefore he discerns the elephant pulling down and wrenching off the branches of a favourite tree, the gorilla, stealing along the bough, strikes the sensitive proboscis of the elephant with a violent blow of his club.*

On the subject of elephants, at least, Owen appears to be well-informed. His characterization of the ape is reliable in another sense. Every detail is more or less askew, resulting in a neat inversion of the truth, a sort of simian anti-portrait. A gorilla "old one" would seldom be seen alone, since the gorilla, like the elephant, is a highly social creature. Its "quest for food" actually amounts to a dreamy perambulation covering a thousand yards or so each day, the bulk of the animal's diet practically brushing up against its flanks. Owen's fiction does foreshadow what would later be learned of other apes—gorillas never wield sticks, stout or slender, but chimpanzees sometimes wave branches threateningly, and fish for termites with peeled twigs. Both the chimp and the orangutan of Southeast Asia might have occasion to "steal along a bough," as would a host of other tree-living primates. But adult gorillas seldom venture into trees. A three- or four-hundred-pound animal prefers solid earth beneath his feet.

The most interesting aspect of Owen's conception of the animal is not found in specific inaccuracies, but in the way that the whole picture begins to gather coherence. There is something oddly familiar about this gorilla. It echoes even louder in another passage of Owen's *Memoir*, in which we are treated to an encounter between a gorilla and some natives:

> *Negroes when stealing through the shades of the tropical forest become sometimes aware of the proximity of one of these frightfully formidable apes by the sudden disappearance of one of their companions, who is hoisted up into the tree, uttering, perhaps, a short choking cry. In a few minutes he falls to the ground a strangled corpse.*

Even without the racist echo of gorilla steps heard in the footfall of negroes "stealing" through the forest, it is clear that the unseen ape in Owen's tree is not so much an animal as a terrible bloodthirsty man—brutish in habit, but gifted with an intelligent and dexterous cruelty. In this regard he followed the lead of previous gorilla-watchers, and like most of

MR. BERGH TO THE RESCUE.

The Defrauded Gorilla. "That *Man* wants to claim my Pedigree. He says he is one of my Descendants."
Mr. Bergh. "Now, Mr. Darwin, how could you insult him so?"

After the introduction of Darwin's theory of evolution, Victorian cartoonists and pundits attempted to satirize the implications of man's link to the apes. Here cartoonist Thomas Nast shows a tearful ape appealing to Henry Bergh, founder of the ASPCA, for protection against Darwin's cruel claims.

them had never actually watched a gorilla in the wild himself. Who would want to hack through malaria-ridden jungle to get better acquainted with such a fiend? The hunters and explorers who approached close enough for a gorilla to notice their presence were shocked by its ear-splitting screams, furious charges, and violent chest beating. These wild demonstrations did little to protect the animal from men armed with rifles, of course, but they certainly helped to confirm the gorilla's sinister reputation.

Human imagination and the spirit of the times took care of the rest. Darwin's theory of natural descent was sharp-edged and new, and its implications cut into Victorian conceptions of an innately moral human ideal.

The gorilla provided a perfect target for a deflected self-hatred—a beastly man who could be held to account for some of the baser facts of being human. Like the other apes, the gorilla soon became known as a criminal who delighted in tearing men to shreds and carrying women off to endure unspeakable fates.

"The apes resemble man in all bad moral traits," wrote Owen; "they are malicious, treacherous, thievish and indecent."

The gorilla suffered prejudices on the other side of the Atlantic as well, but the evils invested in the beast gave off a distinctly un-American odor. In 1897, a baby gorilla arrived in Boston aboard the S.S. *Pavonia* from Liverpool. The first of its species to reach the New World, the young ape ran headfirst into the ethical bulwark of a rising industrial society. According to an announcement in the *News Bulletin of the New York Zoological Society* in October of 1897, the captive gorilla was "sullen and lymphatic, and its objection to exercise so violent and deeply rooted as to suggest the line of descent whence has come that arch enemy of all labor—the American tramp. The gorilla's sullen disposition and pernicious inactivity predisposes the animal to indigestion, loss of appetite and an early death." A decidedly undesirable immigrant!

The news bulletin was correct in one regard: The baby gorilla died within five days of its arrival in the United States. Cornell University purchased the body for $50, and the brain was removed and thoroughly studied by the famed anatomist Burt Green Wilder. Today, the preserved cerebral organs of the gorilla, and of Wilder himself, float side by side in their glass jars, next to the brains of a wife murderer and a professor emeritus of mathematics. The heart of Jumbo the elephant rests in a bottle nearby.

Not surprisingly, one does not hear so much about the moral depravity of gorillas and other animal species anymore. Twentieth-century *Homo sapiens* attributes its domination over the rest of creation, not to God-given graces, but to mental superiority—the ability to manipulate the environment, invent language, learn from an extended past, and conceive an elaborate future. Studies of primates have concerned themselves more with ape intelligence than ape manners. Beginning with the pioneering research of Wilhelm Kohler and Robert Yerkes in the 1920s and 1930s, the apes have endured decades of intelligence testing and retesting, tracing mazes, unlocking boxes, pulling levers, solving simple problems. Chimpanzees have demonstrated insight by joining two short sticks together, making one stick long enough to reach a banana. Chimps and gorillas converse in sign language and even teach it to others of their kind. Orangutans are taught to chip stones into tools in imitation of primitive man. Sometimes the most remarkable demonstrations of intelligence have occurred almost in spite of the experiment's intentions. Chimpanzees demonstrate conspiratorial behavior by escaping from their confines; one chimp props a branch over a fence while the rest scramble over. Released orangs use their wits to proceed in the opposite direction, pirating a canoe in an attempt to paddle across a stream back to the comforts of captivity. A gorilla, taught to speak, learns to lie.

There is no doubt that controlled studies of primate intelligence teach us a great deal about ourselves. They offer us insights into the evolution of insight, the beginnings of humankind, the meaning of mind. Years ago it was discovered that properties in the blood chemistry of gorillas and chimps are much closer to that of humans than to the other great ape, the orangutan. Gorillas and humans are susceptible to many of the same diseases, including tuberculosis and malaria. More recently, comparative studies of higher primate DNA—the molecule of heredity—have revealed an even more astonishing intimacy between humans, gorillas, and chimps. The three species share 99 percent of the same genetic material. In other words, all of our *inherited* humanity (and its role in creating cooked food, agriculture, the wheel, Bach's fugues, Puccini's operas, *The Origin of Species*, the Brooklyn Bridge, underarm deodorant, and laser optics) occupies only one percent of our total DNA. The rest is all ape.

Laboratory studies tell us relatively little, however, about the apes' behavior in the wild. During this journey we have been trying to break through our static notions of other earthlings, but now we encounter what seems to be a large, hairy, slow-moving version of ourselves. We regard the ape suspiciously, like a stranger who appears from nowhere wearing our clothes or laughing our laugh. Elephants show affection by weaving their trunks together, tigers by rubbing flanks. But what do we make of two gorillas or chimps who put their arms around each other's shoulders, hold hands, and even kiss?

Paradoxically, the ape's humanlike ways distract us from the real nature of the animal. When we confront a living gorilla in the zoo, our first thoughts are anthropomorphic: "Oh, a man dressed up like an ape." The animal crouches down, glowers at us, the weight of its torso resting on the knuckles of one hand. "Just like a football player!" Now he struts forward to challenge us through the bars. "A captive barbarian, decked in fur!" We are trapped by our own analogies, and we see merely the idea of a gorilla—a movie monster, a sideshow sham—rather than the heavy-muscled, knuckle-walking commotion staring into our eyes.

Unfortunately, there is all too much in common between a caged man and a gorilla kept alone in a provincial zoo. The two share not only close blood ties, but a similar environment. Left to their own devices, however, gorillas show themselves to be quite a separate achievement of creation. If we wish to understand gorillas, we must go deep into the forest and try to forget, if we can, how much they seem like us.

CHAPTER FIVE

Gorilla Lives

Across Lake Victoria some three hundred miles from the Serengeti, the Virunga Mountains rise shaggily into banks of mist. Six volcanic peaks knit together the borders of Zaire, Uganda, and the tiny country of Rwanda. The tree-covered slopes of Mount Karisimbi, the highest summit, reach almost fifteen thousand feet above sea level. Heavy-girthed *Hagenia* dominate the saddle areas between the peaks, their huge lower limbs padded with mosses and ferns. Among them stand slender, elegant *Hypercium*, draped with veils of lichen. The terrain of the saddle zone is gentle, disturbed only by soft hills and ridges. Travel is easy. Further up the slopes, deep gullies and ravines, swollen with undergrowth, make it hard to penetrate the forest even on foot.

193

Frequent rain and an incessant drizzle add to the discomfort. To live in the Virungas is to be perpetually damp.

If one can tolerate the wetness, the mountains offer escape from the heat and disease of the lowlands. The mountain forest, though rich in vegetation, harbors a relatively modest menagerie of animal life. It is free of snakes, mosquitoes, and other pests. Lions once ranged widely through the mountains, but now are gone. A few forest elephants still browse in the lower regions. Voles, mice, and shrews scurry through the undergrowth. Two species of antelope, the black-fronted duiker and the bushback, graze alone, ducking out of sight at the slightest hint of danger. Buffalo feed through the night, carving wide paths through the growth with their hooves. In the dark the tree hyraxes wail like lost souls, while giant rats scuttle in the soaked earth.

The forest of the Virunga shelters 250 of the world's 400 remaining mountain gorillas, the subspecies known as *Gorilla gorilla beringei*. (The remainder are found in a dark swath of woodland in southwestern Uganda fittingly called the Impenetrable Forest.) In 1959, the ubiquitous George Schaller set up an observation camp adjacent to Mount Mikeno, in the Zairoise portion of the Virungas. Two years later he emerged with the first truly scientific portrait of gorillas in the wild. His studies were later expanded upon and enhanced by Dian Fossey, an American woman who spent the better part of eighteen years observing gorillas from her Rwandan camp of Karisoke, on the slopes of Mount Visoke. Fossey and her colleagues habituated many of the gorillas in the study area to the presence of researchers, following the fates of specific gorilla groups through generations. In 1981, she published a popular account of her research, *Gorillas in the Mist*, which focused international attention upon the handful of mountain gorillas alive in the wild. Through the work of Schaller, Fossey, and her colleagues, we know much more of the mountain gorilla than we do of its more numerous cousins, the western lowland and eastern lowland gorillas. What information we have of these subspecies indicates that their behavior is much like that of their rarer cousins.

Unknown until 1902, the mountain gorilla belongs to that unfortunate club of mammals who stand a good chance of being both discovered and driven to extinction in the same century. Though the gorillas in the Virungas and in the Impenetrable Forest are now protected by law, they are still threatened by poachers, especially in the Parc des Virungas in Zaire. Poachers used to hunt gorillas and hack off their head and hands, for sale as curios to tourists. Owing to a greater public awareness of the gorilla's vulnerability, the demand for gorilla souvenirs has diminished. Infant gorillas are still sought out and sold to zoos, a practice that often requires killing the entire gorilla family as they defend their young. Gorillas are sometimes not the poachers' intended target. Poachers hunt bushback and duiker in the parks for food, setting wire snares along frequently used trails. Should a gorilla stumble into a snare and be found by a poacher, the animal

The Virunga Mountains—one of the last refuges of Gorilla gorilla beringeri, *the mountain gorilla.*

will be butchered or, if young, captured for later sale. Even if the snared gorilla escapes, it may still be too crippled to forage, and will surely die of hunger or infection.

A far greater danger to the mountain gorilla than poaching is the creeping encroachment of human agriculture. There is an inverse relationship between gorilla and human population densities throughout the animal's range. In West Africa, roughly forty thousand western lowland gorillas (*Gorilla gorilla gorilla*) still survive in vast tracts of sparsely inhabited forest. These animals—the subspecies most often seen in zoos—are unprotected and often hunted for food, but they do not face an immediate threat from expanding human settlements.

Three to five thousand eastern lowland gorillas (*Gorilla gorilla graueri*) live in scattered populations throughout the low rain forests of Zaire, surrounded by a mosaic of cultivated land and open savannah. The ancient patterns of agriculture here put the gorillas in a ticklish relationship with their human neighbors. In primary tropical forest, two-hundred-foot-tall buttressed trees form layers of cover above. If too little sunlight penetrates, the ground vegetation will be too sparse for the gorillas' diet. They prefer the "secondary forest," areas burned out for human agriculture, farmed until the soil could no longer support crops, and then left to slowly regenerate. So long as the plow does not return before the land has completed its cycle back to primary forest—a period of fifty years or more—human intrusion into the jungle may actually *increase* the gorilla's range by opening up new areas of its preferred habitat.

Unfortunately, the distinction between cultivated land and secondary forest is not so clear-cut. Crop plants, such as banana and manioc, are only gradually crowded out by the returning forest, and in the meantime a farmer and a gorilla group may fall into fatal competition. Attracted to the area by the abundant ground cover, the gorilla may end up being shot as a raider of crops.

The 250 mountain gorillas clinging to the slopes of the Virungas, finally, are hemmed in by one of the densest rural populations in the world. Rwanda, a country about the size of Maryland, holds six million people, 95 percent of whom are subsistence farmers. The human beings who live on a single square mile bordering the gorillas' home in the Parc National des Volcans outnumber the entire mountain gorilla population in the world. The intensive educational effort of the Gorilla Mountain Project in Rwanda has made the local people more aware of the fragile presence of the gorillas in their midst, and the government has wisely encouraged tourist interest in the apes. But poaching, cattle-grazing, and crop-raising continue on all sides of the Virungas, holding the mountain gorilla's future continually in doubt. Ironically, the long-term interests of the impoverished human population in the region would best be served by assiduously protecting the gorilla's wooded habitat. The forests in the park above serve as a watershed for the farms below, retaining water during the wet season and slowly releasing it during the dry months.

It was the threat of the gorillas' extinction, combined with the density of their population, that led first Schaller and then Fossey and her colleagues to concentrate their research on the mountain gorilla. The animal that emerged from their work bears little resemblance to the monster of Victorian imagination. Far from being a bloodthirsty fiend, the gorilla turns out to be a shy vegetarian, feeding on leaves and stems. Its habits are deeply social. Gorillas live in stable, polygynous groups—"harem" societies of from two to twenty animals. A typical group contains several females and their offspring, led by a dominant older male who mates with all the adult females except, in most cases, his own daughters. This lordly character is called a *silverback* because of the salt-and-pepper cloak of gray across his back and sides. Two, three, or even four silverbacks may live together in a large gorilla group, but one is clearly in charge and very likely is the father of the others. His coloring is not a sign of old age, but of sexual maturity. All young "blackback" males begin to silver around the age of twelve, and the process continues through life.

Female gorilla hair never silvers. The trait is a good example of sexual

dimorphism: pronounced differences between males and females, usually found in species where the males must vigorously compete for the opportunity to reproduce. Like the bull elephant, the male gorilla is much bigger than his mate, averaging 350–400 pounds in the wild; the females are about half that size. A silverback is also endowed with longer canine teeth, and in his maturity develops a distinctive bony ridge down the center of his skull. An anchor for his powerful chewing muscles, this sagittal crest greatly enhances the male's glowering intensity. In moments of anger and excitement the hair on his scalp stands on end, exaggerating the effect. With his nostrils flaring below burning amber eyes, an aroused silverback appears as menacing and ferocious as his reputation would predict. In the vast majority of cases, however, the threat displays turn out to be bluffs. The gorilla will not attack unless he or his family is truly menaced, or the intruder panics and runs.

The silverback is much more than the chief defender of the group. He is the emotional heart of gorilla life, a source of comfort and justice, a gentle father or a stern disciplinarian as the situation demands. Immature animals enjoy his company as much as they do their own mothers', playing near him while he dozes in the long afternoon or squeezing in beside him in his nest at night. In this way he acts as a babysitter, both offering protection and giving the mother a chance to concentrate on feeding away from her young.

The adult females in a group also show much more interest in the silverback than they do in each other. A female's position in the group hierarchy can sometimes be discerned by estimating how close to the big male she feeds, or how much time she spends picking insects from his fur. Those with very young infants stay closest to his side. As among elephant family units, the excitability of sexually mature young males bothers the others in the group, and may pose a sexual threat to the breeding male. The lead silverback will not tolerate their rambunctiousness too close to the center of the group. To maintain order, he struts toward the unruly son, head-hair erect, glaring at the offender. The latter responds with a submissive posture, bowed low over his forearms, rump sticking up, eyes avoiding his father's stare.

Naturally, the relationships among the members of a gorilla group weave a pattern too complex to be accounted for in stereotyped postures or measured in the distance between two animals. Gorillas behave idiosyncratically, each one an exception, in one way or the other, to the rules of gorilla behavior. Over twenty years, the researchers at Karisoke have followed the fortunes of almost a hundred individual gorillas living in half a dozen major groups within the study area. Each family has its own story, the tranquil passing of days shattered by violent interludes, tragic uprootings. Our focus here will be on the gorillas known as Group 5—a somewhat typical, somewhat eccentric family led by a silverback known as Beethoven.

An adult male silverback. Note the pronounced saddle of silver hair across his back and the exaggerated sagittal crest. His lips hide large canines, another expression of sexual dimorphism in gorillas. Though they can be used in fights, the massive canines serve more to intimidate rivals than to inflict wounds.

Dian Fossey first encountered Group 5 in 1967. Following a gorilla trail up a thickly wooded ridge, she was met by a racket of screaming and chest-thumping. The zealous defender was not a silverback, but a young blackback male. As the rest of the animals in the group ran to hide in the foliage, the juvenile climbed into the tree and put on a furious display. He swung through the branches, crashed to the ground before the researcher,

Good maternal practices among gorillas are a matter of instinct and learning. Young females sometimes handle their firstborn infants clumsily; but experienced, successful mothers treat their young with great care.

then picked himself up and took to the trees again. Fossey named the youngster Icarus. Then Fossey spied another, much larger male, who gave his hiding place away by his deep roars of alarm. He turned out to be a proud old patriarch, perhaps as much as forty years old. Fossey called him Beethoven and concluded that Icarus was probably his son. After another half hour's observation, she could see that the group included two more adult males: a young silverback she dubbed Bartók and a blackback, Brahms, pushing toward puberty. Six adult females carrying infants of various ages also peeked out through the leaves.

 Because Group 5 lived close by her camp Fossey made frequent contacts with them, and before a year was out the gorillas were allowing her to approach within twenty feet. Beethoven was clearly in control of his group, enjoying the privileges of leadership as well as its responsibilities. In spite of Bartók's evident sexual maturity Beethoven enjoyed exclusive breeding rights with four females (two females were too shy for Fossey to identify and observe). Bartók fed apart from the rest of the group, and even built his sleeping nest a distance down the slope from the others. From this position, he could serve as a sentry for the group, alerting them to intrusions with his grunts and chest-beating displays. Bartók had no breeding opportunities in Group 5, but by contributing his vigilance to the survival of his relatives, he could still protect something of his own genetic inheritance. Nevertheless, with Beethoven monopolizing the wombs of all the females in the group, Bartók and Brahms drifted away after a few years, foraging for a time on the fringes of the group, much as a maturing bull elephant lingers near his natal family. Soon Bartók and Brahms moved off to become lone silverbacks, who would eventually secure mates of their own.

Of the four mature females in Group 5, Beethoven's favorite was a steady-natured gorilla named Effie. Fossey saw that Effie shared physical similarities with the exuberant, high-flying Icarus, and presumed she was his mother; moreover, Icarus frequently went to Effie for reassurance. Effie also had a two-year-old daughter, Piper. Of all the gorillas in the Karisoke study area, Effie was the most skilled at mothering, "balancing consistent discipline with demonstrations of affection." In 1968 she gave birth to another infant, whom the researcher named Puck.

To his young children, Beethoven was an affectionate father. Fossey once saw him lift Puck off his mother's stomach, hold him high by the scruff of the neck, and casually groom the infant's fur for a while before returning him to Effie's care. Sometimes the big silverback would simply lie about and stare at his newborn. He and Effie would have three more offspring together. Effie's births came about every four years, as close together as is

Because of the extended delays between births and the limited number of breeding females in each group, every birth is important to the genetic survival of the species.

possible for a wild gorilla. A female does not become sexually mature until eight or nine, and six offspring in a lifetime is quite an accomplishment. Possibly, Effie's reproductive success helped her establish her dominant position in the group.

The second-ranking female in Group 5 was Marchessa. Though older than Effie, Marchessa—at the time Fossey first met the group—had only one daughter, called Pantsy because of her wheezing exhalations. A son, Ziz, was born in 1971. (Spindly at birth, he would later figure very importantly in the life of the group.) Marchessa and her children stayed close together during the day's resting periods, but unlike Effie and her children, they were usually found on the perimeter of the clan. Marchessa seemed wary of Effie. Ziz, something of a mama's boy, kept close to her side, whining when she thwarted his attempts to nurse and throwing temper tantrums if she wandered out of sight. Pantsy was much more independent and never hesitated to join in play with Effie's children.

Fossey saw that Beethoven much preferred Effie and Marchessa to a third breeding female named Liza. He paid Liza little attention even when both of his favorites were burdened with infants and therefore not coming into estrus themselves. It is the female gorilla who solicits sexual attention, sidling up to the silverback or standing stiffly on all fours, head and neck raised, fixing an unwavering stare upon her mate. During Fossey's observations, Liza's approaches rarely excited Beethoven, though the two conceived at least two children, Quince and Pablo, before Liza left the group in 1978.

Female emigration from family units, rare among mammals, is a common part of gorilla life. In most cases only younger females who have yet to give birth choose to leave their group. Breeding females like Liza usually stay for life with the silverback who has fathered their children. Perhaps Liza was frustrated by Beethoven's indifference. Whatever her reasons for emigrating (Liza appeared soon after as a member of a neighboring group), they must have been strong. The stress of shifting allegiances to a new family temporarily interferes with a female's ability to reproduce; she also risks trading her mean status in her old group for an even lower position in the new family.

The last of Beethoven's original mates identified by Fossey was named Idano. This shy, elderly female gave birth once in 1969, but the baby soon disappeared and Fossey presumed that it had died. Idano herself became ill three years later, and in spite of her low-ranking status, Beethoven adjusted the group's pace so she could keep up. He also slept much closer to her than usual, and was nesting nearby on the night she died.

The silverback was later equally solicitous to another invalid. Liza's daughter Quince, born in 1970, grew into an amiable, bright-spirited juvenile. She seemed destined to be a good mother. When scarcely more than three herself, Quince was already grooming and cuddling the infants in the family, appearing deeply distressed when Effie or Marchessa denied

Relations within a gorilla group are normally peaceful, affectionate, and cooperative. Juvenile gorillas are the ones most likely to be found cavorting in high tree branches. The much heavier adults sometimes rest on lower branches, but generally remain earthbound.

her a chance to carry their infants about with her. She was barely seven months older than Ziz, but she still came running over to comfort him when he whined.

Quince was about eight years old when her mother left Group 5. Soon afterward she began to grow listless and weak. Fossey discovered bloody tissue deposits in her dung, and it became increasingly evident that the young female was seriously ill. Beethoven slowed the pace of travel on her behalf, and when the other members of the group began to treat her abusively, he defended the invalid from their kicks and charges. About one month later, Fossey found her body lying under a log. The cause of death was identified as malaria.

Why had the other members of the group suddenly turned on Quince? According to Fossey, Quince had been attacked hardest by Effie's daughters during her illness. When hostilities do break out within a gorilla group, the sides often form along matrilinear lines. Full siblings are less likely to quarrel than gorillas who share only one parent.

Quince, however, had always been tolerated and tolerant, and her ministrations were a binding force in Group 5. The apparent cruelty to her might have stemmed from acute frustration. According to David Watts, an anthropologist who spent three years with Fossey at Karisoke, Quince's illness might have prevented her from giving the normal social signals solicited by others in the group. When she failed to respond to their solicitations, her lassitude provoked aggression.

An even more grizzly display of exasperation was observed two years later by Peter Veit, one of Fossey's students. Veit came across Marchessa lying helpless under a tree, apparently close to death (an autopsy later revealed severe cysts in her spleen). Suddenly Icarus—Beethoven's son by Effie—began to hoot and beat his chest. He then dragged Marchessa out from under the tree and began to pound viciously on her chest with both fists. A death rattle sounded from the female a few minutes later and she expired, but Icarus only increased his frenetic attack, jumping on her and pummeling her body. His abuse lasted for hours, and Beethoven did nothing to interfere except when Icarus tried to move the body. When Icarus rested, Marchessa's infant, Shinda, made pathetic attempts to suckle her corpse, and the others in the group gathered around to investigate. They seemed befuddled by the death, probing her mouth and anus and grooming her fur. One of Marchessa's own daughters even tried to mount her. The next day, Icarus was still worrying the corpse with his fists, and when the group wandered away, he was the last to leave. Why Marchessa was the victim of such a strange posthumous assault remains a mystery.

Gorilla groups make no effort to defend feeding territories against other clans, since there is usually enough for everyone to eat. A mutually relished rarity, however, can lead to strained relationships between neighbors. An oaklike fruit tree called *Pygeum*, for instance, bears a favorite gorilla fruit for only two or three months a year. A few ridges on the northwestern slopes of Mount Visoke harbored some of these trees, in an area shared by two gorilla groups. During one season of the fruit, Dian Fossey observed a *Pygeum* skirmish. Rafiki, the well-grizzled, dignified old silverback of Group 8, had established his family's claim to the more prolific trees, forcing Group 9 and their young silverback, Geronimo, to settle for *Pygeum* a little further down the ridge.

The two silverbacks coveted the fruit enough to risk entrusting their 350-pound frames to thin branches high aboveground, filling their hands and mouths before descending to devour it. Meanwhile, Peanuts and Geezer, two juveniles in Group 8, were growing bored with waiting. When they noticed that there were also a couple of young gorillas in Group 9, they made off down the ridge to investigate. Suddenly Geronimo appeared from the rear of his group, grunting loudly and charging at the young trespassers. Peanuts and Geezer came to a screeching halt, stood up, and wrapped their arms around each other in terror. Screaming, they bolted back up the hill. Geronimo followed, only to meet Rafiki himself rushing down to defend his sons. Geronimo wisely retreated, herding his group away from trouble.

That death should so terribly disturb the routine of a gorilla family unit underscores the essential interdependence of its members. The animal's close social bonds can be traced in part to its eating habits. With an adequate supply of food, gorillas can afford the advantages of each other's company without fighting over the choicest morsel or the last fruit on a tree. Raising young is easier with the assistance of family members, and the animals in a group can also rely on each other for defense. Gorillas in their present habitat have little to fear from animal predators, but long-forgotten attacks by lions or leopards might have contributed to the cohesion of gorilla society. Now only man poses a serious threat as a predator, but once an animal is firmly set on a social track through evolution, it is miserable alone. Female gorillas who leave their natal groups quickly seek contact with other units, even though they risk a hostile reception. Solitary silverbacks, too, crave companionship. One lone silverback seemed glad even to have some human company around, and regularly approached the Karisoke researchers. "We are a poor substitute for another gorilla," says David Watts, "but we'll do in a pinch."

The food an animal species eats eventually finds expression in the pattern of its social life. Gorilla families forage in a food-rich habitat. Among their fellow higher primates, the gibbons and siamangs of Southeast Asia feed on fruit which is sparsely but evenly distributed throughout the forests. Though their food supply is spare, it is fairly constant through the seasons. These so-called lesser apes live in monogamous pairs. For mammals this is a very odd arrangement; it is much more common among birds. But with each pocket of fruit at a premium, there is little for a gibbon to gain by foraging with a band of other gibbons. They seek out a single member of the opposite sex, and the pair share in child-rearing and defense of their feeding territories.

Only rarely will gibbons of the same sex meet at the border of a territory and fight. A bonded pair defends their range passively, declaring their presence with elaborate duets of barks, screams, and plunging trills. Behaviorally, the gibbons share many traits with birds. Some species have inflatable throat sacs that act as resonators to carry their calls far into the forest, where they are answered by others of their kind. Between neighboring Kloss gibbons, these bouts of song can last as long as two hours.

Agile and light, gibbons clamber along small branches to reach isolated fruit, and bound quickly from one part of their territory to another. The orange-haired orangutan of Indonesia, also an arboreal fruit-eater, weighs much more and must forage slowly to save energy. Eating alone, a big male orang weighing 170 pounds can easily consume the fruit of an entire fig tree in one sitting. By far the most solitary of the apes, orangutans pair up only to mate. After consorting together for several days, the male and female go their separate ways.

The last of the three great apes is also a fruit-eater. Chimpanzees are genetically very close to gorillas. Like their bigger relatives, the chimps are extremely social creatures. They live in large communities composed of roaming bands so fluid that their membership changes daily, or even hourly. Chimps prefer ripe fruit, but the figs and other staples they depend upon do not all come into season at once. Chimps cover large distances on the ground in their search for ripening fruit, announcing a find to their companions with exuberant hoots and drummings on the buttress roots of trees. A large fig tree will easily satisfy a dozen or more chimps, and there is little need to bicker over a privileged place on

An adult male brown capuchin. Note its massive head muscles and teeth, used to acquire food.

a branch. As the tree yields up its fruit most of the animals slowly disperse again; only the females with infants stay behind to settle down to a more leisurely meal. Chimpanzees also eat enough meat to be considered omnivores, occasionally conspiring to kill a young baboon or gazelle.

Unlike their close relatives the chimpanzees, gorillas never eat meat and consume only a smattering of fruit. The only animal matter they ingest are the grubs and larvae eaten by accident as they browse. It may seem strange that a gorilla weighing four times as much as a chimpanzee can survive on a comparatively meager diet of leaves and vines. In fact, it is the gorilla's huge proportions that fit it to a salad-bar diet. The larger the animal the slower its fundamental metabolism in relation to body size. The additional bulk allows for a bigger gut without greatly increasing the amount of energy needed to support life processes. Surrounded by vegetation, the gorilla can afford to move slowly from place to place without wasting energy ranging over wide expanses. Thus the gorilla's monstrous bulk, which has so enhanced its reputation for ferocity, is really an adaptation to a lethargic, vegetarian lifestyle. A behemoth the size of King Kong would move much too sluggishly to snatch helicopters out of the air or catch up with fleeing maidens.

For real gorillas, the plants with the most protein and other nutrients are still most prized. Mountain forests offer the best of all possible worlds for a gorilla. The low, open canopy allows sunlight to penetrate, and the seventy-two inches of rain a year nourishes a tangled profusion of vines and herbs. For Group 5 and the other Virunga gorillas, the staple food is a scraggly vine called *Galium*, found at all levels of the forest, from the thick ground foliage to the branches of the tallest trees. High in protein, *Galium* stems and leaves are armed with tiny hooks, which make the plant difficult to ingest. Adult gorillas roll the vine up into a ball and eat it, a trick which juveniles must learn through experience. Other favorite foods are wild celery and thistle, nettles and blackberry leaves, bamboo shoots, nar-

Gorillas spend about a third of their time eating. Here a gorilla carefully strips the leaves off a piece of Galium. *High in protein,* Galium *stems and leaves are armed with tiny hooks, which make the plant difficult to ingest. Adult gorillas roll the vine up into a ball and eat it, a trick which juveniles must learn through prickly experience.*

row-leaved ferns, and mistletoes dangling from the branches of moss-laden trees. A gorilla prepares a stalk of thistle by sliding his palm up to gather the leaves into a bouquet, which he then stuffs into his mouth. Stinging nettles, powerful enough to penetrate two layers of clothing, can be dispensed with just as easily.

The mountain gorillas of Karisoke eat fifty to fifty-five different plants; the gorillas in the region of Mount Kahuzi to the south, where plant species are even more diverse, regularly consume over a hundred. Strangely, the Mount Kahuzi gorillas do not eat *Galium*, though the plant grows profusely throughout the region. Tradition plays an important role in food choice, and "cultural" differences have developed between populations that only recently have become isolated by human cultivation. Local tastes are a curious trait among primates—perhaps they arise when young apes sample plants their elders would never touch. If the new plant proves harmless, others may imitate the youngster, until it becomes an accepted part of the regular diet.

Food choice is one area where the young sometimes instruct the old. A gorilla silverback is the living repository of knowledge and tradition, but the youngsters embody the power of innovation. Perhaps the most famous recorded example of this among primates occurred in a group of Japanese macaques on Koshima Island. An infant macaque named Imo began to wash the grit from her sweet potatoes when she was only a year-and-a-half old. Her playmates soon picked up the habit, and later her mother was scrubbing her potatoes too and teaching the behavior to another sibling. Nine years after Imo first washed a potato, most of the monkeys in the group were eating clean spuds. Only the youngest infants and the oldest dominants continued to eat gritty potatoes.

Imo was also the first macaque to "placer wash" her food. When investigators sprinkled wheat kernels on the beach, Imo responded by cleverly throwing handfuls of sand and wheat into the sea: the sand would sink, and Imo harvested the floating kernels of wheat. Once again, it was the older animals who were last to pick up the habit. Such conservatism may seem self-defeating, but it is the dominant's responsibility to protect the others from novelties not so harmless. In another experiment with free-ranging animals, a researcher seven times offered drugged oranges to a group of chacma baboons. Each time the lead baboon tasted the spiked orange first and threw it down, chasing away the infants and juveniles who tried to eat it.

Like other gorilla families in the Karisoke study area, Group 5, spread out over a small patch of greenery, spent most of its time feeding, each animal solemnly occupied with the foliage within reach. When Beethoven got up to move, the group casually followed him to a new feeding area.

Compared to the challenges most mammals endure to keep their bellies full, the gorilla enjoys an enviable abundance of "fast food." But there is more to feeding than simply reaching out and grabbing the nearest tuft. The jungle abounds in toxic plants, many of which must be assiduously avoided; others can be eaten only in small quantities. Gorillas have evolved the physiological machinery to cope with plant poisons, but detoxification, like any biological process, requires energy. Gorillas take great pains to select just the right stem or leaf, sifting through a mass of herbs and vines to pick out familiar items and discarding the rest with fingers and lips.

Not surprisingly, competition for the less plentiful, spicier delicacies in a gorilla diet leads to bickering within the group. One of these is a kind of rare fungus that grows in shelflike projections from certain trees in the forest. This "bracket fungus," once discovered, proves extremely difficult to pry from the tree. Gorillas covet the stuff over almost any other food. The older ones who can manage to pull a chunk free from the bark quickly make off with it to eat in peace. A great deal of screaming and slapping can erupt over a disputed piece of fungus. Once again it is up to the silverback to settle the dispute—most often by commandeering the prize for himself.

Gorillas also develop rare but insatiable cravings for soil, especially during the dry season. Every six months or so they go on earth-eating orgies, possibly to satisfy a need for calcium and other nutrient minerals. Over the years the gorillas of Group 5 have excavated a small mine in one ridge within their range, only big enough for one gorilla to squeeze into among the exposed roots. Beethoven always claimed the right to enter the cave first, and when he emerged, drooling sand, the others descended, feeding in order of rank.

With his authority to claim the best feeding spots, his monopoly on mating, and the attentions paid to him by the others, the silverback leader occupies an exalted position in his group. It would be silly, however, to think of his privileges as absolute. Even an experienced character like Beethoven suffered setbacks in contests of will within the group, especially against high-ranking females. Dian Fossey witnessed one such battle, waged over a comfortable place to sleep.

At night, and frequently during the day, gorillas sleep in nests which they build on the ground by bending stalks of vegetation into a rough clump. Sometimes two or three animals snuggle together in one of these nests. One rainy day, Fossey found Group 5 settling down for a rest. Effie and Pantsy had each carefully constructed sturdy nests out of *Hypercium* branches and were curled up against the downpour. Beethoven had thrown together a rather sloppy nest, and as the rain poured over the silverback it was clear that he was less comfortable than the others. Suddenly he stood up, strode over to Effie's side and glowered at her. She simply turned over on her side and ignored him. "With somewhat of a miffed expression" the silverback next strutted over to Pantsy and tried to intimidate her to give up her nest as well.

"I fully expected Pantsy to ooze submissively out of the far side of her nest in obedience to Beethoven's postural command," Fossey wrote. "Instead, she made it quite clear that he wasn't going to pull rank on her, looked directly at him, and harshly pig-grunted. With as much dignity as he could muster, Beethoven promptly withdrew and plodded back to Effie's nest to stand by her side looking somewhat chagrined."

Eventually Effie allowed Beethoven to cram at least part of himself into the nest behind her, leaving his rump sticking out in the rain. Of course the silverback could have thrown either of the females out of their nests, but the conflict is staged completely on the level of will, with a clear triumph registered for the females.

Pantsy's "pig-grunt" is a common vocalization of gorillas—a series of harsh, staccato grunts. Silverbacks use it in settling squabbles. Pig-grunting can also be a verbal rebuttal or an expression of annoyance. Fossey noted nine distinct vocalizations among the gorillas, the most common being a rumbling purr that she called a "belch vocalization." Besides expressing obvious satisfaction with the warmth of the midday sun or the prickly sweetness of a fine nettle bouquet, belch vocalizations inform others in the group of one's whereabouts—an important function in an environment so stuffed with greenery that full-grown gorillas are invisible only a few feet away. Fossey quickly learned that she could calm a group as she approached by rumbling a bit herself, perhaps nibbling at the same time on a wild celery stalk or a thistle stem.

"It is an extraordinary feeling," she wrote, "to be able to sit in the middle of a resting group of gorillas and contribute to a contented chorus of belch vocalizers."

Beyond the basic social group, a gorilla's relationships with other gorillas are unpredictable. Occasionally two groups will be found browsing quietly within a few yards of each other, the youngsters mingling and playing among themselves. The adults, especially the males, are seldom so sanguine. Trouble between neighboring gorillas usually involves competition for mates rather than food. The males hoot and roar and beat their chests. The displays are more than mere braggadocio: They provide potential combatants with an accurate preview of each other's condition, giving the weaker animal a chance to back down. Adult male gorillas are endowed with inflatable sacs in their upper chest and neck, extensions of their larynx that enhance the resonance of the chest beats. Chest-beating is an excellent way to communicate size and strength over distance.

Some gestures are so typical of a species that we cringe to see them performed, as if the animal were staging a hackneyed imitation of itself. Chest-beating is the gorilla's great cliché. Pounding on the chest, however, is only one element in a string of ritualized expressions and acts that the gorilla uses to "show off" its strength.

First dissected by George Schaller in the late 1950s, the threat

In early infancy male gorillas take an interest in their elders' aggressive postures. By the age of two they have mastered the rudiments of the chest-beating display.

display of a mature male gorilla includes nine separate gestures, some shared with other apes and humans, others belonging to the gorilla alone. The male warms up with a series of soft, clear "hoots,"—lips pursed, head tilted back. These introductory notes begin slowly but quickly gain tempo, fusing into a "slurred growling sound" at the display's chest-beating climax. The gorilla often interrupts his hoots early in the display with a gesture of surprising delicacy: Plucking a leaf from a nearby branch, he places it between his lips, sometimes holding the morsel there for the duration of the ensuing hoopla. "Symbolic feeding" of a single leaf or several handfuls of foliage seems to serve as a warning to other gorillas in the immediate area to steer clear of the displaying male lest they be caught

in the more violent proceedings.

The male then stands up (though never so erect as the postures given to stuffed museum specimens), in the same motion ripping up vines and leaves and tossing them into the air. His hoots gather momentum as the silverback pounds the familiar tattoo upon his chest—a dozen or so staccato beats, not with his fists but with open, cupped palms. The hollow "pok-pok-pok" is remarkably resonant and drumlike, carrying up to a mile through dense forest. Often the silverback further embellishes his display by kicking a leg as he beats— occasionally, in fact, kicking *both* legs at once so that he hovers momentarily in the air. He then runs sideways for a few yards, slapping and tearing the surrounding vegetation. At this stage he poses a real danger to others, not because he would focus an attack upon them, but simply because he is out of control. The performance ends, emphatically, with a single great thump upon the ground with the hand, whereupon the gorilla simply settles back into his calm routine. The excitement of chest-beating is contagious, however, and by the time the original performer has retired, several others in the group will have picked up on his theme and kept the commotion alive.

It is precisely this display of simian ferocity that a human being is most likely to confront first when approaching a gorilla in the wild. With his chest thundering, his hoots fused into a sort of slurring growl, and wisps of plant matter dancing about in the air, it is no wonder that the gorilla managed to keep his shy inner self secret for so long.

Clearly the display serves to intimidate, but the origin of such a stylized ritual, very rare among mammals, is harder to explain. According to Schaller, the chest-beat is a classic example of displacement behavior. When two conflicting impulses—in this case, the drive to attack an intruder and the urge to run away—function simultaneously, the individual will often display a seemingly irrelevant gesture, such as fastidiously sampling a leaf or, as noted in elephants, tossing a log about with one's trunk. Over generations these originally meaningless gestures begin to communicate explicit messages and become reinforced into ritual. Gorillas are not the only primates who exhibit displacement behavior during a conflict, as anyone knows who has slammed a door after an argument or hurled an offending golf club into the bushes.

The display serves as much to impress females as to terrify rivals. For gorillas, mate choice is a female prerogative. A new group often forms, in fact, when a lone male succeeds in getting females to abandon their companions and join him instead. The adult males of the group are certainly aware of what a prowling stranger has in mind, and violence often erupts. Sometimes a solitary silverback will shadow a group for days if he sees an opportunity to entice a mate. His presence causes much anxiety, and frequent scufflings break out.

Serious fights also occur between groups—again, most often over the issue of mates. In 1971, Beethoven acquired a female named Bravado from Group 4, a neighboring family led by a young silverback named Uncle Bert. When the two groups encountered each other across a ravine ten months later, the two silverbacks squared off for two days in a series of staring contests, strutting displays, and lunges. When Bravado reconsidered and returned briefly to her natal group, Beethoven charged into their midst, grabbed the young female by the neck and herded her back to his side of the ravine. Following an even more violent confrontation two years later, Bravado left Group 5 to wander off with two unknown gorillas from beyond the study area.

Most mature males carry scars from such encounters. The gorilla has an impressive capacity to recover from even the most gruesome wound. Fossey twice found silverback skulls with broken canines embedded in their crowns, evidence of battles fought and forgotten. In April of 1976, she came across the scene of a violent fight in Group 5's range. Silverbacks give off a terrifically pungent "fear odor" when frightened and aroused, and the area reeked of it. Broken saplings were everywhere, along with tufts of silver hair and pools of bloody, diarrhetic dung—another sign of excitement.

By following the "flee trail" of dung, Fossey discovered Beethoven lying crippled, with bone and ligaments protruding from his elbow. Icarus too was badly bitten, probably when he came to his father's aid in a battle against an unknown group. For several weeks following the fight, father and son lay propped up against each other during long resting periods, murmuring softly between themselves in apparent commiseration. Icarus's wounds healed rapidly, and he began to leave the aging silverback resting on his own, "his head cocked to one side, listening to his family's vocalizations rather like an old man trying to hear a weak radio set." Over forty years old at the time, Beethoven would need six months to recover from his injuries.

Without Beethoven's active leadership and diplomatic interventions, relations within his family became tense and nervous. According to Fossey, Effie and her daughters squabbled especially violently with Marchessa and her children. Icarus was just beginning to reach sexual maturity, and his awakening curiosity about the females in other groups may have set off the dispute which so gravely wounded his father. Though the young silverback did not take advantage of his father's weakness to usurp his position, he made the group extremely uneasy by wildly running about, perhaps carried away by his temporarily elevated status. Whenever Beethoven lingered too far behind to intercede, Icarus charged and harassed the others, including Pantsy, even though she was probably his mate. Pantsy kept her six-month-old infant, Banjo, tucked close to her chest away from Icarus's unpredictable assaults. Fossey later noticed that Banjo had disappeared, and Pantsy was back playing with the younger gorillas much like a juvenile herself. Such regression is typical of young gorilla mothers who have lost an infant, and probably helps them cement social bonds following the traumatic death of a child. To Fossey, Banjo's sudden disappearance at a time of intense internal stress in the group was deeply suspicious, and she feared the baby might have been a victim of infanticide.

According to David Watts, however, Banjo was probably Icarus's daughter, making it highly unlikely that he would harm her. In any case, her death during Beethoven's long convalesence clearly demonstrates how important an experienced silverback is to the stability of a gorilla group. It could have been much worse. Two years later, Uncle Bert, the silverback of Group 4, and one of his mates were shot and beheaded by poachers. His absence

The leadership of a mature and experienced male is essential to the stability and safety of the gorilla group. Without a silverback the group will eventually disband, the breeding females seeking the problematic security of more stable, albeit strange, neighboring groups.

also left an immature male in charge, but with far more tragic consequences. The "heir apparent" to Uncle Bert was his son Tiger, at the time about eleven years old. Tiger tried to hold the group together, ably regulating the animals' feeding pace and tending gently to an infant orphaned by the poachers. But he was no match for Beetsme, an aggressive male two years his senior.

In the clearing of her camp, the late Dian Fossey and a group of armed guards stand over a pile of slings employed by poachers. Fossey was a fanatical enemy of poachers and, despite great personal danger, frequently took direct action to stop the slaughter.

Beetsme had immigrated to Group 4 and hence had no kinship ties with its members. He tormented the females in the group, especially an older female with a two-month-old infant. In spite of Tiger's efforts to stop him, Beetsme eventually succeeded in snatching her baby away and killing it. Beetsme's triumph over Tiger was a Pyrrhic victory; his leadership was never accepted by the females, and within a few months all had emigrated to join with other males.

Infanticide is not an empty, malicious crime among animals. By killing an infant, the male eliminates a potential rival for his own offspring and speeds the mother's return to sexual availability. Over a fifteen-year-period, Fossey estimated that infanticide accounted for 38 percent of infant mortalities among the gorillas.

A silverback needs more than brute strength to hold his group together. Among his many attributes, Beethoven possessed a good "trap sense"—an acute respect for the wire snares laid by poachers for antelope. Whenever the group traveled through heavily poached areas, Beethoven carefully led them around traps set in the middle of game trails. In 1977, Group 5 had worked their way into a bamboo thicket—a favorite place to browse in season, but also an area dangerously close to human habitation. Fossey was watching the gorillas as they day-rested in an uncomfortably crowded clearing near the park boundary when Beethoven's son Ziz, then six and a half years old, grew restless and wandered into the bamboo, followed quickly by his mother Marchessa and the other gorillas.

Beethoven brought up the rear. Suddenly the thicket erupted with a violent din of gorillas screaming and thrashing, and Beethoven grunting harshly in distress. A few minutes later he emerged into the sunlight, followed by Ziz and the others, and the group headed back toward the familiar slopes of Mount Visoke, comforting each other with soft murmurings. Fossey and her colleagues tried to follow, but were unable to keep up.

The next day the researchers made contact again with the group. They found that Ziz had suffered some ugly wounds. A deep gouge circled his right wrist, his palm was scraped, and long gashes ran down his arm from his biceps to his hand. From the nature of the injuries, Fossey deduced that Ziz had caught his wrist in the wire noose of a snare, setting off the trap that pulled his arm high over his head. Apparently Beethoven freed his son from the trap by working his teeth along Ziz's upraised arm and under the wire.

Through his years as leader of Group 5, Beethoven acquired a keen awareness of the danger of poacher's traps. The group did not lose a single member to poachers during the eighteen years it was under observation. Though much of the credit must go to the antipoaching efforts of researchers and conservation officers, Beethoven's vigilance and trap sense clearly helped keep his family out of trouble. Once, he may even have saved a human follower from the pain of a poacher's noose.

In December of 1984, Jan Rafert and his colleague Mike Catsis were following Group 5 when they heard Beethoven's distinctive scream. Catsis saw the big silverback lunge at two females and their young, and when the observer approached to investigate, Beethoven started screaming at him too. Catsis looked down at his own feet and saw that he was standing in the middle of an unsprung snare. He carefully stepped out of the trap, and Beethoven quieted down. The two researchers quickly searched the area, and in a grassy clearing uncovered two more of the bamboo poles used as springs for snares. As the gorillas watched anxiously, Rafert cut the bindings on one of the poles and started to break the pole in half. As soon as it bowed in his hands, the animals screamed in alarm. Clearly, they recognized the look of an unsprung trap. When the pole snapped in two, they relaxed and returned to their feeding.

By this time Icarus had become a breeding silverback himself. While most mature males leave their natal group to seek mates elsewhere, Icarus chose to stay in Group 5 and take Pantsy as his mate. Beethoven offered little interference to their copulations. If his son had attempted to mate with any of the other mature females, Beethoven would certainly have driven him out. But Pantsy was Beethoven's daughter, and under most conditions male gorillas avoid incest with their offspring. With a clear breeding opportunity close at home, Icarus had little incentive to leave. With

Beethoven back in charge, Icarus's relationship with Pantsy had become quite tender, and the two gorillas often stroked each other and lay side by side staring into one another's eyes.

As Icarus grew into a strong and wary adult, forming his own harem of half sisters from the group, Beethoven began to assume a more passive role. He seemed less inclined to lead the defense of his family, leaving Icarus to chase away intruders by himself. Soon it was clear that the young silverback had taken over the position of dominance. Beethoven continued to receive the lion's share of grooming and gentle attention from the females.

Beethoven was also destined to outlive his son. In the fall of 1983, Icarus led Group 5 on an ill-fated excursion onto the lower slopes of Mount Karisimbi, far from their normal range. Whey they returned to Mount Visoke, Icarus was no longer with them. He was never seen again.

For two years Beethoven shared the leadership of Group 5 with another of his sons—the "mama's boy" Ziz, who had become one of the largest silverbacks ever seen in the study area. (David Watts estimates that Ziz weighs at least four hundred pounds.) Ziz was considerably stronger than Beethoven, and asserted his claim to a favorite feeding spot whenever a conflict arose. Ziz also inherited the breeding rights of Group 5, though not without some grumbling from his father. Ziz mated with his sister Pantsy and half sisters Puck, Tuck, and Poppy, as well as with the aging "super-mother" Effie. For Beethoven to relinquish his favorite clearly showed his age.

Late in 1984 the females of Group 5 were forced to make room for five immigrants from neighboring Group 6. Ironically, among them was Liza, Beethoven's neglected mate who had left six years before. Like the rest of the immigrants, Liza endured a less than enthusiastic reception from the resident females. She assumed a casual indifference, ignoring everyone but Beethoven, Effie, and Ziz, and behaving as if she'd only been off on a short spree.

Each of the other immigrants developed their own tactics for dealing with the pig-grunts and strutting intimidations of the resident females. One named Kwiruka obscured the sexual threat she embodied with regressive behavior, spending most of her time playing with the juveniles in the group. Another called Picasso grew timid and withdrawn. Simba, meanwhile, took just the opposite approach. A bit of a wallflower, she returned in full all the belligerence directed at her by the unwelcoming residents, deferring only to Effie and Tuck. According to Watts, Simba managed to form a close, if somewhat turbulent, friendship with Beethoven's daughter Puck, the two "resting calmly one minute, only to be strutting and thrashing vegetation at each other the next."

The affairs of Group 5 were gradually settled after that grand influx of immigrant females. Some of Beethoven's daughters departed, and new infants were welcomed into the group. Effie's daughter Tuck finally gave

A gorilla family tableau: two subadults tussle in the foreground, while behind them others groom a silverback, an infant near his side.

birth at the age of thirteen, five years after most females reach estrus. The researchers named her infant son Ndatwa—Kenyarwandan for "an accomplishment to be proud of." Earlier, Effie delivered an unprecedented sixth child, a girl named Mahane, which translates into "trouble." A final test of Effie's gift at mothering.

When Ziz took over the breeding rights of Group 5, he also assumed the duties of defense, meeting intruders with his great roars and his chest-beating vigor. Now almost sixty years old, Beethoven lingered behind, indifferent to all the storm and stress of family politics. But the aged silverback was seldom forgotten. When the two males squabbled, his daughters invariably rallied to Beethoven's side. He continued to enjoy as much as three-quarters of the grooming attention in the group, lounging regally under the ministrations of his many daughters, like a Lear whose plans for his dotage had blissfully come to pass.

"In Group 5, Ziz is the general but Beethoven is still king," researcher Jan Rafert said in 1984. The following fall the king died of natural causes, leaving in charge of his group the son he had saved from a poacher's snare eight years before.

At the time of this writing, Group 5 numbers nineteen individuals. As before, they spend most of their time feeding and resting. They still keep mostly to their familiar ground on the south slope of Mount Visoke, borrowing each other's warmth in nests at night. Sometimes the juveniles discover a new toy—a baby antelope to be stroked or prodded, perhaps some researcher's knapsack to haul around for a while and then forget. On bright afternoons the young ones spin through the patches of sunlight, while the adults stretch out on their backs and doze, their great bellies rising and falling to the accompaniment of buzzing flies. Ziz, the silverback, has a few more scars to show for his efforts on behalf of his family. As he sleeps his little son Ndatwa wrestles with his father's fingers.

Of the original group contacted by Dian Fossey in 1967, only Pantsy and Effie remain. The veteran gorilla-watcher is also gone. Deeply protective of the animals she came to think of almost as family members, Fossey had devoted herself increasingly to an implacable, intensely personal crusade against the poachers who threaten them. Once she burned down a suspected poacher's house. When another captured an infant gorilla, Fossey kidnapped the poacher's own child and held it hostage. Her efforts earned her many enemies. On Christmas night in 1985, she was murdered in her cabin.

"Dian readily admitted that she liked gorillas more than human beings," says David Watts. "The real tragedy of her life is that she came to feel much more for the gorillas than they were ever capable of feeling for her. And she never stopped hoping that would change."

Getting

Smart

Homo sapiens is the loneliest species on earth. We build walls and fences against the natural world, and then invite a select guest list of creatures to join us inside. We anthropomorphize our dogs and cats and canaries, and in return they humanize us, offer us companionship, receive our affections, and give us a sense of belonging to an order not of our own contrivance. We pay handsomely for this privilege; Americans spend $1.5 billion a year on cat food alone, and another $200 million dollars on kitty litter.

For the most part wild mammals stay in the wild, the terror and beauty of their ways conveyed in television programs, books, and posters. These dramas can never satisfy our longing to reconnect, to deny our isolation and cross the barrier of species. The great intelligence that severed us from the other earthlings fills us with questions of how they think, what the world looks like through the eyes of a stalking lion or those of a cardinal perched on a backyard feeder. Do lions conspire before a kill? Does the cardinal sing for joy or for territorial imperatives? Does he know the difference? The great apes, with their soft amber eyes and familiar expressions, bear the greatest weight of our longings. The more insight a chimpanzee demonstrates in solving a maze, the fewer twists and turns obscure our own path from the past. The more that a gorilla can mentally distance itself from the present moment, the closer we feel to the rest of the animal world.

For all the amazing revelations of gorilla behavior learned on the slopes of Mount Visoke over the past twenty years, the gorilla who most captures our imagination is Koko, a solitary resident of a mobile home in California. Over the past fifteen years, researcher Francis Patterson has taught Koko to communicate with American Sign Language (ASL). The gorilla has developed a vocabulary of some five hundred signs. When Koko speaks, we hang on her every word. Koko learns to rhyme. Koko learns to make jokes, throw insults, converse with another gorilla. When accused of smashing a sink, Koko learns to lie, though her technique lacks polish. She tries to lay the blame on one of her trainers. Next, Koko discusses ideas of death with a trainer:

> Q: *Where* do *gorillas go when* they *die?*
> KOKO: *Comfortable hole bye.*
> Q: *When* do *gorillas die?*
> KOKO: *Trouble old.*

Koko is only one of several laboratory apes who have learned to communicate surprisingly complex thoughts and emotions. A female chimpanzee named Washoe was taught to "speak" in ASL (the vocal apparatus of apes is not suited to complex utterances) by Alan and Beatrice Gardner in the late 1960s. David Premack, a psychologist at the University of Pennsylvania, taught a seven-year-old chimp named Sarah to use colored plastic tokens for words. After teaching Sarah that the word for apple was a blue plastic triangle, Premack asked the chimpanzee whether the token was red or green, with or without a stem, more round than square. Premack found that Sarah clearly endowed the blue triangle with all the attributes of an apple. Other researchers have used keyboards and computers to demonstrate the verbal skills of chimps.

One of the most fascinating studies in primate communication is being conducted, not in a laboratory, but in the wild. Building on the work of Tom Struhsaker in the 1960s, Robert Seyfarth and Dorothy Cheney began to investigate the vocal repertoire of vervet monkeys in Kenya's Amboseli Park. Struhsaker had discovered that a monkey employed different alarm cries, depending upon what sort of danger is perceived. Furthermore, the other monkeys in its group responded differently to each alarm. The sight of a leopard inspired a loud, raspy bark, and the monkeys all took to the trees. Eagles excited a short, staccato grunt; immediately, all the monkeys within hearing would look up and scan the sky, or scurry for the safety of a bush. Finally, if a monkey spotted a snake, it would chatter at a high pitch, causing its fellows to stand on their hind legs and search the grass.

Struhsaker's observations were intriguing, but were the monkeys really responding to a specific alarm cry, or were they merely alerted to the sight of the prey, and responding accordingly? Seyfarth and Cheney ruled out that possibility when they played tape recordings of alarm vocalizations through hidden speakers to a group of unsuspecting monkeys. The false alarms prompted the same escape reactions caused by the approach of a real predator. Clearly, the monkeys communicate with "words," though what they actually say to each other is difficult to determine precisely. At the sight of an eagle an observant vervet might be screaming, "Look up at the sky!" or he might be shouting "Here comes an eagle!"

Seyfarth and Cheney next applied their technique to the social life of the monkeys. Vervets constantly grunt to each other—soft, low-pitched sounds that accompany their foraging and grooming. The grunts sound so similar that even experienced observers hear them as one sound. Furthermore, the monkeys in the vicinity make no immediate response to their fellows' gruntings. The two researchers thought they could detect tiny differences in the grunts, however, and when they played recorded grunts back to a monkey group, they discovered a surprising variety of reactions. When a monkey was addressed by the recorded grunt of a subordinate, it stared sharply in the direction of the loudspeaker. If a dominant animal's grunt was played through the speaker, the listener walked away. Seyfarth and Cheney found that two other grunts could be loosely interpreted as "a group movement onto an open plain has begun" and "another group is approaching."

"It was almost as if we had discovered another language," says Seyfarth. How much the monkeys are saying to each other remains to be seen. And who knows what messages will eventually be uncovered in the belch vocalizations of gorillas in the wild or in the infrasonic rumblings of elephants as they pass?

Back in the laboratory, the original chimpanzee student Washoe has been tutoring other chimpanzees in ASL, instructing a youngster named Louis in how to sign "come," "food," and some fifty other words without any human interference. Whether the apes can really use language to invent new word combinations, form sentences, and create grammar is still hotly debated. But there is no longer any doubt that they possess the power of the word, what linguist Noam Chomsky, echoing Descartes, called "the sole sign and certain mark of the presence of thought." Indeed, Koko the gorilla scored 85–95 on a standard IQ test, nearly as high as the average human child, in spite of the fact that the questions sometimes showed a distinct human cultural bias. For example, Koko was given four choices when asked where she would run to get out of the rain—"hat, spoon, tree, and house." The correct answer for us would be "house," but Koko was penalized for her perfectly sensible answer of "tree."

But Koko's cleverness brings up a very perplexing question. Back in the forest of the Virungas, gorillas show nothing remotely approaching her mental aptitude. When it rains they run for neither house nor tree, but huddle miserably in the downpour. Faced with a crisis like an unsprung poacher's snare, the gorillas seem capable of reasoning and insight. But their daily feeding routine requires little creativity, or imagination.

"After five years of working with wild gorillas," says Sandy Harcourt, another investigator with the Karisoke project, "I found it difficult to see that they were doing anything requiring more intelligence than the average sheep. Either they don't use their intelligence in the wild, or they were using it in ways too cleverly for me to see."

Evolution shows little patience with waste. If an animal possesses such an extravagant (and energetically expensive) characteristic as intelligence, we are tempted to look for a reason. Twenty-five years ago R. J. Andrew and others suggested that the growth of intelligence in mammals was due to interactions between species. As prey species struggle to elude their predators, only the smarter carnivores survive, demanding even more intelligence from the prey, and so on in a mutually edifying spiral.

This seems plausible enough for mammals generally, but how can it account for the sudden leap in intelligence characteristic of the primates, and the great apes in particular? What does it take to pluck a fig fruit from a bough? It requires a great deal more planning and quick thinking for a tiger to bring down a grazing deer than for a gorilla to glean the choicest morsels from a tangle of vines. It is the ape, nevertheless, who has evolved the superior brain, at least as measured against human standards. What unseen force pressed such huge advances in their minds? Given the direction in which our own intelligence has led us, there is no more important question to be asked.

Traditionally, one of the defining features of human intelligence has been the ability to use and make tools. The toolmaker has harnessed the power to manipulate his environment, to shape his world to his own ends. One day in 1960, Jane Goodall, working in Gombe National Park on the shore of Lake Tanganyika, watched a wild chimpanzee named David Graybeard insert a grass stem into a termite nest, pull it out, and eat the insects clinging to its tip. Over the next few days, David Graybeard and another chimpanzee fished and feasted at the termite mound, sometimes arriving at the site with a reserve of three or four grass stems, repairing their tools by biting off the bent tips. On several occasions they stripped the leaves off twigs to fashion more termite probes—the first recorded instances of an animal other than a human being making a tool. Goodall quickly alerted her mentor, Louis Leakey, and he declared that the time had come either to redefine tools or redefine man.

It is no easy matter to understand the relation of tool use to intelligence. When is a tool a tool? A chimpanzee might scratch his back with a twig, but what of a tiger who rubs his flank against a branch still attached to a tree? Gulls drop clams onto rocky beaches to break their shells. Woolly monkeys defecate into their hands and heave the stuff at human researchers observing them. Baboons and macaques throw stones and branches in defense. Are these animals also tool users?

Obviously tool use depends on manual dexterity, and the primate hand, originally evolved for grasping and moving through the trees, lends itself

Like Jane Goodall's termite-fishing chimps, this young female chimpanzee sits before a termite nest intently repairing her twig. Using skills learned from older, more experienced family members, she has carefully chosen and prepared her tools, bringing them to the termite nest where she will continually modify them throughout the fishing expedition.

nicely to manipulating objects. But primates are not the only tool users in the wild. There is a species of finch in the Galápagos Islands that manipulates cactus spines to pry insects out of bark, sometimes improving on the tool by first shortening or stripping the thorn. Green jays in Texas were observed doing much the same thing with small twigs; one young bird tried the techniques but kept dropping the twig, as if it were imitating its parents but hadn't yet mastered the trick. Male bowerbirds of Australia and New Guinea construct nests to attract mates, lavishly decorating their interiors with colorful leaves, feathers, flowers, bits of plastic, auto keys, and other bright objects. Sometimes they paint the bower walls with fruit pulp. They seem to enjoy their efforts, keeping the bowers scrupulously clean and replacing flowers after they wilt. There is even a species of wasp that hammers dirt into its burrow with a pebble clutched in its mandibles.

Chimpanzees, indeed, have to share their termite-fishing trophies with another species. Elizabeth McMahan of the University of North Carolina discovered an assassin bug in the tropical rain forest that glues bits of termite nest on itself, then lingers near an opening to a nest. Hiding from the soldier termites, the assassin bug reaches in and grabs a worker, sucking the soft insides out of the hard exoskeleton. Mimicry is common in nature, but the assassin bug has another trick up its sleeve. The bug nudges the empty exoskeleton of its victim back into the nest and gently wiggles it. When another worker arrives to dispose of the corpse—responding to its instinct to keep the nest clean—the assassin bug gives a tug and pulls the skeleton back out with the worker attached. This one too is eaten and turned to bait for the next cast into the nest.

The termite-fishing assassin bug demonstrates a remarkable bit of stereotyped behavior, but nothing more: no demonstrable planning, no insight, no choice in the matter. The chimpanzee fisherman, on the other hand, prepares for his angling by breaking twigs off trees and stripping them well before he arrives at the termite nest itself; apparently he has already conceived the notion of termite-fishing before he begins to strip the twigs. But where does one draw the line? According to Donald Griffin, an ethologist at Rockefeller University, "At the level of neurons and synapses, the fundamental units of all central nervous systems, there are only minor differences between insects and anthropoid apes or human beings. . . . To be sure, the central nervous system of a sea otter or chimpanzee is thousands of times larger than that of any insect, but it is arbitrary to assume that an absolute distinction can be made. The differences are more likely to be of degree rather than kind."

Relatives of the land-bound weasel family, sea otters subsist on a variety of bottom-dwelling shellfish. Here a bewhiskered mother and her young float in the Pacific off California. A large, strong adult like this mother will use her teeth and claws to pry open her mussels, while her young will use tools.

Sea otters offer an interesting case of a deliberate use of tools as sophisticated as any found among primates in the wild. Large, sleekly furred members of the weasel family, sea otters live on molluscs, sea urchins, and other bottom-dwelling shellfish. Sometimes an otter tucks a stone under its arm before it dives; abalone and other shellfish that prove too stubborn to be pried loose with claws can be hammered free with the stone. When the otter returns to the surface, it flips over on its back, props the stone on its chest, and slams its prey against it until the shell breaks. The sea otter does nothing to alter its anvil, but it does take the trouble to find a rock of the right size and shape, and may carry an especially good one through an entire feeding session. Most importantly, sea otters use the stones only when less challenging food is hard to find. In some areas, only the young and very old otters carry stones; adults in their prime have no trouble opening mussels with only claws and teeth. The otter is not bound to its tools by blind instinct; it *chooses* to find one as the situation demands.

Why do sea otters use tools, when their freshwater cousins do not? Why do chimpanzees fashion sticks to probe for insects, scratch their backs, or break open hard-shelled fruit, when their relatives the orangutans and gorillas never do? According to John Alcock of Arizona State University, the sea otter and the woodpecker finch share an important historical circumstance with the human being: All three species developed tool use only after they invaded unfamiliar habitats or environmental niches. Of all the otters, only one is adapted to a marine environment. The woodpecker finch is among the most recently evolved of the Galápagos finches. Some anthropologists hold that our human ancestors developed skills with tools only after they left the forest for the savannah and were forced to compete with well-established carnivores. Chimpanzees too may have ventured onto the savannah for a time before retreating again to the forest. Like Robinson Crusoe, the tool users discovered their ingenuity only when tested by a hostile environment.

To be accurate, however, the animal technologists are probably less ingenious than simply observant. Defoe's hero had to use insight, conceive new techniques, find wholly new solutions to survive on his desert island. The other animals probably developed tool use through imitation or trial and error. In 1974, Geza Teleki conducted a curious experiment in Gombe Park, using himself as subject. To test whether the chimps could have devised termite-fishing by using insight, Teleki broke twigs off of trees and tried to fish for himself. Only by trial and error, and by watching a skilled chimpanzee fishing nearby, could the investigator even approach the chimp's proficiency. He concluded that there was no way to imagine beforehand the best way to strip a twig or twiddle it in the termite hole. Other experiments show that young chimpanzees learn to use tools by watching their elders the same way a tiger cub learns to hunt or a polar bear learns to build a den.

Thus the use of tools might be one measure of intelligence, but it may not ultimately explain the gifted mentality of primates. Only one primate developed tool use to such a degree that it began to shape and sharpen its intelligence beyond that of other earthlings. In our species, tool use took on special, unprecedented meanings, gathering awesome importance. The question remains: What makes the higher primates apparently so clever beyond their needs? How does the "belch-vocalizing" gorilla of Rwanda become the loquacious Koko of California? How can the chimpanzee, who travels from tree to tree in the wild feeding on fruit, learn to drive a tractor, ride a bicycle, and even bake a cake?

A possible—and the most intriguing—solution to the puzzle of primate intelligence has been put foward by Nicholas Humphrey of Cambridge University. Humphrey's research interests led him to the Virunga Mountains, where he too was puzzled by the apparent lack of stress in gorilla life. "I could not help being struck by the fact that of all the animals in the forest, the gorillas seemed to lead much the simplest existence," Humphrey wrote.

Based on his various observations of primates, Humphrey proposed what seems at first to be an upside-down theory of intelligence: The more an animal species leaned upon tool-using and other "subsistence technologies" while learning to survive, the less room there would be for individual creativity and invention. Extending an earlier hypothesis of Alison Jolly's, Humphrey proposed that the original function of primate intelligence was not to figure out how to obtain food or avoid predators, but to solve the more demanding riddles of *living in a social community*. So long as he was alone on his island, Humphrey believes, Robinson Crusoe's ingenuity would be only half challenged: "It was the arrival of Man Friday on the scene which really made things difficult for Crusoe," he wrote. "If Monday and Tuesday, Wednesday and Thursday had turned up as well, then Crusoe would have had every need to keep his wits about him."

Primates are not the only social species, but their social interactions are certainly among the most complex. Infants born into a social group have before them a long period of dependency in which to learn through imitating their elders and playing with their peers. Older animals, as well as the uncles and aunts who do not contribute young themselves, are kept on in the group for the knowledge they embody and the contributions they can make to raising and protecting the young. All this improves the odds of survival for the members of the group, but there is a catch. As a society becomes larger and more extended through generations, conflicting desires are bound to erupt among its members. Who breeds with whom? Which monkey can claim the higher branch, safe from predators? Who feeds first?

Society is thus a double-edged knife to shape the intelligent being. On the one hand it provides a "collegiate community" for the long education of the young, and on the other offers plenty of strife and conflict to test one's intellectual prowess. As Sandy Harcourt has pointed out, even the social affairs of monkeys can become exceedingly sophisticated. Time spent by a vervet monkey grooming a more dominant animal, for instance, may be a way of recruiting a useful ally for the future. When the groomer is harassed by another member of the group later on, a glance of appeal might bring its protector over to lend support. The life of the primates is filled with such political dealings.

It is reassuring to think that the key to gorilla intelligence is not a weapon or a tool, but the gorillas themselves. It is woven into the shifting texture of their social lives, in the fitful adjustments to newcomers and new leaders, in the sudden heroism of the emigrating female who must decide when to leave, when to stay. The intruding silverback who beats his chest and thrashes the ground might be acting out an ancient, inherited ritual, but the female who chooses to depart with him acts on what she knows from the past and what she can imagine of the future. It is a mistake, finally, to characterize gorilla life as easeful and arcadian. Gorillas must lean upon and endure other gorillas. As Humphrey says, "the chief role of creative intellect is to hold society together." It is a lesson almost too painfully applicable to our own species.

CHAPTER SIX

The Legacy of the Wolf

I

When gorilla researcher David Watts is away from the field, he carries with him a picture of a young silverback named Ahab. It is a close-up of the animal's face. Ahab's eyes, clear and deeply set, stare resolutely back at the observer.

"The picture keeps me honest," says Watts. "It reminds me of something that I can't publish or explain scientifically. Sometimes when I'm at Karisoke studying a gorilla group, one of the animals will come over and sit down next to me. He takes my head in his hands, turns my face to his, and just stares into my eyes. I am absolutely convinced that he is studying *me*. Who am I? Why am I out there in the rain, day after day?"

231

If what we are looking for on this mammalian journey is some clear and nondefensive recognition passed between the human and the non-human, perhaps we could say we've reached our goal in the gorilla's probing gaze. It would be misleading, however, to end our journey with the great apes. For all their great expressiveness and unpredictable interactions, for all their humanlike gestures of comfort and distress, and even taking into account our close genetic kinship, the apes are not on their way to becoming human. They are the product of very different environmental influences than those that have shaped us. Our paths parted at least five million years ago; the gorillas, orangutans, and chimps stayed in the forest, feeding on its offerings of leaves and fruits, while our human ancestors pressed out onto the plains, and out of necessity took to a more eclectic diet, including meat and bone marrow.

We share our more recent ecological heritage, not with the apes, but with the social carnivores of the open savannah. For much of our past as a species, we too scavenged or chased down our prey, and by relying on our companions, we caught up with the fleeing food and managed to survive. The same harsh circumstances that shaped our minds and behavior also curved the lion's claw, sharpened the hyena's tooth and brightened his eye, and strengthened the social bonds uniting a pack of wild dogs. Simple analogies between animals and humans should always be looked upon suspiciously—*all* species are unique, one to another. There is much

Mankind shares an ecological heritage with social carnivores such as the hyena. Much of our early history was spent on the savannah living in nomadic groups, scavenging from abandoned carcasses, and running down game by using increasingly clever schemes.

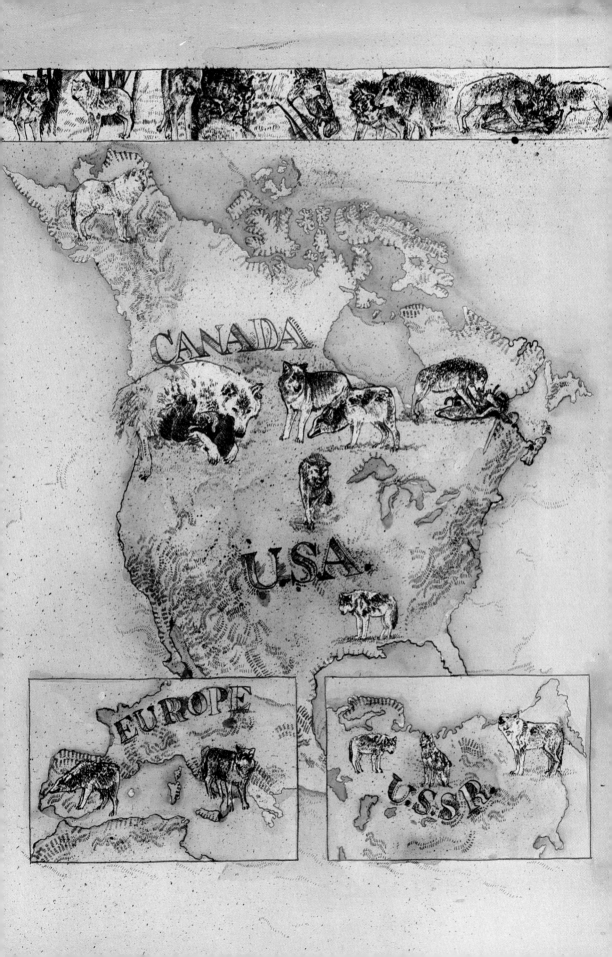

*The wolf is supremely suited to virtually every kind of habitat the earth has to offer.
Deep forest, open tundra, and swampy lowland are all home to the wolf.*

to be learned, nevertheless, by listening to the echoes of our origins in the
lives of the social predators.

As humankind was making its first, fateful strides onto the African
savannah, another social predator was taking hold in the more temperate
climates of the Northern Hemisphere. Two million years ago, the wolf had
developed into its present, supremely well-adapted form, and had become
the most ubiquitous killer on earth, thriving in a range of habitats covering
half the globe. Until recently, the wolf trotted across the top of the food
chain throughout Europe from Portugal to Scandinavia; eastward through
the Balkans and the Middle East to Afghanistan and northern India; north
again to China, Japan, Siberia, and occasionally onto the ice belonging to
no country. In the New World the wolf settled in virtually all of North
America, from Mexico City to Cape Morris Jesup in Greenland, a few hundred
miles from the North Pole.

But in spite of the wolf's ecological success, few people today stand
much chance of seeing one in the wild. This is partly because wolves are
very elusive, avoiding people whenever possible. More importantly, wher-

ever they have failed to avoid men, wolves have been relentlessly exterminated. There are no wolves left in Great Britain, Germany, France, and most of Scandinavia. A few hundred live in the Apennines of Italy, a few hundred more in Spain and Portugal. These populations may soon vanish, genetically, into the populations of feral dogs (pets gone wild) that surround them. The largest wolf populations in Eurasia are in the empty expanses of the Soviet Union (50,000–100,000). Thirty years ago there was a healthy population of wolves in Bulgaria; 15,000 were killed between 1954 and 1969, and now there are only a hundred or so left.

Wolves have fared no better in the Western Hemisphere. In the continental United States the wolf population has shrunk to about 1,200 animals in northern Minnesota, plus some tiny populations in Wisconsin and Michigan. (In April of 1986 a wolf that researchers called Phyllis gave birth in Montana's Glacier National Park. Phyllis is believed to be the first wolf to breed in the western United States in fifty years.)

The best place to look for wolves in North America is in the vast, sparsely inhabited northern forests, and on the tundra beyond. Canada currently harbors some fifty thousand wolves, and perhaps another ten thousand survive in Alaska.

Humankind despises and fears the wolf more than any other mammal. Our myths portray this consummate survivor as the very incarnation of all that is shadowy, treacherous, and evil—the embodiment of a beastliness beyond redemption. Wolves were once so dreaded in Europe that to mention their name was a crime. Myths of werewolves and wolves possessed with satanic intent have infected the folklore of Western society since the Greco-Roman period; fueled a hundredfold by the hysterical repression of the Inquisition, they are still perpetuated in our popular literature and film. A persistent image in Russian folklore is that of a wolf pack foaming at the mouth and snarling at the wheels of a Russian *troika* as it hurtles through the forest. In the carriage is a baron and his wife. One by one the nobleman throws to the wolves his clothing and possessions, then his faithful

footman, and in a last act of desperation, his bride.

In the young American nations, hatred of wolves was no less emotional, though more economically motivated. Wolves were viewed by early settlers largely as "the enemy of the state," the chief obstacle to progress and manifest destiny (excepting, of course, the other indigenous rival, the American Indian). So tolerant a thinker as Rhode Island's Roger Williams regarded the wolf as a "fierce, bloodsucking persecutor." On Cape Cod in 1717 the inhabitants tried to build an eight-mile-long fence across the peninsula to keep the wolves away from their livestock. When the fence didn't work, the citizens hid spring-loaded fishhooks in balls of wax; the wolves ate them and died of internal bleeding. But in the American attitude toward the creature there was more contempt than fanaticism, a sort of seething impa-

Inspired by memories of the bloody rampages of rabid wolves, and fueled by the destructive collisions of this preeminent social carnivore with vulnerable herds of domesticated animals, mankind has developed a special hatred for the wolf. This fifteenth-century German woodcut shows a particularly demonic werewolf attacking an unfortunate man who has strayed outside the city walls.

tience with the wolves' presumption to exist at all. "Really," wrote one sheep farmer in 1892, "it is a stain, a foul stigma, on the civilization and enterprise of the people of Iowa that these wolves remain and are frequently seen crossing the best cultivated farms, and even near the best towns in our state."

There is some justification for our traditional prejudice against the wolf, both as a potential man-killer and as a predator of livestock. In southern Europe, population densities of wolves and men have brought the two species into conflict for centuries. As recently as 1948, a wolf reportedly killed twenty people in a Romanian village. But virtually all wolf attacks, including this last, have been committed by rabid animals. The people killed were not victims of the wolf, but of rabies. There are some exceptions, the most famous and grisly being the so-called Beast of Gevaudan. For three years in the 1760s this beast terrorized a region of the Cévennes Mountains in south-central France, killing at least sixty-four people and possibly as many as one hundred, mostly small children. The Beast of Gevaudan turned out to be a pair of wolves, and according to Canadian naturalist C. H. D. Clark, they were probably not wolves at all, but notoriously vicious dog/wolf hybrids.

In North America, there isn't a

single documented account of a white person killed by a nonrabid wolf. Indians and Eskimos have undoubtedly suffered wolf attacks; ironically, their cultures don't bear the same animosity toward *lupus* as does our own. James Curran, editor of a daily newspaper in Ontario, offered a hundred-dollar reward to anyone who could prove he'd been so much as bitten by a wolf. The reward was never claimed. Before he died, Curran proclaimed that "any man who says he's been et by a wolf is a liar!"

Wolf predation on livestock cannot be so easily dismissed. From the time that swine and cattle were first herded ashore in 1609, the economic interests of colonial Americans and the resident wolves came into conflict. As Americans moved westward, the threat grew even worse, and an entire industry of wolf hunting for bounty grew up around the cattle and sheep concerns. The cattlemen did not imagine their losses; livestock on the open range are a fat and easy catch for an animal trained to hunt much wilier prey. In Montana alone, bounty hunters accounted for the death of 80,730 wolves from 1883 to 1918, and similar figures in other states led to the close extinction of the species in the continental United States by the middle of the century.

Picture a pack of a dozen wolves, loping evenly across a snow-covered meadow in central Canada. In the lead is a big male, broad-faced and heavily ruffed about the neck. His coat is a mixture of brown, silver, and red, and as he moves, his flanks gleam like copper in the late afternoon sun. He walks along with his tail erect, pausing every once in a while to sniff the snow. Behind him, his pack follows in a ragged column. A sharp-snouted, cream-colored female near the front of the line suddenly veers off. Two or three others follow her to where a stand of spruce trees has caused the snow to pile into a shallow drift. The female sniffs the ground beneath a tree, raises her leg, and lets fly a squirt of urine. Her companions approach and nose the spot, tails wagging.

Meanwhile the rest of the pack has moved on; the lead male has his eye on a thicker bank of forest farther along. Suddenly he turns, panting slightly, and looks back at the female and her group lingering under the trees. Some of the other wolves trot by him, as if they were hurrying toward some solemn appointment at the meadow's edge. But then they become aware that the big male has stopped, and they turn to look to him, their lips relaxed, panting. The wind catches their frozen breath and carries it away.

The lead wolf, the alpha male of the pack, looks forward, then back, then forward again. In the group ahead of him, one wolf—gray-flanked, with a saddle of thicker, black hair down his back—takes a few quick steps toward the distant forest, backtracks, then runs on another fifty feet, his tail wagging high. He is long-legged and thin in the face. The big male stares at him, and when their eyes meet, the gray wolf lowers his head, drops his tail, and ambles over to the lead animal's side, licking his face. The lead male ignores him and stares back to the stand of spruce. The creamy-flanked wolf, the alpha female, has curled up on her side in the lee of a snowdrift; two others lie on their backs nearby, playfully nuzzling each other's faces. The big male watches, hesitates, then trots back to join them. The rest follow. Soon everyone has found a place to lie down out of the wind, and they fall asleep.

Wolves are built to roam. Their narrow, keellike chests and turned-in elbows allow their forelegs and hindlegs to swing fluidly in the same line. Dogs aren't built this way, and when standing still, seem sturdier than their wild cousins. Wolves thrive on movement. They cover their territory in a whispering trot, easy and unswaying, like ghosts with a purpose. Like all members of the dog family, wolves walk on their toes, an advantage in running. A large heel pad gives them agility on rocks and steep slopes. At full stride a wolf can reach forty miles an hour, and the last bound onto the rump of a moose can stretch sixteen feet. People are alarmed when

Wolf coats vary in color from an icy blue-white to the deepest black; across a spectrum of silvers, blondes, and beiges, cinnamon reds, rusty browns, and oranges. Surprisingly, hair coloring doesn't seem to serve as camouflage. Black wolves can be found on the Arctic plains, while white wolves have been spotted in temperate regions far to the south.

they find a wolf footprint in the snow: It is nearly twice the size of one made by a dog of the same weight. There is an amazing difference in jaw strength too. A wolf bites with a crushing pressure of five hundred pounds per square inch, double the power of a German shepherd. Animal behaviorist Michael W. Fox was once attacked by a captive wolf, and he found the wounds on his arm "interesting." Though the wolf's canine teeth could not penetrate his thick clothing to tear into his flesh, the pressure of the animal's jaws, combined with the canid's characteristic headshake, severely damaged the muscle tissue and tendons of Fox's arm.

In the wild the force of these jaws is brought to bear on hoofed prey—elk, moose, caribou—often much larger than the wolves themselves. Under such circumstances, hunting in packs is a virtual requirement. A full-grown moose can outweigh a wolf ten to one; few wolves hunting alone could survive an attack on such prey. To conquer moose demands a great deal of experience and communication, a coordinated effort of skilled individuals.

There is no specific time for wolves to hunt. When they are no longer satiated from their last kill, they can be said to be hungry for the next, and when they are moving they always keep a watch out for prey. Toward twilight, while his pack is still resting beneath the spruce, the big male rises, stretches, and opens his nostrils to the evening air. Another male, a huge wolf with a silvery brown coat, is curled up a few feet away. The alpha walks over and nuzzles him awake. The big male rolls over on his back, reaches up and licks the alpha's chin. The cream-colored female wakes and rises to join them. One by one the wolves wake up and gather around the alphas, whining with excitement, tails wagging feverishly. This "group ceremony" is an integral part of the positive bonding that holds the pack together. Characteristically, it precedes any change in activity. A couple of juveniles bound off toward the line of trees on the horizon, and the rest follow, their strides falling into step.

It has long been part of the semimythology of wolves that they use a variety of hunting strategies, including flank attacks and elaborate ambushes. Documented observations, however, are pretty sparse—hardly surprising, since there are only a hundred or so confirmed observations of any kind of wolf kill, and no single researcher has personally witnessed more than a dozen. The wolves will occasionally herd elk onto lake ice, where the prey lose their footing and are easily dispatched. One winter on Isle Royale in Lake Superior, wolf biologist Rolf Peterson happened upon evidence suggesting some careful planning: The carcasses of five moose lay at the bottom of a rocky cliff, while a pack of wolves loitered on the rim above. It would appear that the wolves had herded the moose over the edge.

One should be wary, however, of assuming a conscious strategy on the part of wolves—their hunting, as far as we can tell, is not so much strategic as responsive. How they go about a kill depends largely on what kind of prey they are after, and how the quarry behaves. Wolves have an

Long shadows of the winter sun stretching across their shoulders, a wolf pack travels along the frozen shores of a lake in northern Minnesota.

uncanny ability to chart the course of a migrating herd and to set off across long stretches of territory to intercept them. Memory is enormously important. If a pack wounded a moose in some alcove of their territory two months previously, they will keep checking the area. Perhaps the moose has died. Perhaps he is weak enough now to succumb. The wolves follow no predetermined pattern of predation. Are the caribou due back this way from their spring migration? Is the moose going to make it across the lake before we can catch up? Can we take a shortcut across that sandy spit? If he turns to fight, what is the risk, what should we do?

Group memory probably plays a part in this. Barry Lopez, in his book *Of Wolves and Men*, writes of an old she-wolf shot with a tranquilizer gun in south-central Alaska. The researchers found that her teeth had been worn down to stubs, useless for hunting. And yet the wolf was fat and healthy. In all probability she was being provided for by the other members of her pack. Wolf-pack structure does not usually allow for freeloaders, but perhaps the old wolf could make more important contributions than her teeth—her experience, and her knowledge of where and when the pack should move to have the best chance of success. Interestingly, highland Eskimos and other nomadic people similarly tolerate the old ones staying on because of the information they embody.

The fact that dogs, wolves, and coyotes interbreed in the wild has long confused wolf counters and classifiers. When is a wolf really a wolf, and what sort of wolf is it? In 1945 a taxonomist identified twenty-four separate subspecies of wolf in North America alone—too many to be useful, really. Nowadays people usually differentiate only between the tundra wolf and the timber wolf in North America, depending on the creature's habitat. Both are of the species *Canis lupus*, the gray wolf.

Elsewhere distinctions are made according to peculiarities of behavior as well as form: The smaller Asian, or Iranian, wolf rarely howls and apparently hunts alone or in very small packs. The Chinese wolf is likewise a more solitary predator. The wolf closest to our collective consciousness, the European gray wolf, is slightly smaller than its American counterpart and can survive in closer proximity to human beings. Because sheep, chickens, and garbage are easier prey than moose and caribou, the European wolf tends to live in smaller social groups.

Here a captive Mexican wolf, Canis baileyi, *sprints across his breeding compound.*

Wolves are keen appraisers of the condition of prey animals. At the slightest hint of weakness, the pack will close in for the kill.

The wolf pack led by the big reddish male reaches the end of the meadow and moves on. Its members climb a ridge, pause momentarily on the crest, and then clamber down into the darkening woods. They travel through the night, their purposeful gait carrying them ten, then twenty, miles across frozen lakes and on into taller timber. Occasionally the alpha male or female stops to sniff at the base of a tree and leave a squirt of urine behind. The others traipse over to investigate. Sometimes one of the wolves shoots off after a hare, a bird, or perhaps some imagined prey. The others ignore him and lope on.

It is almost daybreak before the alpha female, drifting off to the left of the others, catches the scent of moose. As soon as she senses the prey she freezes rigid and points, her tail stiff behind, her nose quivering toward the scent. The big male sees his mate's tense attitude and runs over to her. When the others catch up, the pack feverishly falls over itself again in another group ceremony, touching noses, whining, their tails wagging so hard that their haunches sway back and forth and knock into each other. After everyone has had a chance to lick everyone else's face, the wolves dash off in the direction of the scent, and soon pick up the moose's fresh footprints in the snow.

Fifteen minutes later the pack has the prey in sight. Respectful of the moose's sensitive nose, they circle around to approach upwind. They stalk to within ten yards before the moose hears their breathing, and jerking up his antlers, wheels around to face them. No one moves. Though they have been discovered, the wolves make no rush to attack. Instead, they stop short, staring back into the widening eyes of the prey.

What the moose does now is of intense interest to the wolves. They know that a healthy bull who backs up against a thicket, lowers its head, and charges is a formidable enemy. Moose cows are no easy kill either, and they are ferocious in defense of their young. One researcher once watched a moose cow defend her calf from a wolf pack for more than a day—even though the wolves had already killed the calf. Eventually the wolves conceded defeat and left.

The pack is not desperately hungry, and if the moose continues to stand his ground, they will probably give up and go on their way. But not all moose who stand up to a pack are capable of defending themselves. Perhaps the moose in not *able* to run. Elk, caribou, moose, and other wild ungulates are plagued by a variety of crippling parasites. Perhaps the animal's lungs are clogged with cysts of hydatid tapeworms. Wolf biologist David Mech once found a moose with fifty-seven of these lung cysts, each the size of a golf ball. Another researcher found a mule deer at the point of death, covered with seven hundred winter ticks. Additional afflictions might be nagging at the animal—a wound that won't heal, arthritis, or simple old age. Wolves are adept at reading weakness; the slightest hobble in an animal's step, a thinness of body hair, or perhaps a waft of stale breath, is all that is needed to trigger the wolf's attack.

The condition of the prey animals killed by wolves has been carefully studied by biologists and wildlife managers. Most, but not all, now agree that wolves tend to kill aged, injured, and ill animals, thus helping to maintain the general fitness of the prey population. Young animals are also vulnerable, and by limiting their numbers the wolves serve to keep the size of the population in check and perhaps eliminate inferior gene combinations. It isn't true, however, that wolves take *only* vulnerable animals. Perfectly healthy caribou can find themselves cornered; even the nimblest stag can trip over a root.

Suddenly the moose pivots on its hindfeet and bolts. At the sight of running prey, the wolves attack. This is the most critical point in the hunt. If the wolves can bound within snatching distance of the moose, their chances of bringing it down are good; otherwise the chase could be long and futile. Moose are the most difficult prey; even after the wolves have made a successful stalk, they stand only a 5 percent chance of making a kill. While chases can last twenty minutes, most times the wolves give up after only a minute or two, having covered less than a mile. A hungrier wolf is less concerned with his energy budget. Naturalist Robert Aghook, a Nunamiut Eskimo, once watched a wolf pursue a caribou through hard-packed snow for six miles. When the snow turned to loose powder both animals slowed to a walk, the wolf keeping a constant distance between himself and his quarry. As they reached a steep slope, the stretch of pow-dered snow ended. The wolf put on a spurt, caught up to the exhausted caribou, and brought it down. After a run like this, a wolf may be too tired to eat for a long time.

This time, the wolves are lucky. The moose, though still in his prime, is slightly hobbled from an encounter with another pack two weeks before. The alpha male is the first to grab hold, latching his jaws onto the moose's rump. This is the best point of attack: There are no vital organs in the rump, but it is out of the way of flashing hooves and meaty enough to give purchase to several wolves. Running prey are never hamstrung by wolves. "The Achilles tendon in a moose is so thick and strong you could hang a truck from it," says Rolf Peterson.

The moose tries to continue running, but finds himself heavily bur-dened with wolves. While the alpha male keeps his hold on the rump, other animals attach themselves to the moose's flanks. The prey twists and bucks, lashing out with his hooves. For a moment he shakes free, knocking one of his assailants senseless with a kick. But as the moose heads toward a frozen creek, two other members of the pack cut him off. One lunges and grabs hold of the moose's nose, dragging his head down. The moose heaves him away into a bush. The alpha female, a white blur, leaps and buries her teeth in the moose's neck. She too is shaken off, but she leaves behind a deep, reddening hole just above the victim's shoulder. The moose, bleeding from several wounds, twists around to face the nearest wolves, lowers his rack, and paws the snow. Suddenly the predators cease the attack. They stand just out of range of the moose's kicks, panting, eyes fixed on the prey. They know enough not to take unnecessary risks. The moose is theirs.

After a few minutes, some of the wolves lie down and rest. Others lap at the bloody snow. A trio of younger males cavort among themselves, chasing one another about, catching up and rolling each other over on the ground. The moose stands still and watches; if he tries to lie down, two or

Wolves begin to feed immediately after killing an animal, tugging at the carcass from all directions.

three wolves quickly rise and menace him again. It may take a long time for the moose to die. An hour later most of the wolves have moved off in search of other game, leaving a couple of individuals behind on a death watch. After another hour the moose collapses, and the hungry predators move in. With their prey too weak to resist, they begin to feed while the moose is still alive. By this time the great deer has succumbed to shock; pain-numbing endorphins are pouring through its brain, and the animal seems blissfully detached from the proceedings.

Soon the other wolves return and join their companions at the moose's side. The meal proceeds with a good deal of growling and snapping at companions who try to squeeze in closer to the carcass. But when the alpha wolves arrive at the moose, the others make way for them to feed. Upon the health of these animals rests the safety of the pack; by allowing them a privileged position at the carcass, the other pack members further their own chance of survival.

A full-grown moose provides meat enough for everyone, and the animals eat until their stomachs bulge. A wolf's alimentary system is aptly designed to accommodate its feast-or-famine diet. The stomach is huge—

capable of holding twenty pounds of meat gorged at a single sitting—and digestion is quick. Since raw meat is much easier to process than cellulose, there is no need for complicated stomachs or bacterial helpers like those that assist the plant-eating elephants and gorillas. Nor does the wolf require any fancy grinding surfaces on his teeth; he simply bolts his food down in huge chunks. Wolf saliva contains no digestive enzymes, but serves as a lubricant. Digestion of the raw meat takes place in the intestines and is 95 percent efficient, compared to the 40 percent efficiency of the elephant, who must eat almost constantly.

For all the messiness of the kill and the wolf's unmannerly gorging, the end product of its digestion can be surprisingly discreet. Wolves take in a certain amount of indigestible hide, hair, and bones along with the usable flesh, especially after the carcass has been well picked over. As the indigestibles move through the intestines, they arrange themselves so as to protect the intestinal walls from puncture. Wolf scats from the first feeding on meat are loose, black, and stinking. But the later scats are perfect little parcels—hair wrapped around the outside, a bundle of splintered bones within.

II

Biologists call the social organization of a wolf pack a *dominance hierarchy*. Dominance among social animals is sometimes misunderstood to be some rigid exertion of strength, a sort of might-makes-right credo governing the affairs of lesser earthlings. Dominance, however, is not based on strength alone, but rather upon the *assessment* of one's strength by other animals in the group. The cinnamon-flanked alpha male in our pack may be physically inferior to others in his group, but unless he betrays signs of weakness, they will not challenge his authority. It is not in their interest to do so, at least not in the short term. If the alpha animal had to constantly fight off challenges from subordinate wolves, he would quickly tire and lose the ability to lead cooperative ventures, the lifeblood of the pack.

Wolf packs are essentially nuclear families, the alpha wolves either parents or older siblings to the rest of the animals. Within each pack there are really two hierarchies, one among the males and one among the females. In the male hierarchy, another high-ranking animal, called the *beta*, is heir apparent to the alpha position. In pack politics the beta plays the role of a chief minister, serving as a buffer between the alpha and the lower-ranking members of the pack, keeping order among them so that the alpha does not have to constantly settle petty skirmishes himself. Below the beta in the hierarchy come the wolves who have recently reached maturity or who have fallen from prominence, perhaps because they grew too old. The lower end of the hierarchy holds the sexually immature juveniles. Sometimes a wolf may be of such low status that it is actually thrust from the security of the pack and becomes an outcast, a peripheral wolf who follows the pack at a safe distance.

In captive wolf packs, there is often an animal for whom social stability brings nothing but woe. At the bottom of the dominance hierarchy dwells the scapegoat, or omega wolf, an unenviable creature who frequents the fringe of pack life and suffers attacks from the other wolves. The scapegoat is most fiercely harassed during peaceful times, presumably as an outlet for pent-up aggression. Typically, the beta wolf in the pack will brew up a fight, in which the lower-ranking wolves gladly join, encircling the scapegoat, closing in, lunging at the animal's hindquarters. The alpha wolf rarely participates in the abuse of the scapegoat, and will even break up fights on its behalf. The scapegoat is often a deposed alpha himself, an animal who has suffered a sudden plunge from "riches to rags."

Packs living in zoo or park enclosures will usually assign the scapegoat a strip of ground near the outside of the enclosure, closest to the humans. The social freedom of the scapegoat is narrow indeed—if the animal should so much as defecate outside of his assigned area, the other wolves could find that sufficient grounds to attack. Scapegoating is probably rare in wild packs. Outcasts can choose to keep away from the others, living on leftovers and begged indulgences. If violently harassed, they may venture off on their own. Their chances of survival alone are slim, but why not leave, if staying becomes an even more perilous proposition? The mental ter-

Two wolves assert their dominance by "standing across" the forequarters of a lower-ranking wolf in a prone, submissive posture. Judging by the expression on the submissive wolf's face, the question of dominance has yet to be settled. Radical upheavals in rank are not unusual.

rain of wolves is crowded with such rocks and hard places—always the alternatives to be pondered, crucial choices to be made. Sometimes the outcast will try it alone for a while, then return to the pack. Perhaps things have changed; the pack may need more wolves for defense or extra help in rearing the pups. Maybe the outcast will be accepted back into the safety of the pack.

Throughout the hierarchy, each individual's freedom is limited by the degree to which other, higher-ranking wolves take exception to it. This doesn't mean that the individual is locked into his or her place; the social order can change, and any disruption is an opportunity for movements, reversals, new relationships. Alphas grow old or die in battle with other packs; brothers and sisters wander off on their own and return to find themselves less highly regarded. Meanwhile the pack order adjusts, and a new status quo is established. The rank order itself should not be looked on as a simple chain of individual relationships—wolves are much too complicated for that. There are personal friendships and alliances to be taken into account. Littermates often seem to stick together, touch more, protect each other. Skirmishes between pack members are rarely private affairs; everybody else gets worked up over a fight, and takes a natural interest in the outcome.

Unfortunately, studying the subtle alliances, coups, and twists of fortune in a wild wolf pack is next to impossible—wolves don't stand around waiting to be documented, and can only be observed at a distance, usually from airplanes. Ever since animal behaviorist Rudolph Schenkel's discoveries in the 1940s, however, people have been observing the intricate patterns of relationships among wolves in captive packs in zoos and enclosed parks. This scrutiny has revealed a rich complexity in the animal's social life. Keep in mind, however, that captivity exaggerates some habits, and leaves others in shadow. Dominance hierarchies in prisons, for example, are much more pronounced than those among human populations generally.

Through the winter months, the coppery male in our fictional pack leads his companions in a continual peregrination of their three-hundred-square mile territory, checking for hoof tracks in the snow and the scent of prey carried on the wind. Sometimes the cream-colored alpha female takes the lead, and at other times the big, silvery-brown wolf, the beta of the pack, ambles ahead, the rest following. Even lower-ranking animals may occasionally lead the pack in its wanderings, but when it comes to a decision—whether to forge a rushing stream or when to veer off across an open plain—the wolves look to their leaders. Once near the edge of their territory, they climb to the top of a hill and see below a lone wolf loping down the far slope. The two big males, joined by a pair of younger wolves, take off after the intruder, silent and intent, their eyes gleaming. The lone wolf hears them coming and dives into the trees; the others chase him for half a mile before returning to the pack.

Lone wolves are not always so fortunate. In 1970, some wildlife photographers saw a lone black wolf feeding on a caribou carcass in Alaska's Mount McKinley National Park. The wolf left the carcass, and suddenly four gray wolves appeared and began to chase him across a wide river bar. The lead attacker wolf caught up and grabbed the black wolf by the neck, pulling him down. The other three grays arrived and all began biting the struggling wolf. Then they backed away, their tails wagging slightly. The black wolf jumped up and ran about frantically, and the others renewed the attack, more vigorously this time. Their victim raised his head once, and then died. The gray wolves sniffed about the area of the fight, and left.

Wolves are supremely territorial. A pack will defend its territory against all trespassing wolves, whether they are members of a neighboring pack encroaching because food is growing scarce in their own range, or a lone wolf hurriedly passing through. Pack territories expand and contract with the season, the density of prey, the size of the pack, and the number of other wolves in the area competing for space. Lone wolves don't have any range of their own, and must often trespass across the territories of others or else risk living in the dangerous, human-infested areas nobody else wants. These solo travelers—vanquished leaders, young rovers in search of a mate—are those most likely to be killed by other wolves or by men. In 1980 one young loner was caught, tagged, and radio-collared near International Falls, Minnesota. He lost his collar soon after, but a year later was shot outside of Nipawin, Saskatchewan, in Canada, 550 miles away, a distance record matched by few other land mammals.

The internal affairs of the pack are managed with little overt violence. Peace is kept through a repertoire of signals and body gestures, clearly understood by all. A subordinate wolf, nosing his way past the beta male to get at a prey carcass, hears a snarl and looks up into the beta's bared teeth, wrinkled forehead, perked-up ears. There is no mistaking the meaning of this threat display. Quickly the upstart appeases the higher-ranking wolf with a submissive, closed-mouth grin, flattening his ears back and lowering his head. What's going on in a wolf's netherparts is also a good indication of its rank. Alphas hold their tails high and present their anus for the olfactory inspection of a lower-ranking wolf. The wolf's body is littered with scent glands, seats of self-expression—glands on the tail, glands in the anus, glands between the toes. A subordinate clamps his tail over his anus and curls away, a posture known as "anal withdrawal," a muffling of self.

The body language of submission in wolves derives some of its vocabulary from the individual's early relationship with its parents. A mildly submissive gesture is to nuzzle and nip at the mouth of a higher-ranking wolf. More extreme, "passive submission" is communicated by flopping over on one's back. Both of these gestures have their roots in puppyhood: Wolf pups nip at their parent's mouths to stimulate them to regurgitate food for them to eat, and they first expose their bellies so that their mother or father can lick them clean, a gesture that often stimulates the pup to urinate. Submissive posturing carries with it all the positive emotion of that early bond. It is an expression of affection, reverence, a declaration of one's dependence and good intentions. Domestic dogs, overbred for loyalty to their human masters, sometimes grovel obsequiously. But there is nothing neurotic in the wolf's ecstasies of self-effacement. On the contrary, they are essential to the harmonious spirit of the pack; the absence of submission in the wrong situation could start a serious fight.

Generally speaking, the longer an alpha wolf maintains his or her position, the stabler will be the affairs of the pack. Trouble starts when either of the alpha animals is removed. Not only is the pack now leaderless, but the opportunity suddenly emerges to breed with the remaining alpha, an enormous incentive to compete. Eric Zimen, who has contributed much to the understanding of wolf social dynamics with his studies of captive packs in the Bavarian Forest and elsewhere in Germany, once withdrew the alpha male from his pack in order to see how the rank order would be affected. What followed was a political drama lasting over a year. The departed alpha, a wolf Zimen called Grosskopf because of his big head, had been a tolerant animal, and during his tenure relationships among three subordinate wolves—Näschen, Wölfchen, and Alexander—had been generally friendly. As soon as Grosskopf was removed, however, play among the three abruptly stopped, and the struggle for dominance commenced.

Näschen was the first wolf to claim the upper hand, but his authority was precarious from the start, since Alexander continually snarled back at him. In January a real fight broke out, Alexander and Wölfchen joining forces to topple the presumed alpha Näschen, who withdrew without being seriously wounded. Alexander immediately took on all the trappings of dominance, holding his tail high, strutting about with an alpha's proud, stiff-legged walk. For a time peace prevailed, with Alexander at the top of the hierarchy, Näschen in second place, and Wölfchen in third. But soon Wölfchen began to snap at Näschen too, and with Alexander as an ally, he took over the middle position.

As Alexander gathered increasing authority over the other wolves, Zimen began to notice a change in his relationship to his human keepers as well. Alexander had always been a friendly, good-natured wolf, but now he was growling menacingly whenever Zimen entered the wolves' enclosure. One day Alexander suddenly jumped at the biologist and put his paws on his shoulders, baring his teeth. "Whenever I moved he snarled more loudly," Zimen remembers. "His big white teeth came alarmingly close, and I did not feel at all comfortable."

Zimen managed to keep his poise, talking calmly to the wolf until he finally removed his paws and walked off. With a parting snarl he lifted up a leg and urinated—another gesture of dominance used only by alphas. "To avoid completely losing face," Zimen says, "I did the same. Then I strutted proudly around the enclosure, walked slowly to the door, and left."

Toward the end of the summer, the lower-ranking wolf, Wölfchen, began to show "expansionist tendencies" toward Alexander himself. Aggressive, tense encounters between the two animals gradually overshadowed more friendly styles of play. Wölfchen developed a penchant for following close behind the alpha wolf, nipping at his heels. The alpha responded with intimidating grimaces and countering attacks, but Wölfchen persisted.

On October 1, a year after the departure of the tolerant Grosskopf, the final battle took place. Wölfchen made a sudden charge at Alexander, fixed his teeth in him, and shook. Alexander squealed in pain, and Näschen ran over and rather half-heartedly snapped at Wölfchen. Hearing the commotion, a keeper arrived and trained a powerful spray from a water hose on the battling wolves in an effort to separate them. But Wölfchen kept his grip on Alexander. Finally Alexander struggled free and retreated, seriously wounded, to his kennel. He did not reemerge for three weeks. His absence only helped Wölfchen consolidate his authority, and by the end of autumn the young wolf—who had begun as the lowest member of the hierarchy—had established himself as the alpha of the pack. Soon after, the three animals were playing peaceably together again.

In the wild, internal conflicts within a wolf pack are most likely to erupt during the breeding season. Toward the end of March, the cream-colored alpha and the other adult females in our northern pack begin to feel the coming of estrus. Everyone is on edge. Table manners at a kill site begin to deteriorate; game is becoming harder to find, and when a deer is killed, the wolves scramble for the best pieces of the carcass. Relationships among the mature females come unglued; two sisters, normally close companions, growl and snap at each other, then gang up and harass a younger female who comes too near. For some reason the alpha female can no longer tolerate the sight of another high-ranking female, a handsome, eager-faced wolf, with a coat of mottled red and tan. The alpha chases her off. For weeks she lingers on the fringe of the pack, scared to come closer, scared to depart. Some of the young males begin to approach older females, sniffing and licking their hindquarters and attempting some clumsy mounts. The females are unimpressed by such adolescent pawings, and turn to snap at their suitors. The older males watch and bide their time.

As the height of estrus approaches, the high-ranking males show more interest in the dominant females. The big beta wolf suddenly seems to have reverted to childhood; he prances in front of the alpha female, then lowers his forelegs to the ground, his hindquarters erect, tail wagging. His lips are relaxed in a "play grin." The female responds by playfully grabbing his snout, but then coquettishly moves off. When she sees the alpha male returning from a brief excursion, she greets him in a wagging, whining curl of affection, then flings her forelegs up on his shoulders. The male responds by sniffing her genitals and mounting her side, at the same time eyeing the beta wolf, who lowers his tail and retreats.

Aggression within a pack reaches its peak during breeding season in the spring. The body language of threat and submission helps to maintain order in the pack.

The human imagination has always harbored a fascination for the sexuality of wolves. Historically, we have bestowed upon them an insatiable carnality. Rapacious wolves crop up everywhere in our myths, from the suggestive undercurrents in "Little Red Riding Hood" to the grotesque perversions attributed to werewolves during the Inquisition. In French idiom the expression "She has seen the wolf" *(Elle a vu le loup)* refers to a woman who has lost her virginity, while in many Western languages a "wolf" is a man who preys upon the affections of women.

Real wolves hardly live up to such a reputation. During their single yearly estrus, they form solid, deeply affectionate bonds that endure well beyond the breeding season and may last for years. More importantly, the social structure of the pack actually discourages matings between most of its members. Subordinate wolves rarely mate, even though they are physically able and inclined to do so. Experience has taught them that the higher-ranking animals in the pack will not permit subordinates to copulate or even to engage in flirtatious play. Dominant males and dominant females each preserve the order of their hierarchies, occasionally crossing over to suppress a particularly presumptuous member of the opposite sex. Very low-ranking, peripheral animals who dare to approach a member of the pack sexually are ganged up on and attacked. The most vigilant defender of wolf chastity is the alpha female; a cold look from her is enough to curl the tail of the most eager young wolf. Even if a male should manage to mount a subordinate female, he may still fail to mate, because his partner is trembling too hard from fear of the alpha female's retribution.

With all this policing going on, it is not surprising that few courtships reach their natural conclusion. Those that do take a strange turn, found only among wolves, dogs, and other canids. One evening near the height of estrus, the big alpha male approaches his mate, and after the two exchange some affectionate face licks and some exploratory sniffings, he mounts her and inserts his penis. Immediately it begins to swell, while his partner's vaginal sphincter muscles constrict. The wolves are locked together in a "copulatory tie," a virtually unbreakable physical bond. Their mating gives rise to a sudden outburst of excitement among the other wolves, who squeal and whine and run circles around the pair. A few minutes later the male pivots on his penis and faces to the rear, but his penis is not released. Next the female decides to lie down for a while—but still the pair remain joined.

A copulatory tie between wolves lasts about twenty minutes, the male ejaculating all the time. Its function is mysterious; perhaps, as David Mech has suggested, it helps to strengthen the vital psychological bonds between two newly mated animals. Sometimes the other wolves in the pack take advantage of the breeders' temporary vulnerability to harass them. Sometimes the alphas' copulation will excite subordinates to mate as well. But one should never underestimate the vigilance of alpha females; they have been known to go after a pair of courting subordinates while locked in a copulatory tie themselves, dragging their helpless mate behind like some oversized appendage.

The sexual dynamics of a wolf pack pose an intriguing evolutionary mystery. Why is it that most often only one pair in the pack breeds, when the other adults are also physiologically quite capable of doing so? In the past, the phenomenon has been attributed to group selection—the apparent tendency on the part of some members of a social group to sacrifice their individual interests for the good of all. According to this theory, a population of wolves that did not evolve mechanisms for limiting its growth would soon outgrow the environment's ability to support them, and the population would die out. Those populations, on the other hand, that developed natural ways of stemming their growth—in this case, social constraints on having more than one litter in a pack at a time—would survive better and pass on the traits that enable them to evolve those behaviors in the first place.

Many biologists today, however, question how group selection can really evolve. Evolution is blind; the genes that motivate an individual's behavior cannot know what behavior would be best for the future of the group as a whole. And if it is the self-sacrificing wolves who forgo their chance to breed, how then are they to pass on the genes that predisposed them to act so unselfishly? To get out of this bind, some biologists explain the wolves' apparent altruism by invoking kin selection. Though the subordinates do not themselves mate, their protective behavior toward younger siblings, nieces, and nephews helps ensure that their common genes will survive.

Recently, wolf researchers Jane Packard, Ulysses Seal, and David Mech have come up with an alternative solution to the breeding dilemma, relying on straightforward natural selection to explain the subordinate wolf's seeming unselfishness. According to Packard and her colleagues, there are no non-breeders in wolfdom—only those who breed and those who haven't yet had a chance to do so. All wolves are mo-tivated by an innate drive to reproduce, but to do so they must first rid themselves of their subordinate status.

To become a breeder, the individual can follow one of two strategies. Take, for example, an adult female, a daughter of the reigning alpha female. She has the opportunity either to abide in her mother's pack and wait for her chance to take over the alpha position, or to journey off by herself in search of a mate and a chance to start a family of her own. The criteria she uses to make that crucial decision are difficult to determine, but wolves are extremely canny "politicians," always on the lookout for a weakness or some gap in the status quo. Perhaps the young female notices a slight limp becoming more evident in her mother's stride, and so decides to stay and see what develops. Or perhaps she does make a tentative attempt to start out on her own, and finds her ambitions frustrated by the number and ferocity of the packs surrounding her territory on all sides.

Whatever her reasons for choosing her strategy, the outcome of that choice is bound to be influenced by conditions within the pack and in the population outside. Imagine a situation where the wolf population in the area is overcrowded, while moose and other prey are scarce. If the young female chooses to leave, she will have to roam far for food, and she stands a better than normal chance of being killed by a neighboring pack. Since her mother, the alpha female, is one of the principal warriors in her pack, stressful times like these will expose the mother to increased danger. If the alpha were to be killed or wounded in a confrontation with another pack, the young female and her sisters might then have an opportunity to breed themselves. Under these circumstances, she would probably do well to stay with her natal pack. This does not presume any conscious intention on the part of the wolf, only that her genes are disposing her to act in one way or the other, and that their "decision" will have consequences for her future.

Under different environmental conditions, our nonbreeding female might lose out by abiding with the pack. If the population density of wolves is low but there is an abundance of prey, packs tend to be stable and relatively free from strife. The incumbent breeder is likely to remain in power, enjoying ever-greater authority as she continues to breed. Now is a good time for the younger female to leave; she will be rewarded for the risk she takes with an excellent chance of settling with a lone male in a moose-rich territory, unmolested by other wolves.

And so it goes, each wolf gambling on the course of action that will most likely lead to a successful litter of cubs. There are, of course, many other factors influencing social organization—for instance, the need to keep the pack as close as possible to the optimum size for hunting. Packard's theory of "deferred reproduction" is new, still awaiting evidence from the field. In the meantime, there is one intriguing bit of circumstantial evidence: While only some 60 percent of the adult wolves in the wild copulate and produce a litter each year, an examination of the placental scars of dead females showed that almost all had produced a litter at some point in their lives. Whether a wolf breeds or not may just be a matter of time.

The usual result of these complex constraints on mating is to limit successful breeding within the pack to one couple per year, almost always the alpha pair. When the pups are born sixty-three days later, they will be able to live through their early, vulnerable days without competition for food from other litters. Ironically, the discovery of the apparent pair-bonding of wolves has led people to think of them as tirelessly monogamous—an impression of wolf sex diametrically opposed to the animal's previous reputation for lustful excess. But wolves, especially the females, may not be quite so faithful as commonly supposed. Unquestionably the alpha female shows a preference for her long-term mate, but she may occasionally copulate with the beta wolf, as well as with other high-ranking wolves.

The wolf's polyandrous practices—one female enjoying the reproductive attentions of more than one male—probably serves to tighten social bonds within the pack. The closer the bonds between the alpha female and the other members of the pack, the better the chance that they will pitch in and care for her pups when they are born. Her occasional sexual partners may even be deceived into thinking that they have sired the brood themselves, and will be all the more solicitous. By cementing her relationships with high-ranking males and meanwhile discouraging the breeding hopes of her daughters and sisters, the alpha female emerges as the most prominent wolf in the pack.

With all the struggles for power taking place during the breeding season, it might seem that wolves are governed by some sort of Machiavellian drive to rule, and that little trust should be placed in one's brother or sister. Individual ambition undoubtedly plays a role in the affairs of the pack, but the challenges, the skirmishes, and shifts in the dominance hierarchy take place within the overwhelmingly cooperative context of a nuclear family sharing a common purpose: the hunting of large game. Shared purpose encourages extremely tight social bonds strengthened and expressed by a web of interactions—snout nuzzles and crotch sniffings, laying-on of paws, play rituals, and so forth.

By the end of the breeding season, the males in our northern pack are a little ragged. The alpha has lost a chunk off his left ear, an injury suffered while coming to the aid of a lower-ranking wolf in a scuffle. The thin-faced wolf with the long legs now walks tenderly, his right hindfoot badly chewed in a fight. But now, as spring approaches, the animals can be found licking each other's wounds, sometimes for hours on end. The animals closest to each other in the hierarchy—and thus the most likely to have inflicted the wounds on each other in the first place—are the ones doing the most licking, all part of the reassurance, the essential bonds of trust.

Early in May, the alpha female begins to prepare a den for her pups. She finds an abandoned fox den in a clump of cottonwood trees near the summit of a hill. Fifty yards away a brook, swollen from the spring thaw, coughs and chortles downslope. The brook will provide water for the female when her cubs are born. With her forepaws she remodels the den to wolfish proportions, digging deeper and scooping out a tunnel in the sandy soil nearly ten feet long. At the end of the tunnel she excavates an ample chamber for her pups. Sometimes her mate, or some other females, help her to dig or scratch separate tunnels into the den. Those who are not busy or away on the hunt lie on the hilltop above, a good place to watch for intruders. The movements of the pack begin to pull inward, more and more circling about the den site as spring progresses.

Three weeks later the alpha gives birth to five pups in three hours, licking each one clean as she pushes it free, eating the afterbirth and cord while she waits for the next. The pups are dark balls of fur—blind and deaf, pug-nosed and squealing. In another three weeks they've waddled out from the den and are soon romping about. The pups will bond quickly with any wolf who pays attention to them. Five months later, their attitude will suddenly change, and they will invariably back away from strangers. This turnaround in disposition—well-known to anyone who has tried to raise wolf pups in captivity—happens at about the same time that the pups

A female wolf moves her pups one by one, carrying them in her mouth from one den site to another. Wolf pups benefit from their parents' affectionate care and the solicitous attention of the whole pack. But harsh conditions and unpredictable resources weigh heavily on wild wolf populations, and over half of the pups born will die within six months.

begin to roam farther, following the pack on hunts. It makes perfect sense: If the pups were to indiscriminately befriend strange wolves they encounter from other packs, the whole fabric of wolf society would unravel.

In the meantime, all the wolves in the pack show an abundance of fondness and toleration for the pups. Wolves love to play—pups, juveniles, even the adults. German biologist Eric Zimen once watched some young wolves in British Columbia frolic in a lake for five hours, chasing after each other, jaw-wrestling, playing King of the Castle on a rock sticking out of the water. Wolves play with sticks and bones much like domesticated dogs. Barry Lopez once saw a tundra wolf "winging a piece of caribou hide around like a Frisbee for an hour by himself."

In puppyhood, play helps the youngster develop muscle coordination. Many of the inherited patterns of play—the chasing and pouncing—are distinct prototypes of hunting behavior and will be useful later on. Play is also a chance to test one's strength and, by extension, assess the strengths and weaknesses of others. For young wolves it becomes a forum for establishing a place in the ranking order which they will join as juveniles. Noticeably absent from bouts of adult play are the alpha wolves, who prefer to stand about with an air of distant reserve. Their reticence is very much a part of the political life of the pack. Play is a showcase of one's condition;

Through playful fighting, wolf pups establish their own very unstable order of rank.
Usually a strong male of the litter emerges as the "little alpha."

perhaps the alpha is getting on a bit, developing just a twinge of arthritis. Why give the others a chance to put him to the test?

"Wolves are always looking for a weakness," says biologist Fred Harrington. "If the alpha wants to keep a good thing going, he is best off keeping his information to himself."

Early in July the alpha moves her pups one by one to a new area, the first in a series of "homesites" that will serve as the focal point of pack life through the summer. Quickly the grass and leaves are flattened all around by wolf beds and by the pups' continual games. A web of trails leads to and from the site. In summer, the wolves tend to split up and hunt alone or in small groups, keeping in touch with each other through howls and scent marks left on the trails. Movements in the summer resemble the spokes on a wheel, with the homesite serving as the hub.

Wolves and human beings are among a tiny minority of mammals who readily share food. While the alpha female stays at the homesite with her pups, the others in the pack, especially her mate, return from the hunt with tidbits for those left behind. Most often they eat the food at the kill site and bring it home in their stomachs. The pups greet the returning adults with gleeful nips on their mouths, the wolves regurgitate the semidigested meat, and the pups eagerly gobble it up. The adults seem to enjoy this exchange as much as the pups, and if their stomachs are empty when the pups whine for more, they readily set off again to hunt, even in the middle of the day.

Summer is a binding time for the pack. Soon after the birth of the pups, the young eager-faced female chased to the pack's periphery during breeding season begins to creep a little closer to the center of things. One day she approaches to within a few feet of the den and sniffs. She looks at the alpha wolf lying by the entrance, quickly averting her glance so as not to offend. When she reads no threat in the alpha's face she edges closer still, curling sideways as she walks, her tail pressed down against her anus. The alpha merely raises an eyebrow, then lets her head drop back on her forelegs. While not exactly a warm welcome, the gesture is enough to reassure the young wolf that her presence will be tolerated. Cautiously, she pokes her head into the den and disappears inside. Within a couple of days, the former outcast has found a niche for herself in the heart of the pack, serving as a "dry nurse" for the pups and even daring to snarl and chase away some young males when their own curiosity leads them to the opening of the den.

Now, with summer progressing, the young female takes on new responsibilities. The alpha female, restless and bored with her confinement to the homesite, begins to join occasionally in the hunt. The young female stays behind to protect the pups from danger. In the past, some researchers have suggested that this sort of familial generosity, common among wolves, represents a sort of primitive morality, a gesture of altruism acted out on behalf of the group. But there are other more likely explanations for the female's apparent unselfishness. By bonding closely with the alpha's pups she has managed to regain and even raise her status in the pack. The attentiveness of nonmating "helpers" in the raising of cubs can also be attributed to kin selection: Since the helpers are directly related to the pups, by contributing to the pups' survival through a difficult time they are also protecting the genes that they share with them.

Some recent studies by David Mech and his colleague Fred Harrington of Mount Saint Vincent University in Nova Scotia, however, suggest that seemingly unselfish siblings may actually be "looking out for Number One" more than has been supposed, at least in times when food is scarce. Mech and Harrington cite a study reporting that the pups in one pack were left alone up to 73 percent of the time. When adolescent wolves did return to the homesite, there was a suspicious regularity to their comings and goings, which the researchers believe might have been deliberately timed to coincide with the return of older, more skillful hunters. Food brought back for the pups by the older wolves might in fact end up in the jaws of an opportunistic yearling. The juveniles might also return to the homesite simply to gather information, to see who has been where, and what he or she has found.

There is good reason, furthermore, to think that the parent would actually encourage the theft of their babies' sustenance. If food is scarce, why waste time feeding a gaggle of newborns—over half of whom will probably die anyway—when the same food could be used to protect the investment already made in full-grown yearlings? As for pitching in on defense, the wolves left behind at the homesite are often the weakest ones in the pack, hardly capable of fending off a hungry grizzly bear who may come sniffing around the den. In another study, in fact, the primary "babysitter" turned out to be a female so timid she may have been afraid to venture out beyond the homesite.

III

One bright fall morning our alpha male, fat with the summer's largess, his nostrils filled with the scents of earth, wolf, fungus, squirrel droppings, and matted leaves, gets it in his mind to sing. At first he tests the air with a thin, shivery whine, and when he finds it good he wags his tail, points his muzzle at the sky, and lets loose a full-throated howl. With lips drawn back and eyes shut, he shapes his notes with his cheek muscles and lets them fall like long, floating streamers flung from the branches of the tallest spruce. Immediately the silvery-brown beta wolf hops up from his leaf bed. As the alpha's song rises again, the beta joins in, a few intervals above, the two howls curling into each other but never touching, the sounds threaded and looped between each other's overtones. Now more of the pack picks up the mood, and a half dozen muzzles point at the drifting clouds above, all flinging their songs up in a burst of wailing joy. For a full two minutes the howls possess the sky, and as the notes fall they stir the hills for miles around with a tingling presence, as if it were the spirit of the wilderness itself that had spoken and left its breath on every leaf.

The choiring of a wolf pack in full voice cannot be heard with equanimity. When asked to describe such a concert of howls, one trapper wrote, "Take a dozen railroad whistles, braid them together, and then let one strand after another drop off, the last peal so frightfully piercing to go through your heart and soul."

"Hearing a howl increases whatever you already feel about wolves," says Fred Harrington. "It brings you closer to the animal if you already like it, but if you hate the wolf, you'll hate them all the more when they start to howl."

For a social carnivore like the wolf, howling is an excellent way to keep in touch with one's companions over distance, particularly at night, when visual signals are useless. Less social canids—foxes, for instance—haven't any sort of far-flinging call to compare with it. On a clear night in open country, a howl can be heard as far as 10 miles away by human ears; to the sharper-eared wolves, the sound may blanket an area of 140 square miles or more. After an individual has made a kill, a howl can call the others to the feed. In summer, howling in and around the homesite keeps everyone aware of where the pups are—a necessary piece of information if the mother decides without warning to move her litter to a new den location while everyone else is out hunting.

But group howls serve a deeper purpose than merely conveying information. They help to cement the bonds between the members of the pack and confirm the order of things. This is especially important when the pack wakes up from a nap, grows restless for the hunt, or whenever there is a decision to be made. High-ranking wolves, though not necessarily the alphas, most often initiate howling ceremonies, and only the outcasts on the periphery refrain from joining in. Everyone else is pleased to get into the act, approaching the initial howler with tails wagging and a general excitement of limb and gait that seems to say, "What a good idea!" Barry Lopez once saw a wolf "with an air of not wanting to miss out, howl while defecating."

By advertising their presence with howls, a pack of wolves also alerts strangers to their territorial claim. Neighboring packs sometimes engage each other in howling jousts that last for hours. Nomadic packs have even more reason to howl to other wolves than a pack established at its summer rendezvous site, which is already well-defined with scent marks. A tundra pack following a herd of caribou, for instance, might well create with their howlings a sort of acoustical domain for themselves: "We have come; we are many; keep your distance or dismay."

But this can pose something of a dilemma. What if, in fact, the many are few? It is something of a fundamental law in wolfdom never to betray a weakness. Wouldn't the territorial howl of a pack of three wolves lose something of its imperative majesty if, let us say, it fell on the ears of a nearby pack of twelve? ("We have come; we are weak; come and kill us.") Fred Harrington has recently studied smaller packs to learn if they howl less often or at pitches that do not carry as far as those of larger packs. So far his results are inconclusive, but along the way Harrington has come up with an interesting theory about the nature of the howl itself.

When an individual wolf joins in a howl, the sound immediately begins to interact acoustically with both the howls of its fellows in the group and the environment itself. Wolves never sing in unison; the pressure waves of the different voices intermingle and collide, creating harmonic effects. What one hears is a cascade of broken moans and yips, creating the impression of far more howlers than actually exist. The sound reflecting off the features of the terrain further adds to the piling up of frequencies, and if these echoes reach the ear at the same time as the original notes, the brain— or at least the human brain—simply balks and refuses to process a sensation of voice number at all. Harrington believes that this environmental reinforcement may cloak the true strength of a howling pack. Lying around their homesite at night, the wolves in our pack might perk up their ears when they hear a chorus of cries in the distance. They cannot know that the "pack" they hear is really only two wolves in duet, ably accompanied by an exposed granite rock face and a quiet lake surface glistening in the moonlight.

The choiring effect, however, cannot be achieved with a single voice. The cry of a lone wolf, etched across the skyline at dusk, seems like the voice of anguish itself—a long, mournful arc rising in intensity and pitch, as if the wolf were flinging up a piece of its soul in the hope that it might catch hold of something and be pulled out of its isolation. A solitary wolf does not howl to advertise territory, because it has none to protect. Nor does the lone wolf howl to affirm social bonds; it has none to affirm. A loner's soaring moans only advertise its solitude—a dangerous thing to do, especially if packs roam the area. But it must still run the risk. A lone wolf howls most during the breeding season to attract the company of another loner, so that the pair can establish a family and territory of their own. The loner must carefully weigh the hope implicit in his howl against the fear of exposing himself as an intruder and a threat to the pack. In Eric Zimen's study of captive wolves in the Bavarian Forest, he found that loners often initiated howls, but they always directed their furtive appeals away from the resident pack, out beyond the fence that closed them in. There is no hope of an answer for these captive outcasts; the Bavarian Forest has been empty of wild wolves for two hundred years.

Like most wolf specialists, Zimen is a good howler himself. Scientists seldom roar to lions, trumpet to elephants, or converse in shrill squeaks with mice; yet it is an accepted, useful practice in the field to locate wolves by howling. There is, of course, a solid scientific purpose behind this. Wolves do respond to human howls, and often approach to investigate. Tape recordings of real wolf howls are also piped into the wilderness to attract the animals or excite them to answer. Curiously, the wolves seem to prefer the raw, flawed performance of a human howler over the sterile precision of a tape recording.

By all acounts howling is one of the more enjoyable parts of field research (especially if a clutch of grad students is along to really let loose a chorus of howls). Apart from the obvious gratification in contacting one's research subjects, howling brings a peculiarly personal reward. According to Fred Harrington, cold, clear nights unruffled by winds are best for howling. Cup your hands over your mouth and let the sound pour out; the howl carries away, reflects off the surface of a lake, and glances off the shoulder of a hill. Your howl and its echo, merely a split second apart, roll away across the terrain. "You hear the sound ring through the forest," says Harrington, "and you suddenly feel a wondrous sense of accomplishment, as if you've just filled a tremendous space."

With that human howl echoing off through the wilderness, consider once again the wolf and the human as social carnivores, territorial hunters. For both species, long-range vocalizations that penetrate the distance and the dark would be an effective way of staying in touch with one's own—a

Wolf country in northern Minnesota. The howl of a wolf can be heard over an area of 140 square miles. Some scientists believe that howling employs a complex grammar, with varying intonations and emphases signaling different intentions. A lone wolf howls in high pitches, a language of friendly intention shared by many mammal species. Human adults, for instance, invariably raise the pitch of their voice when talking to infants.

means of announcing one's location and recognizing the promixity of others. Not having the advantage of a nose like the wolf's to aid in communication, early hominids probably relied even more on vocalizations flung through distance. According to psychologist Roger Peters, who studied wolf communication with David Mech in Minnesota, natural selection might have favored those of our ancestors with "the ability to produce distinctive patterns of sounds as an aid in individual recognition, just as it has favored the ability of individual wolves to produce distinctive odors." Through the generations, vocalizations refined into distinct voices could then produce even more distinct sounds, until something like a *name* emerged from the throat. According to Peters, the individuality of every human voice, apparent even over the telephone, might be "an adaptation to a way of life that placed a premium on quick identification of fellow hunters."

No wonder Harrington felt such a sense of accomplishment in his howl. As it joined its echo and carried away through the forest, the howl bore with it a declaration of self, a hope of penetrating the darkness and reaching another.

For the wolf, the sense of smell is an even more important medium of self-expression. The wolf's nose is approximately one hundred times more sensitive than our own. With this exquisite receptor, the wolf has evolved a system of communication based on the subtle exchange of odors—a social diction that governs all the affairs of wolves, from reproduction to interpack strife. The vocabulary of this language is imbedded in bodily secretions, primarily the richly articulate products of digestion. A pile of feces or a urine mark crossed with another in the snow are the very texts of wolf society.

One of the ritual privileges reserved for the alpha wolves is the characteristic habit of urinating with a raised leg. All the other wolves, male and female, urinate from a squat or semisquat position. According to David Mech and his colleague Russell Rothman, the dominant pair in the pack carry on a sort of hormonal dialogue during the breeding season, urinating successively on the same spot. "Double scent marks" draw the delighted interest of the lower-ranking pack members, who squeak and wag over the mark as if it were an ancient codex discovered in the backroom of a second-hand bookshop. The bonded mates are equally enthralled by their crossed splashes of urine in the snow.

Mech and Rothman suggest that double-marking in canids and other species is a part of the familiarization of courtship, a crucial exchange of information about each other's reproductive state. To commit to copulation and breed successfully the couple must be fully in tune with each other, both behaviorally and physiologically. By "reading" the hormones borne in the urine mark, the wolves respond by producing additional hormones that will balance their cycles, gradually reaching a mutual rhythm that allows them to mate. Not surprisingly, bonded pairs who know each other well double-mark much less than newly acquainted wolves.

To a lone wolf, meanwhile, finding a pack that *doesn't* leave double scent marks during the breeding season may be the chance of a lifetime. David Mech once came upon a pack which had recently lost its alpha female. With no other adult females to take her place, the alpha male went about his raised-leg urinations alone. His marks were soon discovered by a solitary female, who, instead of fleeing from the pack, persevered alongside until she was eventually accepted by the alpha male and mated with him. Her ability to read the meaning of the uncrossed mark, amid all the tracks and squat urinations left by the pack, won her the coveted alpha position.

Wolf packs define the borders of their territories with scent marks, primarily performed by the alpha male and female of the pack. Much like solitary tigers, wolves leave most of their scent marks at crucial junctions between territories, keeping the marks fresh by making periodic rounds of their domain. Wherever they perceive a mark, either their own or that of a strange wolf, the alpha wolf raises its leg and overwrites its own signature on the spot. In so doing, a buffer zone is created between territories. In normal times, when prey is adequate within the home range, the packs avoid conflict and steer clear of the buffer zones.

For any earthling seeking to elude the packs—notably lone wolves and the wolf's prey—these buffer zones are the safest place to linger. David Mech noted in Minnesota that white-tailed deer who lived in the buffer zones formed a reservoir of animals that could survive long enough to maintain the deer population and eventualy repopulate the wolf core areas. White-tailed deer once found refuge from Indian hunters in Minnesota in the same way—living in the border areas between warring tribes where hunters were less likely to venture.

A gray wolf rubbing its urine into the snow to mark its territory.

A wolf's howl can communicate over long distances, but the pungent scent mark he leaves behind on a rotting log extends over time. Wolves sometimes defecate on poison baits or near wolf traps—possibly as a warning to other wolves who come later to investigate. Scent marks also serve as memory joggers, reminders for the wolf and his companions. Fred Harrington recently discovered that wolves, like red foxes, use scent marks to keep track of food caches. Previously it had been supposed that after stashing a quantity of food, canids would leave a scent mark on the cache to enable them to find it again. But if the fox or wolf that hid the food could find it by sniffing for its scent mark, couldn't any other sensitive nose do the same? Harrington observed that in fact a thrifty wolf leaves a scent mark only after it has *emptied* the cache—a reminder that although food odors linger, there is no food left in that particular store. J. D. Henry, who has observed the same behavior in red foxes, noted that a fox who neglected to "close" an empty cache with a scent mark wasted considerable time rummaging through the barren cupboard when he next returned.

Generally speaking, relationships between the wolf and its much smaller cousin, the fox, are mutually beneficial. Foxes sometimes raise their litters in abandoned wolf dens, while wolves commonly remodel abandoned fox dens to rear their pups. Scavenged wolf kills are a main source of food for the smaller canid, though a fox who tampers with a wolf kill before its owner is through eating may find himself eaten as well.

Wolves are not above stealing a fox's food cache, all the time aware of the fox's designs on their own hidden stashes. Sometimes a wolf will go to great lengths to outwit its relative. Wolf biologist Adolph Murie happened upon a wolf trail one morning in Mount McKinley National Park. Judging by the blood and hair littered along the trail, Murie could tell that the wolf was carrying the remains of a lamb. He soon noticed that the wolf tracks were joined by those of a fox, who had obviously picked up the scent of the dead lamb and was trailing the wolf to see what might be found. The biologist decided to follow the hungry fox, as it in turn tracked the lamb-burdened wolf.

Murie hadn't gone very far when he noticed that the wolf had begun to carve a very unwolflike trail through the brush—backtracking, jumping off the trail, and looping about. The researcher concluded that the wolf had become aware of the fox tailing behind him, and was taking evasive actions. At one point the wolf deliberately waded through a shallow stream, and Murie could make out where the fox had stood in the streambed, perplexed, trying to pick up the scent of his quarry. In time the fox and then the biologist discovered where the wolf had left the stream, and they set out after him again.

The wolf, meanwhile, had excavated a cache, dropped in a piece of the lamb, covered it with lichen and snow, and proceeded on his way.

The wily red fox—neighbor, cousin, and frequent beneficiary of the wolf—speaks the same pungent language of scent marks that orders the wolf's life.

But his precautions were all for naught—by the time Murie arrived the fox had already robbed the stash, leaving behind only a few shreds of lamb's wool. Murie caught a glimpse of the thief making off with something in his mouth, still in pursuit of the wolf. Apparently the wily wolf had elected not to put all his eggs in one basket, and had continued on with part of his kill to another hiding place. No use—the even wilier fox emptied this one too, before going on his way.

Wolves leave four kinds of scent marks: raised-leg urinations, squat urinations, defecations, and dirt scratchings. Dirt scratchings may be both a visual way of communicating one's dominance over others in the pack, and a way of leaving odorous messages by means of sweat glands on the wolf's feet. The significance and meaning of a pile of feces is enhanced by anal-gland secretions mixed with the droppings. Naturally, urinating and defecating also serve to void the unused products of digestion; the whole business of communicating with excreta may have evolved from the simple fact that the places a wolf would most need to remember—denning areas and kill sites—are places littered with wolf droppings.

The language of scent-marking suits purposes ranging from the oratory of territorial imperative to the intimate dialogues of pair-bonding. But the most intriguing communication may be going on between these extremes. Even within a pack's core territory, pack members leave some sort of scent

A timber wolf investigates a scent left on a tree trunk. Much like a tiger, a wolf will scent-mark conspicuous landmarks to help define the limits of his pack's territory.

mark about every 250 yards. The function of these frequent marks away from the territorial border is still not entirely understood, though it seems probable that wolves, and canids in general, use the marks to orient themselves amid a home range too large to scan from any one place.

In his field research in Minnesota, psychologist Roger Peters noticed a suspiciously familiar method to the placement of the orienting marks. The wolves chose to mark the most conspicuous landmarks, such as trees and outcrops, and even more so the pathways and intersections that defined their peregrinations. The most noticeable *visual* landmarks therefore became *olfactory* signposts as well, "vivid entities," according to Peters, set off from their unanointed surroundings. In essence, the wolves were carving a pattern of sensory signposts out of their territory, fixed points and routes that allowed them to create mental representations of the terrain. With the aid of these "cognitive maps," the wolves could traverse their range using shortcuts and multiple approaches to a particular area, rather than dumbly follow predetermined paths. In other words, the pattern of scent marks allowed them to travel *insightfully* from one place to another, adjusting their routes according to constant calculations made between their present location and established points of reference.

Such cognitive maps would be useful to any territorial animal. But consider how much more important they would be for the *social* carnivore, who not only has to remember spatial relationships, but who must share a common understanding of the terrain with companions. Human beings, too, make continual, unconscious use of cognitive maps to orient themselves. Peters participated in a study wherein some hikers, having traveled through some natural terrain, were asked to sketch maps of the country they had passed through. Without exception, the human hikers gave definition to the terrain by drawing the same sorts of landmarks that the wolves "drew" with urine and feces: forest edges, paths, intersections, distinctive landmarks.

That we share a sense of physical terrain with the wolf should not come as any great revelation—no free-ranging social group could survive for long if its members were perpetually lost. But imagine if a species were to apply this map-drawing talent to other, more abstract sorts of terrain. Lacking the wolf's formidable jaws to bring down prey, early human hunters would have relied even more on cooperation among individuals to succeed in the hunt. Their need to communicate information about events in the terrain would be all the greater. From a common mental image of terrain— and a reliance on sounds and gestures to describe particular routes and locations—there may have emerged something like a symbolic language: "Mammoth by the big water." Over generations, the ability to communiate locations on cognitive maps of actual geography perhaps led to the more sophisticated ability to find one's way among mental points of reference in time and space apart from the actual terrain: "This mammoth bigger than last one. Nork better come too, and bring his spear."

From there, another intellectual step would have brought us to the brink of analytical thought, negotiating through a *symbolic* landscape of choices, outcomes, and pitfalls: a group leader planning a strategy for the next morning's hunt; a cook marshaling spices for a meal; a doctor deciding a course of treatment for a patient. It is all a matter of speculation, of course, but our very patterns of thought might be the legacy of our earlier triumph, shared with the wolf, in making sense of the terrain around us.

Epilogue: Coming Home

Twenty thousand years ago both wolf and man roamed the plains that covered Eurasia and North America, hunting down the hoofed prey. Our common environmental heritage has left its traces in shared habits of being. The nuclear family forms the center of wolf society and most human societies, the "heads of household" bringing food home to distribute among dependents. In both species leaders emerge from the group, consolidating their authority through strength, charisma, and political savvy. Group members cement their bonds through ritual gatherings and song, at the same time remaining deeply suspicious of foreigners and intruders. If one believes Roger Peters' theory of the origin of cognitive maps, wolves and men even enjoy some common ways of knowing, a sense of a world articulated with deliberate reference points, notches carved in the blank face of nature, imprints of self left behind.

For the few human societies still organized around subsistence hunting, the connection between the ways of wolves and the ways of men are more than speculation. Until recently the Nunamiut Eskimos of the Brooks mountain range in northern Alaska were seminomadic hunters who roamed the tundra looking for caribou and other game, much like the wolves who inhabit the same territory. Over centuries the Nunamiut have become deeply familiar with the ways of the wolf. They know that to find wolves they must watch the sky for ravens, who follow the packs and scavenge their kills.

271

They know that to locate a wolf's den you must watch the movements of the older members of a pack, ignoring the pointless peregrinations of yearlings. They know that black wolves are more nervous than light-colored ones; that rabid wolves walk with muscles tensed and so leave a track with spread toes; that a female whose mammae have shed hair has recently given birth.

Like the wolves, the Nunamiut depend on stamina, cooperation, and insight into subtle changes in the environment. Wolves do not see static shapes very well, but are quick to pick up movements. Eskimos are far better than most people at discerning subtle movements—a white Arctic hare disappearing into its burrow or the tip of a wolf's tail skipping along the top of a ridge, half a mile away. The Eskimo and the wolf hunt through long months of darkness, and even when there is light to see by, the horizon fades into the general whiteness all around. Northern landscapes lack definition; the Eskimo's cognitive maps of his terrain are not furnished with visual landmarks, but with collections of relationships—shifts of light, the sound of his tread in the snow, the voice of the wind against his parka, sudden movements on the peirphery of his field of vision.

The Nunamiut have never developed a loathing for wolves, even though they are in direct competition with them for food. Certainly the Eskimos will kill wolves for furs and profit, but never for sport, never out of righteousness or fear. The Eskimos regard the wolf as a creature to be respected and emulated for his great prowess in the hunt, an animal devoted and loyal to his kind, as the Eskimo is to his own companions.

But the more human societies have moved *away* from a hunting culture, the more we hate the wolf and deplore what it stands for. In the West, the legacies of the wolf have long been assimilated into more complex social structures and behaviors. Primitive impulses that might threaten civilized society have been neatly shunted into the safe context of sport. We still gather around our alphas and cheer them as they run forth to attack "the enemy," but our cries only carry to the other side of the stadium. Hunting, for so long a subsistence activity practiced by all, is now a nonessential recreation in the United States, and in Europe it has for centuries been the exclusive privilege of the upper class.

Humankind abandoned subsistence hunting gradually. By ten thousand years ago agriculture had taken its place as the dominant mode of life. After that point, *Homo sapiens* flourished at an astounding rate, quickly usurping the wolf's place as the most widespread of mammals and ultimately assuming a baffling and unprecedented control over the future of the other earthlings. The total human population ten thousand years ago had been estimated at between five and ten million. Eight thousand years later there were three hundred million of us, and now there are four billion. In an amazingly short time the former hunter-gatherer has seized nature and turned it upside down. Where the natural order of things would dictate that a species either adjust to its ecosystem or perish, now it becomes the fate of the ecosystem to adjust to humankind's interests or disappear.

From this perspective, the analogies between the lifeways of humans and those of other species seem grossly trivial. To the extent that wolves think like people, they are far behind our achievements, mere clumsy beginners; in the comparison they actually lose much of their grace and real stature. Conversely, to the extent that wolves think in purely wolfish ways, they are beyond us, out of reach of our ability to imagine a world perceived by senses we hardly possess. Try as we might to bring this journey home to ourselves, the footing underneath slips away into analogy and abstraction. Wolves and apes do not really think like people. Tigers do not dance. Polar bears have no names for snow.

It is one of the greatest ironies of all history that humankind rose to its exalted position on earth by manipulating an alliance with the wolf and turning it to profound ends. Domestic dogs have been part of the human landscape for at least twelve thousand years. Most experts believe that *Canis familiaris* is a descendent of a small Asiatic wolf, *Canis lupus pallipes*, though how and why humans and wolves should have entered into such an intimate cross-species relationship is anybody's guess. Perhaps they began by scavenging each other's kills, or perhaps they formed some sort of hunting alliance, humans benefiting from the wolves' superior senses, the wolves profiting from the greater intelligence and manipulative skills of the humans. As the climate cooled with the advent of the Ice Age, the two species may have huddled together for warmth. Some biologists believe that the wolf was tolerated as a sort of camp garbage-collector, lurking on the fringes of human homesites and devouring the trash and human feces.

Gradually, human beings discovered that the pups of these canids could be coaxed into an even closer association; if adopted early enough they would bond to their human companions and could then be trained to sniff out game, flush it from hiding, and bring it to bay. Through this strange symbiosis, the first domestication of one animal by another, humankind was able to control the actions of other wild animals, herd them in ordered patterns, keep them close, manage their lives. The advent of animal husbandry was the first step taken by humankind away from a passive acceptance of the conditions of nature. First reindeer and later sheep, cattle, pigs, and goats all became domesticated not by men, but by men and dogs.

When left to breed without interference from humans, *Canis familiaris* looks very much the same all over the world: a small canid weighing some thirty pounds, with a pointed nose, twisted tail, and short fur. Very early on in the man/dog relationship, however, people discovered that this prototypical dog could be improved upon by controlling the breeding of individuals to encourage desirable traits. In effect, the human was able to pluck the wolf from the wilderness and humanize it, throwing a spotlight on those parts of the animal's nature compatible with human civilization and leaving the rest in shadows. The wolf's imposing teeth were shrunk to a manageable standard; even the largest Great Dane has small teeth relative to its skull size. The traits of loyalty, sociability, and intelligence were en-

couraged, as well as the wolf's disposition to defecate in established areas
away from the homesite. Breeding could produce dogs designed to serve
specific functions: setters built for sniffing out game, huskies to pull heavy
loads, greyhounds for chasing down prey, guard dogs, sheep dogs, bird
dogs, even dogs with no other purpose but to adorn the laps of their owners.
Ironically, many breeds, such as the Irish wolfhound and the Hungarian
komondor, were developed specifically to attack and destroy wolves.

The American Kennel Club now recognizes 128 distinct, true-breeding
dog types, many of them resembling a wolf about as much as the gardens
of Versailles resemble a stretch of open tundra. But what unites them all
and ensures them a place in our homes and our hearts is their supreme
faithfulness—a refinement of the wolf's natural disposition to form tena-
cious social bonds. As animal behaviorist Konrad Lorenz writes:

> *To love one's brother as one does oneself is one of the most beautiful
> commands of Christianity, though there are few men and women able
> to live up to it. A faithful dog, however, loves its master much more
> than it loves itself and certainly more than its master ever can be able
> to love it back. There certainly is no creature in the world in which
> "bond behavior," in other words personal friendship, has become an
> equally powerful motivation as it has in dogs.*

The dog has become by far the most popular pet in Western house-
holds, an animal treated with all the love and affection accorded a member
of the family. There are some fifty-seven million dogs in the United States
alone—one dog in every third American home. But how many would be
allowed to stay if they were suddenly to lose their most remarkable trait—
a sense of conscience? Captive wolves can be every bit as devoted to their
masters as dogs, but they still make poor pets. Wolves lack comprehension
of the stick; they cannot understand punishment as a consequence of bad
behavior. If a pet wolf were to chew up his owner's boots and be whipped
for it, the animal would simply become hysterical and confused. Dogs are
more "morally fit" to abide with us. If the pet coonhound tips over the
trash can in the kitchen while his master is out at a movie, he will suffer
the awareness of having done wrong—or at least will know that his behavior
will have some unpleasant repercussions. When the dog's master returns,
he does not have to see the bacon wrappers and crusts of bread strewn
about the floor before he knows the dog has misbehaved. He has only to
look down at the miserable ball of fur and contrition slinking out the door.

Dogs are in fact capable of a whole range of emotions—guilt, joy,
anxiety, jealousy, love, even petty revenge. (The guilty coonhound no doubt
knocked the garbage over in the first place because he was annoyed at
being left alone.) Indeed all mammals probably have such emotions; the
brain centers governing these feelings are virtually identical in humans and
in animals. Dogs, however, communicate them better to humans, and therein
lies the difference. We have bred this animal for faith and patience and

brought it into our homes to be treated as friend, confidant, child, therapist, and alter ego. We share good news with our dogs, feed them, bring them presents, seek their company when lonely, deny ourselves trips for their sake.

In return the dog bestows upon its owner a peculiar sense of grace. More than any human can possibly manage, the dogs countenance our transgressions and forgive all our failures. They don't mind if we are poor, old, or fat, and they always listen to our point of view. Stutterers don't stutter when they talk to their dogs. Blood pressure, which rises whenever we talk to another person, drops below resting level after we've stroked and patted our pets. People who own pets are less likely to die of heart disease than people without them, regardless of whether they are rich or impoverished, married or single.

After paying witness to the extravagant accomplishments of polar bears, tigers, wolves, and the other great earthlings in the wild, it may be something of a disappointment to end this journey with Fido and Spot. One could easily argue that domestic dogs belong more to man than to nature. They no longer need to struggle to survive, and for this alone they suffer a severe loss of animal dignity. Much as we appreciate the dog's devotion, we also hold the dog in deep contempt. Idiomatically, a *dog* is anything inferior or unattractive. *Doggerel* is bad verse; *to go to the dogs* is to descend to the lowest level of existence. *Every dog has his day* implies that he is pretty miserable most of the year, while *to die like a dog* deprives a man's life of all its worth.

It is essential to remember, however, that whatever the dog is to us, whether a paragon of love and trust or a creature of the lowest ignobility, we have made it so ourselves. The dog is the product of generations of unnatural selection. When left to breed without management, it returns within a few generations to its generic form. Feral dogs—pets gone wild—quickly assume more wolfish behaviors, living in packs where food is abundant in rural areas, foraging alone in the streets of cities. Like wolves, they do not share the domestic pet's habit of barking. Their breeding cycle reverts to one short season per year, instead of the two annual estrus periods common among their kept cousins. It is theoretically possible, in fact, for every one of the hundreds of breeds of dogs to mate with a wolf, though differences in size could pose a problem. In some areas, such as the Apennines of Italy, so much interbreeding has gone on in the wild that it is almost impossible to say what is a dog and what is a wolf.

Still, it is difficult to comprehend what the distant howl of a wolf would mean to a Pekinese curled up in the backseat of a Cadillac parked on Fifth Avenue, or even what message it would convey to the mongrel terrier who passes by on the sidewalk, following its destitute mistress as she pokes about in garbage cans. Our peculiar bond with the dog nevertheless connects us, inextricably, to the wilder earthlings beyond the city streets and neighborhood yards. A dog can be appreciated for its unremitting trust at any time; less common are those moments when we are caught off guard by an apprehension of the dog's profound otherness, the innate worth of the animal harbored in its heartbeat, the rich and sentient life shooting through its synapses and quickening its soul. Perhaps you whistle to your coonhound as he trots through a garden down the block; with an insouciant flip of his tail he ignores you and jogs off, leaving you exasperated, but incongruously uplifted. Some days later you are walking the dog along the boulevard at dusk when he suddenly tugs hard against the leash, muscles straining, his nostrils in the grip of some arcane aroma. The feeling returns: He is himself, an equal, not your dog but *dog*, worthy of something more than uncritical affection. You unsnap the leash and off he goes, galloping into the shadows.

The deeper ties between our two species cannot be removed. The dog that pulls against the leash is bound to us by a history that has gathered perilous consequence. In our fever to reinvent the planet we have incurred an appalling responsibility over the fate, not only of domestic animals, but of bears, badgers, elephants, hyraxes, koalas, and all the other earthlings who live in our vestibules and in the wilderness that hangs from every door. We have reached the point where we can uproot species and erase ecosystems as thoughtlessly as we can weed the back lawn or pave the driveway. All animals, even those who live their fierce and exuberant lives far beyond our awareness, are now, like the dog, utterly dependent on our ability to envision a future for them. This does not lessen their greatness, but it certainly cries out a challenge to our own.

Acknowledgments

Writing is supposed to be a lonely business, but for this book I enjoyed many close and committed companions. I owe a great debt to three who were with the project from start to finish: Sarah Fitzgerald, whose sound advice and tireless research provided both raw material and a renewing source of inspiration; Hazel Hammond, who took it as a personal mission to seek out and bring back the most beautiful animals on film; and Leonard Mayhew, who believed in the book even before I did, encouraged its sometimes painful growth, and continued to coax it into shape after my work was done. I would also like to thank the many others at WNET, New York, who helped the book along: George Page, David Heeley, and Julie Leonard of the *Nature* production team; Jowill Woodman, who created the beautiful maps that adorn each chapter; Hap Hatton, who stepped in as photo researcher when he was needed; and interns James Braly, Clayton Shaw, Dominick Pesola, John McKinley, Derik Perry, and David Cheifetz. In a real sense, this book is a tribute to the beauty and wisdom of the *Nature* public television series which is produced by WNET and is presented in association with The Nature Conservancy and with the long-standing support of the American Gas Association.

Scientific articles on mammals seldom betray the devotion and respect that the authors hold for their subjects. I am deeply grateful to the investigators who gave their knowledge, time, and patience to help me reclothe their findings in flesh and fur. Those who reviewed chapters include Ian Sterling, David Smith, George Schaller, Virginia Hayssen, Pamela Parker, Cynthia Moss, Joyce Poole, David Watts, and David Mech. I thank them for their margin comments, even—in fact especially—the darkly scrawled ones like "Absolute nonsense!" and "Who told you *this*??"

Other investigators kindly gave their time in interviews and/or read sections of the book. For "Denning in New Jersey" and "Creature of Light": Gary Alt, Steven Amstrup, Charles Jonkel, Jack Lentfer, Pat McConnell, Ralph Nelson, Richard Pais, and Ian Sterling. For "In Praise of Prey" and "Tiger with Deer, Tiger with Tigers": Bruce Bunting, Albert Franzman, Steven O'Brian, Rob Peters, George Schaller, Ulysses Seal, John Siedensticker, David Smith, and Mel Sundquist. For "Diversions Down Under" and "Milky Ways": Virginia Hayssen, Pamela Parker, and Hans-Dieter Sues. For "The Gregarious Giant": Iain and Oria Douglas-Hamilton, S. K. Eltringham, Cynthia Moss, Katy Payne, and Joyce Poole. For "The Familiar Stranger" and "Gorilla Lives": Sandy Harcourt, Russ Mittermeier, Jan Raefert, David Watts, and Cathy Yarborough. And for "The Legacy of the Wolf": Fred Harrington, David Mech, Jane Parkard, Rolf Peterson, and Ulysses Seal. Tom Lovejoy provided timely guidance and somehow managed to find the time to review the whole manuscript—probably on a typical Monday morning en route to Borneo or Brazil.

For editorial acumen and sheer patience, I want to thank Rob Nieweg and Charles Levine at Macmillan, and special thanks to Ed Novak, who took over at the crucial final stage. My agent Victoria Pryor supplied both moral support and a keen critical interest in the book, for which I am ever grateful. Judy Ashmore at the Marine Biological Laboratory Library cordially helped with data searches. My thanks to my friends Jelle Atema, Isja Lederhendler, and Jon Weiner. John Pfeiffer gave me ideas, contacts, and directions, but I thank him most of all for the liberating good spirits his friendship brings to all who know him.

Finally, I am enormously grateful to Christine Kuethe, who knew that she would have to share the trials of a man chased by wild animals and grisly deadlines, and still consented to marry him. This book could not have been completed without her many suggestions and her unwavering trust.

Bibliography

POLAR BEAR BIBLIOGRAPHY

Amstrup, S. C. "Masters of the Northern Ice." *Alaska*, 1984, pp. 32–77.

Breummer, F. "How Polar Bears Break the Ice." *Natural History* 93(12) [1984]:38–46.

———. "White Whales on Holiday." *Natural History*, 1986, pp. 41–50.

Davids, R. C. *Lords of the Arctic*. New York: Macmillan Publishing Co., 1982.

Freeman, M. R. "Polar Bear Predation on the Beluga in the Canadian Arctic." *Arctic* 26 [1973]:162–63.

Furnell, D. J., and Oolooyuk, D. "Polar Bear Predation on Ringed Seals in Ice-Free Water." *Canadian Field Naturalist* 94(1) [1980]:88–89.

Gray, D. R. "Musk Ox." *Canadian Wildlife Service*, 1975.

Hansson, R., and Thommassen, J. *Behavior of Polar Bears with Cubs in the Denning Area*. Vol. 5. Edited by E. C. Meslow. Calgary, Can.: International Association for Bear Research and Management, 1983, pp. 238–45.

Heyland, J. D., and Hay, K. "An Attack by a Polar Bear on a Juvenile Beluga." *Arctic*, 1976, pp. 56–57.

Hummel, M. *Arctic Wildlife*. Toronto, Can.: Key Porter Books, 1984.

Jonkel, C., and Hanson, G. "The Eighth Continent." *Western Wildlands Summer* 9(2) [1983]:33–36.

Killian, H. P. L. "The Possible Use of Tools by Polar Bears to Obtain Their Food." *Arbok: Norsk Polarinst*, 1974, pp. 177–78.

Kolenosky, G., and Prevett, J. P. *Productivity and Maternity Denning of Polar Bears in Ontario*. Vol. 5. Calgary, Can.: International Association for Bear Research and Management, 1983, pp. 238–45.

Kolz, L. A.; Lentfer, J. W.; and Fallek, H. G. *Polar Bear Tracking Via Satellite*. Proceedings of 15th annual Rocky Mountain Bioengineering Symposium thesis, 1978.

Latour, P. B. "Interactions Between Free-Ranging, Adult Male Polar Bears (*Ursus maritimus phipps*): A Case of Adult Social Play." *Canadian Journal of Zoology* 59 (1981):1977–83.

Lentfer, J. W. *Polar Bear* (Ursus maritimus) *Carnivora*. Baltimore, Md.: Johns Hopkins University Press, 1982.

Lewin, R. A., and Robinson, P. T. "The Greening of Polar Bears in Zoos." *Nature* 278 (1979):445–47.

Miller, G. D., and Wooldridge, D. R. "Small-Game Hunting Behavior of Polar Bears (*Ursus maritimus*)." *Canadian Field Naturalist* 97(1) [1983]:93–94.

Mowat, F. *Sea of Slaughter*. Boston: Atlantic Monthly Press, 1984.

Nelson, R. A. *Winter Sleeps in the Black Bear: A Physiological and Metabolic Marvel*. Mayo Clinic Proceedings 48 (1973).

———; Folk, G. E., Jr.; Pfeiffer, E. W.; Craighaid, J. J.; Jonkel, C.; and Steiger, D. L. *Behavior, Biochemistry, and Hibernation in Black, Grisly, and Polar Bears*, Vol. 5. Edited by E. C. Meslow. Calgary, Can.: International Association for Bear Research and Management, 1983, pp. 284–90.

Perry, R. *The World of the Polar Bear*. Seattle: University of Washington Press, 1966.

Phipps, C. J. *A Voyage Towards the North Pole: 1773*. New York: State Mutual Book and Periodical Service, Ltd., 1981.

Ray, G. C. "Learning the Ways of the Walrus." *National Geographic*, 1979, pp. 565–80.

Reeves, R. R., and Mitchell, E. "The Whale Behind the Tusk." *National History* 90(8) [1981]:50–57.

Speller, S. W. "Arctic Fox." *Canadian Wildlife Service*, 1977.

Stirling, I. "A Group Threat Display Given by Walruses to a Polar Bear." *Journal of Mammology* 65(2) [1984]:352–53.

———. "Midsummer Observations on the Behavior of Wild Polar Bears (*Ursus maritimus*)." *Canadian Journal of Zoology* 52 (1974):1191–198.

———, and Archibald, R. W. "Aspects of Predation of Seals by Polar Bears." *Journal of Fish Reserve Board* 34 (1977):1126–129.

Teal, J. J., Jr. "Domesticating the Wild and Wooly Musk Ox." *National Geographic* 137 (1970):862–79.

TIGER BIBLIOGRAPHY

Brahmachary, R. L. "On the Pheromones of Tigers." *American Naturalist* 118 (1981):561–67.

Breedon, S. "Tiger! Lord of the Indian Jungle." *National Geographic*, 1984, pp. 748–73.

Carey, J. "Mangroves . . . Swamps Nobody Likes." *International Wildlife* 12 (1982):21–27.

Chakrabarti, K. "The Sunderbans Tiger." *Bombay Natural History Society* 8(2) [1984]:459–60.

Deans, N. L. "Journey Through a Mangrove Swamp." *Oceans*, 1982, pp. 31–37.

Halle, M. *Operation Tiger*. World Wildlife Fund Monthly Report, 1983.

Jackson, P. "Maneaters." *International Wildlife*. 15(6) [1985]:4–11.

———. *Tigers and Men*. World Wildlife Fund Monthly Report, 1983.

Lovejoy, T. E. "The Blue-Eyed Eagle of the Philippines." *Frontiers*, 1973.

MacDougal, C. *The Face of the Tiger*. London: Rivington Books, 1977.

Mukherjee, A. K. "The Sunderbans of India and Its Biota." *Journal of the Bombay Natural History Society* 72(1) [1975].

Schaller, G. *The Deer and the Tiger: A Study of Wildlife in India*. Chicago: University of Chicago Press, 1967.

———. "Predators of the Serengeti" Series. *Natural History* 81(4):38–49; 81(3):60–69; 81(4):38–43 [1972].

Seidensticker, J., and Hai, M. A. *The Sunderbans Wildlife Management Plan: Conservation in the Bangladesh Coastal Zone*. Sunderbans Wildlife Management Committee, 1984.

Shorey, H. H. *Animal Communication by Pheromones*. New York: Academic Press, 1976.

Smith, J. L. D., and Mishra, H. R. *Management Recommendations for the Chitwan Tiger Population*. Dept. of National Parks and Wildlife Conservation, Nepal, 1981.

Sunquist, M. E. "The Social Organization of Tigers (*Panthera tigris*) at Royal Chitwan National Park, Nepal." Smithsonian Contributions. *Zoology* 336 (1981).

———, and Sunquist, F. "The Tiger Singles Scene." *Natural History* 92 (1983):44–51.

"Tiger's Eyes Dimmed as Slaughter Draws the Gaze of Spectators." *China Post*, 1984.

MARSUPIAL BIBLIOGRAPHY

Beaglehole, J. C., ed. *The Journals of Captain James Cook*. Cambridge, Eng.: Hakluyt Society Press, 1955.

Croft, D. B. "Behavior of Red Kangaroos (Macropus rufus) [Desmarest, 1822] in Northwest New South Wales, Australia." *Australian Mammalogy* 4 (1980):5–58.

Darwin, Charles. *Voyage of H.M.S. Beagle*. 2nd ed. New York: D. Appleton & Co., 1878.

Friend, T. "The Numbat—an Endangered Species." *Australian Natural History* 20(10) [1982]:339–43.

Frith, H. J., and Calaby, J. H. *Kangaroos*. Melbourne, Australia: F. W. Cheshire, 1969.

Gilbert, B. "Nasty Little Devil." *Sports Illustrated*, 5 October 1981.

Gould, Stephen Jay. "Bligh's Bounty." *Natural History*, September 1985.

———. "Sticking Up for Marsupials." *Natural History* 86 (1977):10–15.

———. "To Be a Platypus." *Natural History* 94(8) [1985]:10–15.

Griffiths, M. E. "The Life of the Echidna." *Australian Natural History*, September 1972.

Guiler, E. "Tasmanian Devils—Australia's Ugliest Marsupials." *Australian Natural History* 20(12) [1982].

Hayssen, V.; Lacy, R.; and Parker, P. "Metatherian Reproduction: Transitional or Transcending?" *American Naturalist* 126 (1985):617–32.

Hopson, J. "Queer Mammal of Ducklike Bill and Reptilian Walk." *Smithsonian* 11 (1981):62–69.

Kirsch, J. A. W. "The Six-Percent Solution: Second Thoughts on the Adaptedness of the Marsupialia. *American Scientist* 65 (1977):276–88.

Sharman, G. B. "Adaptations of Marsupial Pouch Young for Extrauterine Existence," in *The Mammalian Fetus in Vitro*, edited by C. R. Austin. London: Chapman and Hall, 1973, pp. 91–146.

Stonehouse, B., and Gilmore, D., eds. *The Biology of Marsupials*. Baltimore, Md.: University Park Press, 1977.

Strahan, R. *The Complete Book of Australian Mammals: The National Photographic Index of Australian Wildlife*. Salem: Merrimac Publishers Circle, 1984.

———, and Thomas, D. E. "Courtship of the Platypus (*Ornithorhynchus anatinus*). Australian Journal of Zoology 18(3) [1975]:165–78.

Tyndale-Biscoe, H. *Life of Marsupials*. New York: American Elsevier Publishing Co., 1973.

ELEPHANT BIBLIOGRAPHY

Bowser, H. "When Elephants Roamed the Range." *Science Digest* 91(6) [1983]:60–67.

Croze, H. "The Serona Bull Problem." *East African Wildlife Journal*. 12 (1974).

Dublin, H. "Cooperation and Reproductive Competition Among Female African Elephants," in *Social Behavior of Female Vertebrates*, edited by S. K. Wasser. New York: Academic Press, 1983, pp. 291–313.

Douglas-Hamilton, I., and Douglas-Hamilton, O. *Among the Elephants*. London: Collins, 1975.

Douglas-Hamilton, O. "African Elephants—Can They Survive?" *National Geographic*. 158(5) [1980]:568–603.

Eltringham, S. K. *Elephants*. Poole, Eng.: Blandford Press, 1982.

Hanks, J. *The Struggle for Survival: The Elephant Problem*. New York: Mayflower Books, 1979.

Krikken, J. "An Interesting Case of Camouflage in African Dung Beetles of the Genus *Drepanocerus*." *Entomologische Berichten*, 1983.

Moss, C. "Oestrus Behavior and Female Choice in the African Elephant." *Behavior* 86 (1983).

———. *Portraits in the Wild*. Chicago: University of Chicago Press, 1982.

———. "Social Circles." *Wildlife News* 16(1) [1981].

———, and Poole, Joyce. "Relationships and Social Structure of African Elephants," in R. Hinde, ed., *Primate Social Relationships*. Boston: Blackwell Scientific Publications, 1983.

Payne, K. "Infrasonic Calls of the Asian Elephant." Author's MS.

Poole, J. *Male/Male Competition in the African Elephant*. Ph.D. thesis, Cambridge University, 1981.

———, and Moss, C. J. "Musth in the African Elephant *(Loxodonta africana)*." *Nature* 292 (1981):830–31.

Styles, T. E. "The Birth and Early Development of an African Elephant at the Metro Toronto Zoo." *International Zoo Yearbook, 1982*.

GORILLA BIBLIOGRAPHY

Dixon, A. F. *The Natural History of the Gorilla*. New York: Columbia University Press, 1981.

Fossey, D. *Gorillas in the Mist*. Boston: Houghton Mifflin Co., 1983.

————. "Making friends with the Mountain Gorillas." *National Geographic* 137 (1970):48–67.

————. "The Imperiled Mountain Gorilla." *National Geographic* 159 (1981):501–22.

Goodall, J. *In the Shadow of Man*. Boston: Houghton Mifflin Co., 1971.

Greenberg, J. "The Sophisticated Sounds of Simians." *Science News*, 8 June 1985.

Gribben, J. "The One-Percent Advantage." *Science Digest*, August 1982.

Harcourt, A. "All's Fair in Play and Politics." *New Scientist*, 12 December 1985.

————, and Stewart, Kelly. "Apes, Sex, and Societies," *New Scientist* 76 (1977):162.

Janzen, D. H. "How to Be a Fig." *Annual Review of Ecological Systematics* 10 (1979):13–51.

Jolly, A. *The Evolution of Primate Behavior*. 2nd ed. New York: Macmillan Publishing Co., 1985.

Maple, T., and Hoff, M. *Gorilla Behavior*. New York: Van Nostrand Reinhold Co., 1982.

Patterson, F., and Linden, E. *The Education of Koko*. New York: Holt, Rinehart and Winston, 1981.

Schaller, G. *The Mountain Gorilla*. Chicago: University of Chicago Press, 1963.

Seyfarth, R. M. "Talking with Monkeys and Great Apes." *International Wildlife* 12 (1982).

Stewart, K. J., and Harcourt, A. H. "Gorillas: Variation in Female Relationships."

Toner, M. "Loulis, the Talking Chimp." *National Wildlife*, February/March 1986.

Veit, P. G. "Gorilla Society." *Natural History*, March 1982.

Watts, D. "Composition and Variability of Mountain Gorilla Diets in the Central Virungas." *American Journal of Primitology* 7 (1984):323–56.

WOLF BIBLIOGRAPHY

Allen, D. L. "How Wolves Kill." *Natural History* 80 (1979):46–51.

Clarke, C. H. D. "The Beast of Gevaudan." *Natural History* 80 (1971):44–51ff.

Crisler, L. *Arctic Wild*. New York: Harper and Bros., 1958.

Fox, M. W. *Behavior of Wolves, Dogs and Related Canids*. New York: Harper and Row, 1971.

————, ed. *The Wild Canids*. New York: Van Nostrand Reinhold Co., 1975.

Harrington, F. H. "Urine Marking and Caching Behavior in the Wolf." *Behavior* 76 (1981):210–88.

————, and Mech, D. L. "Wolf Howling and Its Role in Territorial Maintenance." *Behavior* 8 (1979):207–49.

————, and Paquet, P. C., eds. *Wolves of the World: Perspectives of Behavior, Ecology and Conservation*. Park Ridge, N.J.: Noyes Publications, 1982.

Henry, J. D. "The Use of Urine Marking in the Scavenging Behavior of the Red Fox." *Behavior* 61 (1977):82–105.

Lopez, B. H. *Of Wolves and Men*. New York: Charles Scribner's Sons, 1979.

Mech, D. L. "Wolf Pack Buffer Zones as Prey Reservoirs." *Science* 198 (1977):320–21.

————. *The Wolf: The Ecology and Behavior of an Endangered Species*. Garden City, N.Y.: Natural History Press, 1970.

Packard, J. M.; Mech, D. L.; and Seal, U. S. "Social Influences on Reproduction in Wolves," in *Wolves in Canada and Alaska: Their Status, Biology and Management*, edited by L. Carbyn. Ottawa: Canadian Wildlife Report Series 45 (1983):78–85.

———; Seal, U. S.; Mech, D. L.; and Plotka, E. D. "Causes of Reproductive Failure in Two Family Groups of Wolves." *Z. Tierpsychology* 68 (1985):24–40.

Peters, R. "Communication, Cognitive Mapping, and Strategy in Hominids," in *Wolf and Man: Evolution in Parallel*, edited by R. Hall and H. Sharp. New York: Academic Press, 1978, pp. 95–107.

———. *Dance of the Wolves*. New York: McGraw-Hill, 1985.

———, and Mech, D. L. "Scent-Marking in Wolves." *American Scientist* 63 (1975):628–37.

Ricciutti, E. R. "Dogs of War." *International Wildlife*, 1978, pp. 37–40.

Rothman, R. J. "Scent-Marking in Lone Wolves and Newly Formed Pairs." *Animal Behavior* 27 (1979):750–60.

Stephenson, R., and Ahook, R. "The Eskimo Hunter's View of Wolf Ecology and Behavior," in *The Wild Canids*, edited by M. W. Fox. New York: Van Nostrand Reinhold Co., 1975.

Woolpy, J. H. "The Social Organization of Wolves." *Natural History* 77 (1968):46–55.

Zimen, E. *The Wolf: A Species in Danger*. New York: Delacorte Press, 1981.

ADDITIONAL SOURCES

Austin, C. R., and Short, R. V. *Reproduction in Mammals: Hormones in Reproduction*. Cambridge, Eng.: Cambridge University Press, 1972.

Blackburn, D. G.; Hayssen, V.; and Murphy, C. J. "The Origins of Lactation and the Evolution of Milk." Unpublished MS.

Caufield, Catherine. *In the Rainforest*. New York: Alfred A. Knopf, 1985.

Fogle, B., ed. *Interrelations Between People and Pets*. Springfield, Ill.: Charles Thomas, Publisher, 1981.

Forsyth, A., and Miyata, K. *Tropical Nature*. New York: Charles Scribner's Sons, 1984.

Fox, Michael W. *The Dog: Its Domestication and Behavior*. New York: Garland STPM Press, 1978.

Gilbert, Bil. "A Man and His Dog." *Discover*, May 1985.

Griffin, Donald. *Animal Thinking*. Cambridge, Mass.: Harvard University Press, 1984.

———. *The Question of Animal Awareness*. New York: Rockefeller University Press, 1976.

Humphrey, N. K. "The Social Function of Intellect," in P. P. G. Bateson and R. A. Hinde, eds., *Growing Points in Ethology*. Cambridge, Eng.: Cambridge University Press, 1976.

Konner, M. "The Nursing Knot." *The Sciences*, 1985, pp. 10–12.

MacDonald, D., ed. *The Encyclopedia of Mammals*. New York: Facts on File, 1984.

Paris, R. C. *Recent Evidence of Black Bear Denning and Parturition in New Jersey*. Bulletin of the New Jersey Academy of Science 30(2) [Fall 1985].

Pringle, H. "Giant Bear Barred Entry to Alaska." *New Scientist*, 9 January 1986.

Rensberger, B. *The Cult of the Wild*. New York: Anchor Press/Doubleday, 1977.

Weiner, J. *Planet Earth*. New York: Bantam Books, 1986.

Wilson, E. O. *Biophilia*. Cambridge, Mass.: Harvard University Press, 1984.

———. *Sociobiology*. Cambridge, Mass.: Harvard University Press, 1975.

Wittenberger, J. F. *Animal Social Behavior*. Boston: Doxbury Press, 1981.

Photo and Illustration Credits

285

Index